Criminology and criminal justice

Criminology and criminal justice

by J. E. Hall Williams LLM (Wales)
Hon LL D (John F. Kennedy University, California)
of the Middle Temple, Barrister
Reader in Criminology, University of London
Law Department, London School of Economics
and Political Science

London
Butterworths
1982

England   Butterworth & Co (Publishers) Ltd
London   88 Kingsway, WC2B 6AB

Australia   Butterworths Pty Ltd
Sydney   271–273 Lane Cove Road, North Ryde, NSW 2113
           Also at Melbourne, Brisbane, Adelaide and Perth

Canada   Butterworth & Co (Canada) Ltd
Toronto   2265 Midland Avenue, Scarborough, M1P 4S1

New Zealand Butterworths of New Zealand Ltd
Wellington   33–35 Cumberland Place

South Africa Butterworth & Co (South Africa) (Pty) Ltd
Durban   152–154 Gale Street

USA   Butterworth (Publishers) Inc
Boston   10 Tower Office Park, Woburn, Mass. 01801

ISBN Casebound   0 406 59320 5
         Limp   0 406 59321 3

c c

312396

Limp cover illustration: *le Raboteur*, Mary Evans Picture Library

Photo typeset by Macmillan India Ltd, Bangalore
Printed and bound in Great Britain
by Billing and Sons Limited
Guildford, London, Oxford, Worcester

To the London School of Economics and
Political Science which gave me the opportunity
and the facilities to embark on this venture,
and enlarged my field of study in a way which
has enriched my life.

Preface

In this book I have attempted to provide a straightforward guide to the complex subject of modern criminology, and in addition to relate this to the needs of the criminal justice process and to discuss the way courts and the administration may make use of the information which criminology can provide about offenders and their offences. Clearly the book is aimed primarily at the needs of law students, both undergraduate and graduate, who are coming to the study of criminology for the first time. Increasingly programmes of law studies make room for course teaching in criminology. In London we have a splendid tradition dating back to 1945 when Hermann Mannheim introduced the teaching of this subject for the LL M degree. Recently, however, we have found room for it to be taught at undergraduate level, where it has proved an attractive option. Books which approach the subject from the viewpoint of psychology or sociology are not entirely suitable for students in these courses, and rarely cover the whole subject matter of theoretical criminology as here conceived. Recently some books have been written on certain aspects of the criminal justice process, but so far there has been no attempt to combine these two different aspects of the subject – the theory about crime or the knowledge which exists about the explanation of criminal behaviour, and the use that can be made of that knowledge in the practical business of the administration of criminal justice. I am conscious of the difficulties of this endeavour and would not claim to have solved the difficult problem of relating these rather disparate fields of study. I hope, however, that this work will mark out some of the dimensions of the relationship which I have described, and point the way towards a more practical use of criminology in the future.

The Notes attached to several chapters provide additional reading material and commentary on selected aspects of the subject which it was felt useful to expand. To have dealt with these topics in the text would have interrupted the discussion. I had in mind particularly the needs of advanced students such as those taking graduate courses like

..

the LL M in criminology. They might also provide useful sources for essays and projects. There is a bibliography of all books referred to, which includes references to government reports and official papers. There is also a list of cases and statutes.

There are no doubt many more subjects which might have been treated in a book of this kind, including the criminology relating to specific crimes, and white collar crime. To keep the book to a manageable length, however, these have been excluded and the text confined to a well-rounded, general discussion of the subject. As it stands, I hope it appeals to those for whom it was primarily intended, law students and their teachers in criminology. It may also attract some interest among other students in criminology whose main field is psychology, sociology or social administration. It might also be read by practitioners in the criminal justice process, lawyers, judges, magistrates, clerks, police officers, probation and prison staff. I should be very pleased if that were so.

My warm thanks are due to the London School of Economics and Political Science for making it possible for me to prepare this book by granting me sabbatical leave from January 1981, to my colleagues in the Law Department who cheerfully suffered my absence which placed extra burdens on them, to my secretary Mrs Jane Heginbotham whose patience and skill were sorely tried, but who week after week typed what I had prepared, and in the final stages coped with numerous amendments, and to my wife who bore with my presence working at home for many months without complaint in order that I should achieve my target, and many times rallied my confidence when the task seemed too much. Also my thanks are due to two colleagues, both former students of mine, who readily agreed to read the draft and provided copious comments which were invaluable and greatly appreciated – Dr Eugene Trivizas, Sociology Department, the University of Reading, and Mrs Margaret Wilkie, Law Department, Polytechnic of Central London. They are in no way responsible for the views here expressed which are my own. Nevertheless I am extremely grateful to them for so many sound comments and criticisms.

Eryl Hall Williams
London School of Economics and Political Science
1 January 1982

Acknowledgments

Mr John C. Alderson CBE, QPM, Hon LL D
Dr John Bowlby
Professor A. D. M. Clarke and Mrs Ann M. Clarke
Professor H. J. Eysenck and Mrs Sybil B. G. Eysenck
Dr David P. Farrington
Professor John Gunn and the Academic Press Inc. (London) Ltd
Professor W. L. Linford Rees
Mrs Sarah McCabe and Mr Frank Sutcliffe
Professor Michael Rutter
Mr David Steer
Drs Ian Taylor, P. Walton, J. Young and Routledge & Kegan Paul Ltd
Mr D. A. Thomas
Professor Nigel Walker
Professor D. J. West
John Wiley & Sons Ltd in respect of Dr M. P. Feldman, *Criminal Behaviour: A Psychological Analysis* (1977)
The Baroness Wootton of Abinger
The Controller, Her Majesty's Stationery Office in respect of:
    Figure 2.6, page 61, Criminal Statistics (England and Wales) 1978 Cmnd 7670
    Figure 2.1, page 43, Criminal Statistics (England and Wales) 1979
    Figure 2.2, page 54, Criminal Statistics (England and Wales) 1979
    Report of the Commissioner of Police of the Metropolis 1963, Cmnd 2408 (July 1964) figures from p. 70
    and other official publications listed in the Bibliography on p. 243
The Institute for the Study and Treatment of Delinquency in respect of articles appearing in the British Journal of Delinquency and the British Journal of Criminology
The University of Chicago Press, in respect of Map No. 8, page 54, and Figure 1, page 69 of C. R. Shaw and H. D. McKay, *Juvenile Delinquency and Urban Areas* (revised edn., 1969)

Contents

Table of statutes

List of cases

Abbreviations

Acta Psychol	Acta Psychologica
Am Jo Psychiatry	American Journal of Psychiatry
Am Jo Soc	American Journal of Sociology
Am Soc Rev	American Sociological Review
Amer J Hum Genet	American Journal of Human Genetics
BJC	British Journal of Criminology
BJD	British Journal of Delinquency
BJ Educ Psychol	British Journal of Educational Psychology
BJ Med Psychol	British Journal of Medical Psychology
BMJ	British Medical Journal
BJ Psychiat	British Journal of Psychiatry
Biol Rev	Biological Review
Crime LR	Criminal Law Review
Hofstra L Rev	Hofstra Law Review
JCJ	Journal of Criminal Justice
J Ment Sci	Journal of Mental Science
J Psychol	Journal of Psychology
Jo Crim L & Crim'ogy & Pol Sci	Journal of Criminal Law, Criminology and Police Science
Jo Soc Issues	Journal of Social Issues
Jo Res Crime & Delinq	Journal of Research in Crime and Delinquency
Jo Roy Stat Soc	Journal of the Royal Statistical Society
LQR	Law Quarterly Review
MLR	Modern Law Review
Populat Stud	Population Studies
U Chi L Rev	University of Chicago Law Review
U Toledo LR	University of Toledo Law Review
Yale L Jo	Yale Law Journal

Chapter 1

Introduction

1 The nature of criminological study

Criminology is concerned with the scientific study of crime. It is essentially a multi-disciplinary study. The study of crime is carried out by many scholars from the point of view of their different disciplines, and sometimes (though rarely and with difficulty) through inter-disciplinary studies. The most common approach to the study of crime is to start from the point of view and follow the interests and emphases of one's own particular discipline. Indeed any other approach is fraught with danger. So we have the subject studied by psychologists, sociologists, statisticians and medical scholars, including psychiatrists and psycho-analysts. No one discipline dominates the field, though in recent years, especially in the United States and to a lesser degree in Europe, sociology has made a fair bid to claim pre-eminence.

Criminology is essentially concerned with the *scientific* study of crime. This excludes from the scope of the subject certain kinds of popular journalism or criminal biography such as the accounts of famous murders. Some journalistic accounts of criminal careers, such as the superb observations of Tony Parker[1], deserve recognition however, and criminologists have sometimes themselves studied criminal career patterns[2].

Criminology should not be confused with the science of criminal detection or forensic science and forensic pathology. There is no direct connection between the detection of crime and the study of crimes and criminal behaviour carried out by criminologists, though there may sometimes be an indirect connection. Forensic scientists and

---

1 Tony Parker and Robert Allerton, *The Courage of his Convictions* (1962); *The Unknown Citizen* (1963); *The Twisting Lane* (1969); *The Frying-Pan* (1970).
2 Clifford Shaw, *The Jack-roller* (1931); *Brothers in Crime* (1938); *The Natural History of A Delinquent Career* (1931); E. H. Sutherland, *The Professional Thief* (1950).

pathologists serve the needs of the police and the courts in crime detection and crime prevention. Indirectly, however, their work may throw some valuable light on criminal behaviour in ways which will be of interest to the criminologist, e.g. regarding the patterns of homicide, the battered baby syndrome and the study of alcoholism and drug abuse in relation to crime. The criminologist is concerned more with how and why crimes come to be committed rather than who did it, and providing proof of guilt.

Criminology is best seen as a social science concerned with those aspects of human behaviour regarded as criminal because they are prohibited by the criminal law, together with such aspects of socially deviant behaviour as are closely related to crime and may usefully be studied in this connection. The main focus of the criminologist should remain on *criminal* behaviour as an aspect of social behaviour, including the way people come to be perceived and dealt with as offenders. The study can best be viewed as limited by the range of behaviour currently dealt with as criminal because it is prohibited by the current criminal law.

The list of crimes is not immutable, however, and historically many changes have occurred in the list of criminal prohibitions. In our time changes have been made or are seen as desirable in order to reflect changes in public sentiment or judgments of public needs and values. The criminologist may properly be concerned to study fringe areas, 'deviant' behaviour which is not actually criminal, in order to throw light on the gaps in the criminal law or to show that some closely related types of behaviour which are regarded as criminal should no longer be so defined. The sociologist describes such behaviour as socially deviant behaviour, and sometimes studies aspects of socially deviant behaviour in their own right, as it were. Studies of alcoholism, drug abuse, gambling and sexual behaviour provide examples, as do studies of certain 'white-collar' business or economic activities. Such studies may throw light on the true nature of the behaviour in question and whether the criminal law should or should not intervene.

When we say that criminology should limit its scope to the study of conduct which is criminal because it contravenes the criminal law in one or more of its prohibitions, we do not mean that in studying such behaviour the criminologist must stick slavishly to the legal definitions and descriptions of what is a criminal offence. Sometimes criminologists find it useful to go outside the strict legal definitions in order to study a particular type of behaviour, e.g. Donald R. Cressey's study of embezzlement, *Other People's Money* (1953), McClintock's studies of robbery, violence, and criminal statistics, and the author's studies of incest and serious heterosexual offences[3].

A word of warning must be uttered about the tendency of some criminologists to stray too far from the focus or field of interest described thus far, and to include in their discussion a much wider range of conduct which is in their view anti-social, immoral and contrary to the public interest, and to make public condemnations of such behaviour as criminologists. Certain aspects of the discussion of 'white-collar' crime frequently partake of this character. There is a danger here of intellectual and indeed moral confusion. Simply because one disapproves of certain behaviour does not make it criminal if the law still permits it, however reprehensible the behaviour may be. Lawyers will be familiar with the distinction between tax avoidance, which is legal, and tax evasion, which is criminal. Criminologists would be well advised to confine their observations and studies to the consideration of behaviour already legally defined as criminal. This subject is large enough by any standard[4].

At the same time one should recognise the so-called 'over-reach' of the criminal law, so vividly described by Morris and Hawkins[5] and Herbert L. Packer[6]. Here the discussion usually focuses on areas of private morality including sexual behaviour, such as homosexual behaviour, prostitution and drug abuse, and pornography. In England and Wales the Wolfenden Committee on Homosexual Offences and Prostitution (1957) authoritatively stated the considerations which should govern the law's intervention in such matters[7]. The criminal law has been used in recent years to help regulate such subjects as the pollution of the environment, marine broadcasting by 'pirate' radio stations, and many other matters of public interest and social concern. The extent and range of criminology's interests and concerns

3 F. H. McClintock and E. Gibson, *Robbery in London* (1961); F. H. McClintock, *Crimes of Violence* (1963); F. H. McClintock and N. H. Avision, *Crime in England and Wales* (1968); J. E. Hall Williams, 'The neglect of incest: a criminologist's view' Medicine, Science and Law (1974) Vol. 14, No. 1, pp. 64 et seq.; 'Serious Heterosexual Attack' Medicine, Science and Law (1977) Vol. 17, No. 2, pp. 140 et seq.

4 See the author's contribution to a *Dictionary of the Social Sciences* (1964), eds. Julius Gould and William F. Kolb, on the subject of *Crime*, p. 148, cited with approval in T. C. N. Gibbens and R. H. Ahrenfeldt, *Cultural Factors in Delinquency* (1966), who say 'there is nowadays substantial agreement between criminologists' about this.

5 N. Morris and G. Hawkins, *The Honest Politician's Guide to Crime Control* (1970).

6 Herbert L. Packer, *The Limits of the Penal Sanction* (1969).

7 Report of the Committee on Homosexual Offences and Prostitution Cmnd. 247.

includes all the various aspects of criminal behaviour, though of course individual criminologists have their own special interests. Criminology includes the study of the general crime situation in this country, and also the study of regional differences observed between different parts of the country, and local differences. The variation in the incidence or distribution of crime between, say, the north of England and the south, between urban areas and rural areas, is of great interest. The study of crime extends to comparing the incidence of crimes on a comparative basis, between different countries in the west, the east-block countries, Africa, Asia and South America and Australasia. The variations in the incidence of different types of offence and offender must also be studied, e.g. the enormous differences in the incidence of homicide in different countries, and the differences observed in the incidence of crimes against the person and crimes against property. Clearly cultural traditions and patterns of behaviour, and levels of economic development, are relevant here. What is needed desperately in criminology is some reliable means of classifying offences and offenders for the purpose of study. A typology of crime is needed, classifying and subdividing criminal behaviour in the same way as the natural scientist has done in developing a taxonomy in relation to his subject. Some attempts have been made in this direction by criminologists but so far to little effect[8].

The criminologist has traditionally been concerned to discover the causes of crime insofar as they can be known, or, to put it less debateably, the explanation for criminal behaviour – to discover what factors are associated with criminal behaviour, to explore the nature of such behaviour with a view to explaining it – but not of course justifying it. Nowadays the concept of cause should generally speaking be avoided: this is because in the social sciences it is now regarded as outmoded and unacceptable to speak in such terms; since everything is related to everything else we can never know the causes. But there are still some distinguished criminologists who insist on the search for a causal theory. Without a causal theory, it is argued, criminology becomes empty rhetoric. Sutherland and Cressey are of this opinion[9]. Certainly it may not be sufficient simply to demonstrate statistical relationships between certain factors and criminal behaviour. It is also

8 A useful discussion is to be found in T. N. Ferdinand, *Typologies of Delinquency: A Critical Analysis* (1966). See also M. Q. Warren, 'Classification of Offenders as an Aid to Efficient Management and Effective Treatment' 62 Jo Crim L & Crim'ogy & Pol Sci No. 2, p. 239 (June 1971) and R. Hood and R. Sparks, *Key Issues in Criminology* (1970) pp. 114 et seq.
9 E. H. Sutherland and D. Cressey, *Principles of Criminology* (10th edn., 1978).

abundantly clear that attempts in the past to develop single-cause theories of criminal behaviour have been highly unsuccessful. Such 'monolithic' theories belong to the stone-age period of criminology, according to Nigel Walker[10]. The history of criminology is littered with the corpses of dead theories about crime, and a great deal of effort has been expended in disproving them. Such negative truths are not, however, without value. Even negative kinds of knowledge, i.e. knowing that such and such is not true, provide some assistance in building up a picture of the nature of crime and expanding our understanding of offenders.

Probably the basic error lying behind the failure of the monolithic theories has been the assumption that there is such a thing as 'criminal behaviour' or 'criminality', viewing it as some kind of pathological entity. Lady Wootton[11] has warned against the adoption of such a simplistic approach. It is like trying to explain the cause of headaches by a single explanation, she says. No medical man would dream of searching for a single explanation. The varieties of criminal behaviour are probably just as numerous as the types of headaches. We should not expect a single explanation.

We can continue the medical analogy a little further. In medicine a distinction is made between the *epidemiology* of a disease or illness and its *etiology*. By *epidemiology* is meant the study of the geographical distribution of a disease or illness, in terms of the places where it is rife or endemic and the places where it is rare or non-existent, and the pattern of its distribution within one country or compared between different countries. Thus typhoid fever is more likely to occur in certain places than others, and the spread of different types of cancer is now being studied. The biologist and botanist speaks of habitat and environment, or the ecological conditions which favour certain varieties of plant and animal life. On the other hand, when one speaks of the *etiology* of a disease or illness one is describing its causes or origins. Scientists never cease in their search for causes. Here another medical point can be made. The doctor nowadays does not always have to know the causes of a medical condition before he can treat it. Modern drugs can be applied which are known to be effective for certain conditions however caused. If one does not work, another can

10 Nigel D. Walker, 'Lost Causes in Criminology' in *Crime, Criminology and Public Policy* (1974), ed. R. Hood, pp. 47 et seq.; *Behaviour and Misbehaviour: explanations and non-explanations* (1977) Chap. 13, 'The Criminologist's Stone'.
11 Barbara Wootton, *Crime and the Criminal Law: Reflections of a Magistrate and Social Scientist* (2nd edn., 1981).

be tried. Here the connection between criminological study and 'treatment' of offenders must be faced. One is bound to say that there is no necessary connection between criminological knowledge and the measures applied by society in dealing with offenders or protecting its members from crime. Indeed this has been one of the major criticisms of criminology expressed in recent years, particularly in the United States. Criminology has also been under attack for being based on a scientific model which is said to be inappropriate for such a 'human' study. It may be useful to go into this a little deeper.

James Q. Wilson, in his book *Thinking About Crime*[12], eloquently expressed the view that all the advice and experience of criminologists made available to successive governmental commissions of inquiry in the United States was of little use in formulating policy, and the recommendations of those commissions had not led to the reduction of crime or an increase in public safety. Indeed crime had actually increased in the period under review. He argues persuasively that the apparatus of crime control, involving as it does considerable areas of police discretion, plea bargains by prosecutions and defendants, and judges' 'softness' over penalties for crime, contributed substantially to the perpetuation of criminal behaviour and its growth. There has been too little emphasis on policy-related crime studies, such as studies of deterrence, crime prevention, and other aspects of crime control. This critique may be loosely characterised as the voice of the right in criminology.

Against this one can counterpoise the voice of the radical left, as expressed in the writings of the self-styled 'new criminologists'[13]. American sociological writings of the sixties and seventies led to the growth of a new school of criminology dedicated not to the 'positivist' and traditional study of causes, but to the study of the processes whereby persons became known offenders by being dealt with as such by the police and the courts, to the study of the response of society to criminal behaviour in its definition and identification, regarding the offender not so much as the 'object' of study as the 'subject'. This approach has been coupled with an almost total rejection of traditional criminology on the grounds of its positivism and scientific pretensions and its deterministic assumptions. That there is scope for a funda-mental re-appraisal of goals and methods cannot be denied in the light of the accumulating evidence of the way the system actually works in

12 James Q. Wilson, *Thinking About Crime* (1975).
13 Exemplified in Britain by I. Taylor, P. Walton and J. Young, *The New Criminology* (1973); *Critical Criminology* (1975), eds. Taylor, Walton and Young.

practice. It is also undoubtedly true that there have been too many naive assumptions. deterministic approaches, and much scientific posturing. It may be a trifle harsh, however, to dismiss all previous generations of criminologists as misguided or deluded. What is required surely is a more balanced view of the subject taken as a whole, which involves assimilating the lessons of interactionist sociology and the new criminology without at the same time losing sight of the path by which we have come and the insights and findings of so-called traditional criminology to date.

As for the demand that criminologists should cease to pretend that they are not inspired by value judgments of certain kinds, one is bound to point out that there has been no such pretence by some of the greatest figures in the field in the past, such as Hermann Mannheim[14]. It was never in doubt where his sympathies lay, and the idea of an antiseptic value-free criminology was not one of them. One difficulty which criminlogists must face, however, is that when it comes to making recommendations for practical action, there is very little they can say derived from their scientific studies, and they are left to draw conclusions which derive more from their own particular system of values or political or social philosophy than from any other source. This is a feature identified by James Q. Wilson with regard to American criminologists. There is no great harm in this situation provided it is made clear that the sources of these ideas or suggestions derive more from their personal philosophy than from their scientific studies. Criminologists frequently confuse their role as scholars with their wishes as penal reformers. On such occasions, when they intervene in public debates, it would be more honest to reveal the value system to which they are committed before making value judgments which are not wholly derived from the results of research.

One might conclude from this discussion that criminology should be abolished. Its raison d'etre has been demolished from the left and from the right. It no longer has a leg to stand on. That is not the view taken here. There is indeed a viable future for criminology, as Marvin Wolfgang once said[15]. It lies in the careful and patient exploration of the phenomena of crime, as experienced in all societies but particularly in our own, with as much objectivity as can be mustered, but with a careful selection of objectives and a realistic assessment of the results.

14 H. Mannheim, *Comparative Criminology* (1965), 2 vols.
15 M. E. Wolfgang, 'The viable future of criminology' in *Criminology in Action: inventory of contemporary criminology: its principal fields of application* (1968), ed. D. Szabo.

Only in this way can society be informed and instructed, guided and advised, about the massive and elusive nature of the crime problem.

Increasingly in modern criminology one sees the connection with certain other types of study, for example, in the field of anthropology, human geography, urban sociology, biological medicine, and so on. It may well be the case that the insights and ideas of criminologists were too narrowly based in the past and failed to link up with and derive benefit from these wider studies. There is no longer any excuse for such isolation. Indeed at least one modern criminologist (Paul Rock) sees some reciprocal benefits flowing the other way in that general sociology may derive great benefit from the work of sociological criminologists[16]. Clearly there is room for a mutual exchange in exploring such a complex concept as crime, and such puzzling behaviour as that of offenders. We can no longer afford the luxury of study in isolation from one another's work. This isolation has developed as a result of increasing specialisation, but was not always the case in the past, when knowledge itself was more limited but what was known was more generally shared.

Notes. The scope of criminology

1 The scope of criminology has been the subject of some discussion by scholars. Generally see: H. Mannheim, *Comparative Criminology* (1965) Vol. I, Chap. 1, and H. Mannheim, *Group Problems in Crime and Punishment* (1955) Chap. 12. Also helpful to a beginner is L. Radzinowicz, *Ideology and Crime* (1966); L. Radzinowicz and J. W. C. Turner 'The Meaning and Scope of Criminal Science' in *The Modern Approach to Criminal Law* (1948) pp. 12–46.

2 On the multi-disciplinary nature of modern criminology, see T. Sellin, *Culture Conflict and Crime* (1938) pp. 3–4, and his article 'The Challenge of Criminality' in *International Annals of Criminology* (1962) p. 17. Also Mannheim (1965) p. xiii.

3 On the relation of criminology to the science of criminal detection, forensic science and forensic medicine, see Mannheim (1965) pp. 16–17.

4 On confining the study of crime to that which is legally prohibited as a criminal offence, different views are held. Thus T. Sellin, H. Mannheim and Terence Morris prefer not to see criminological study thus restricted: T. Sellin (1938); H. Mannheim (1965) pp. 14–15; T. P. Morris (1957). For the opposite view, see Paul W. Tappan, 'Who is the Criminal?'

16 Paul Rock, *Deviant Behaviour* (1973).

12 Am Soc Rev 96 (1947) reprinted in *The Sociology of Crime and Delinquency* (1962), eds. M. E. Wolfgang, L. Savitz, N. Johnson, pp. 28 et seq.

5 On the desirability of using the concept of cause, see Mannheim (1965) pp. 3–12; L. T. Wilkins, *Social Deviance* (1964) p. 133; Lady Barbara Wootton (1981).

6 On the value of such negative 'bricks' of knowledge, see Mannheim (1965) p. 9.

7 On value-free criminology, see Mannheim (1965) p. 11.

2 The history of criminology

Sutherland and Cressey[17] consider that the 'systematic study of crime rates and criminal behaviour is of rather recent origin'. It had its beginnings in the middle of the nineteenth century and accelerated towards the last quarter of the century, so that it is now well over a hundred years old. If this is considered recent, then that statement is correct. What is certainly true is that progress in this study has been slow and one can hardly claim great achievements thus far. Perhaps the explanation for this lies in the complexity of the subject, which involves studying almost every aspect of human development and behaviour. No rapid results can be expected in a study so complex.

The Classical School

The starting point for a discussion of the history of criminology must be to refer briefly to the concepts of the so-called Classical School of criminal justice philosophy. This developed in the latter part of the eighteenth century, under the influence of Beccaria and Bentham, and asserted that in broad terms the punishment should fit the crime, being no more nor less severe than was necessary to deter the criminal and prevent the crime. The assumption made was that criminal behaviour was essentially a rational act, chosen because of a calculation made of the relative risks and gains involved. The tariff of penalties should be adjusted so as to make the risk unacceptable but should not go further and extend to the infliction of the unnecessary suffering. Beccaria advanced his theory in 1764 in his famous book *Dei delitti e delle pene*,

17 E. H. Sutherland and D. R. Cressey, *Criminology* (10th edn., 1978) p. 54.

which was, as Jerome Hall put it, 'an avowed polemic'[18] written by an Italian nobleman philosopher who felt that the existing scale of penalties was too harsh, and pleaded for a rationalisation of the system of criminal justice and a mitigation of the penalties. This was essentially a humanitarian cry of protest against the severity of the penal law. Radzinowicz has described it as the manifesto of the liberal approach to criminal law, and he identifies eleven different characteristics of this approach[19].

Jeremy Bentham in 1780 in his *Introduction to the Principles of Legislation* linked this classical theory of punishment with his utilitarian principle. Under Bentham's influence these ideas gained widespread support and extensive publicity. The notion that crimes deserve punishment fixed in proportion to the harm which has been done also had the support of many philosophers. There has always been, and still is, much philosophical interest in the problems of punishment, and many books have been written about the matter[20].

The early precursors

Early scientific work on crime derived from two sources. First, there was the work of certain Belgian and French statisticians and sociologists who began to interest themselves in the phenomena of crime. *Quetelet* (1796–1874) was a Belgian mathematician/sociologist, who was one of the first to see that statistical method could be applied to the study of crime[1]. He was able to demonstrate that a certain regularity existed in the pattern of crime, over the years. In his treatise in 1835 he produced statistical tables together with a commentary. One famous remark of his is worth quoting. He said 'there is a budget which is defrayed with terrifying regularity by the prisons . . . and the scaffold, and it is one which, above all, every effort must be made to reduce'.

A. M. Guerry was a French lawyer who in his book in 1833 originated the term 'moral statistics' in connection with crime figures, and carried out the earliest ecological studies (or area studies) of crime, an approach which later came to have great significance. Taft says that

---

18 Jerome Hall, *General Principles of Criminal Law* (1947) p. 543. See also the essay by Elio Monachesi on Beccaria in *Pioneers in Criminology* (1960), ed. H. Mannheim, p. 36.
19 L. Radzinowicz, *Ideology and Crime* (1966) pp. 7–8 and 22.
20 H. L. A. Hart, *Punishment and Responsibility* (1968); T. Honderich, *Punishment: the supposed justifications* (1969); Sir Walter Moberly, *The Ethics of Punishment* (1968).
1   Radzinowicz (1966) pp. 31–32.

to these scholars belongs the credit 'for the specific application of quantitative methods to the study of crime'[2], and Radzinowicz regards Quetelet and Guerry as marking by their methods and conclusions a clear transition from the classical liberal to the deterministic position[3]. The second major influence in early criminology came from the medical field. Here not only were there influential theories developing in the early part of the nineteenth century concerning physiology but psychiatry in its embryonic state was looking at mental factors in relation to human behaviour. The work of F. G. Gall, Pinel, Esquirol, Morel, Prichard and Maudsley deserve mention in this connection. Considerable interest was being shown in the possibility of linking physical and mental characteristics with regard to criminal behaviour. Indeed it has been suggested that certain English prison doctors anticipated the theories of the Italian school of criminal anthropology, which, as we shall see, came to dominate the subject in the late nineteenth and early twentieth century. The idea that the criminal possessed certain physical characteristics which distinguished him from normal human beings was first advanced by these scholars[4].

The Italian School

The Italian School of criminology originated with the work of *Cesare Lombroso* (1835–1909), whose principal work *L'Uomo Delinquente* (The Delinquent Man) was published in 1876. In this work Lombroso put forward the thesis that criminality was largely inherited and that criminals could be identified by the shape of their heads and certain other anatomical features. Lombroso was an Italian army physician who later worked in mental hospitals and prisons. He noticed certain similarities in the physical types of these populations, comparing delinquent soldiers, mental patients and prisoners. By measuring their skulls and making careful notes of certain anatomical details, he concluded that there were certain criminal types who inherited their criminal tendencies, and who could be identified by the possession of

2 D. R. Taft, *Criminology* (3rd edn., 1956) p. 77.
3 Radzinowicz (1966) p. 35.
4 C. H. S. Jayewardene 'The English Pre-cursors of Lombroso' BJC Vol. 4, p. 164 (October 1963); A. Lindesmith and Y. Levin, 'The Lombrosian Myth in Criminology' 42 Am Jo Soc 653 (1937). The same authors, 'English Ecology and Criminology of the Past Century' 27 Jo Crim L & Crim'ogy & Pol Sci 801 (1937). T. Sellin, 'The Lombrosian Myth in Criminology' 42 Am Jo Soc 896–897 (1937) reprinted in Carson and Wiles (1971) pp. 19 et seq.

certain physical features, described as *stigmata*. Eventually Lombroso was forced to modify his theory and abandon the more extreme claims. His work was severely attacked by French and German sociologists, and as we shall see, eventually disproved by independent researches in Germany and Britain. Nevertheless his influence remained considerable.

Not only are there still vestiges of an anthropological approach towards the study of crime and modern attempts to link physique and criminal behaviour which take a much more sophisticated form, but to Lombroso more than anyone else belongs the credit for arousing interest in the scientific study of crime. He forced attention away from the discussion of the offence, to concentrate attention on the offender himself and his personal characteristics. As Kenny put it, 'the great principle of this new school was to study not the offence but the offender'[5]. Radzinowicz describes Lombroso's book as 'the first systematic and persistent attempt to enquire into the personality of the offender and to formulate the thesis of the individual causation of crime'[6]. It is true, as he says, that others had conceived the same notion. The work of F. J. Gall and the early nineteenth-century physiognomists produced quite a vogue for the subject of phrenology, which even survived as an entertainment in Edwardian times in charity fetes[7]! We now know that the subject is very much more complicated than these simplistic explanations would suggest. Today we can surely recognise, as Radzinowicz suggests, 'that the Lombrosian doctrine has now been relegated to the status of a myth, and can safely be placed, together with the theories of his forerunners, in the historical repository of criminology'[8].

The widespread acceptance of the Lombrosian approach owed much to the work of his disciples *Garofalo* who wrote a book in explanation and support of Lombroso in 1885, and *Enrico Ferri* (1856–1929). Both made extensive modifications to the more extreme claims of Lombroso, and recognised the part played in crime by environmental influences. Indeed Ferri's classic work was entitled *Criminal Sociology*[9]. Later Italian scholars such as *Di Tullio* have added a

5 C. S. Kenny, in *The Modern Approach to Criminal Law* (1948), eds. J. W. C. Turner and L. Radzinowicz, p. 5.
6 Radzinowicz (1965) p. 46.
7 See the letter to The Times, 6 March 1958 from Professor L. Dudley Stamp, commenting on the article published 4 March 1958 entitled 'Inventor of Phrenology: The Bicentenary of Dr. Gall, who related character to the skull'.
8 Radzinowicz (1965) p. 46.
9 First published in 1884. An English translation was published in 1917 and republished in 1967.

psychiatric dimension to the discussion which still has a powerful anthropological flavour with all its talk of 'the criminal personality'[10]. Jerome Hall remarks that it was Ferri who 'supplied the zeal and oratory . . . which established the Positive School as a vital force in criminology'[11]. We shall hear more about 'positivist' criminology in connection with the attacks upon it emanating from the radical school of modern criminologists[12]. For the moment we should note that several other schools of thought about the explanation for crime emerged during the early part of the twentieth century. There were the mental testers, like H. H. Goddard[13] who believed that low intelligence and feeble-mindedness provided the explanation for criminal behaviour. Then there were the psychoanalysts and their supporters who applied Freudian theory and other analytical theories to the study of crime. *Aichhorn*[14] led the way in 1925 with his classic book entitled *Wayward Youth* but there were others.

Psychology has contributed to criminology in the twentieth century not only through the psychoanalytical approach, but also through the researches and writings of scholars like H. J. Eysenck[15] and G. Trasler[16] in Britain, and Bandura and Walters[17] in America. Different versions of what has come to be known as 'learning theory' have been developed and applied to the explanation of criminal behaviour. The sociologist E. H. Sutherland[18] may also be regarded as having adopted and developed a learning theory not based primarily in psychology but in sociology.

The greatest contribution to criminology in the twentieth century has undoubtedly come from sociology. Interest in the environment of the offender has taken many forms, from the simply geographical to the more sophisticated modern interactionist theories and viewpoint. Efforts to study crime from a multiple factor approach have been severely criticised but still command powerful support[19]. Finally we may mention the studies designed to provide an instrument capable of

10 B. Di Tullio, *Horizons in Clinical Criminology* (1969).
11 Jerome Hall (1947) p. 548.
12 See I. Taylor, P. Walton and J. Young, *The New Criminology* (1973).
13 H. H. Goddard, *Feeblemindedness* (1914).
14 A. Aichhorn, *Wayward Youth* (1925).
15 H. J. Eysenck, *Crime and Personality* (1977).
16 G. Trasler, *The Explanation of Criminality* (1962).
17 A. Bandura, *Social Learning Theory* (1977); *Aggression* (1973); A. Bandura and R. H. Walters, *Social Learning and Personality Development* (1963).
18 E. H. Sutherland and D. Cressey, *Principles of Criminology* (10th edn., 1978).
19 See, for example, the comment in D. J. West and D. P. Farrington, *Who Becomes Delinquent?* (1973) p. 201: 'However unfashionable or inconvenient, a multi-causal theoretical approach seems necessary'.

being used to predict the onset or recurrence of criminal behaviour. Prediction studies, as they are called, which are linked with the name of Glueck and Hermann Mannheim and Leslie Wilkins, have also been severely criticised[20].

This sketch of the history of criminology should end with the realisation that no simple or easy solutions have yet been found to the vexed problem of criminal behaviour. Much remains to be done. The shape and direction of modern criminological research is not necessarily concerned with uncovering the causes of crime. More often it is concerned with explaining its characteristics with a view to a better understanding of the criminal process, and with exploring the criminal justice system itself and the way it operates. This may possibly help in terms of crime prevention or protection against crime, but it is submitted that such understanding and knowledge of the crime problem needs no such practical justification since it alerts us to hitherto hidden and unrealised dimensions of the subject, and adds significantly to the total store of human knowledge.

Notes. The history of criminology

1 The early precursors
F. G. Gall (1758–1828) advanced the theory that each human function had an organic seat in a particular area of the brain. This 'faculty-phrenology' is now discredited. See W. A. Bonger, *An Introduction to Criminology* (1936) pp. 45–46.
Pinel (1745–1826) was a French doctor of medicine who first emphasised the importance of mental disease in understanding crime: Bonger (1936) p. 44.
Esquirol (1772–1840) a pupil of Pinel's, wrote a treatise on mental diseases: Bonger (1936) p. 45.
J. C. Prichard was the author of a treatise on insanity in 1835.
H. Maudsley (1835–1918) wrote treatises entitled *Physiology and Pathology of Mind* (1867) and *Crime and Insanity* (1872): Bonger (1936) pp. 57–58.

2 The Italian School
On *Lombroso*, see the essay by Professor C. S. Kenny, 'The Italian Theory of Crime: Cesare Lombroso' in *The Modern Approach to Criminal Law* (1948), eds. L. Radzinowicz and J. W. C. Turner; H. Mannheim, 'Lombroso and his

20 S. and E. Glueck, *Predicting Delinquency* (1959); H. Mannheim and L. T. Wilkins, *Prediction Methods in Relation to Borstal Training* (1955); F. H. Simon, *Prediction Methods in Criminology* (1971), Home Office Research Studies No. 7.

Place in Modern Criminology' *Group Problems in Crime and Punishment* (1955) pp. 69; M. E. Wolfgang, 'Cesare Lombroso' in *Pioneers in Criminology* (1960), ed. H. Mannheim, pp. 168.

On *Garofalo* see Jerome Hall (1947) p. 547, who described him as 'the first theoretician of the School, . . . and a judge and scholar of definitely speculative bent'. See also F. A. Allen, 'Raffaele Garofalo' in *Pioneers in Criminology* (1960), ed. H. Mannheim, p. 254. On *Ferri* see T. Sellin, 'Enrico Ferri' in *Pioneers in Criminology* (1960), ed. H. Mannheim, p. 277.

3 The views of the Italian School were bitterly attacked by, among others, the French sociologists Lacassagne (1843–1924) and Tarde (1843–1904). *Lacassagne*, who was professor of juridical medicine at the University of Lyons, emphasised the importance of the social milieu. To him is ascribed the wellknown aphorism that 'Societies get the criminals they deserve'.

Gabriel Tarde, a French jurist and sociologist, published his book *La Criminalité comparée* in 1886. In his view criminality was not an anthropological but a social phenomenon, dominated in exactly the same way as other social facts, by imitation. See Bonger (1936) p. 80.

Chapter 2

Physical and constitutional factors

The way in which the tenets of the Classical School came under attack from the exponents of the Positive School of criminology during the latter part of the nineteenth century has already been described. Mention has also been made of the criticisms expressed against the beliefs of the latter on the ground that the view of crime as a largely inherited tendency was untenable. In this chapter, after discussing the Lombrosian theory of crime in more detail, we shall show how, although the theory in its purest form did not survive, there were other scholars who developed variations on the same theme of the relation of physical endowment to criminal behaviour which gained some support, and are still adhered to in some quarters at the present day. We shall also examine and evaluate the modern biological evidence tending to support the view that genetic factors do play a significant role in criminal behaviour.

Physical endowment

The Lombrosian theory in its purest form involved the belief that criminals were a distinct physical type, which could be recognised by the possession of certain distinct physical traits or characteristics, known as *stigmata*. They were mainly measurements of the cranium and observations of the shape of the ears, the facial bones, the shape of the forehead, the nature of the lips, hair and teeth. Possession of five of the eighteen characteristics was a sure sign of a criminal type. On this view, crime was essentially inborn or inherited; the criminal man, the *l'uomo delinquente* in the title of Lombroso's book, was seen as an atavistic creature – an anthropological throw-back to primitive man. Lombroso was persuaded to modify his position and recognise the relevance of environmental factors, probably under the influence of his colleagues Garofalo and Ferri. Vold points out that he 'never claimed that "the born criminal" constituted more than 40 per cent, probably less, only about a third of the total criminal population'[1]. Lombroso developed a classification of criminal types which attributed considerable influence to mental illness as well as constitutional endowment. This was in line with his background as an army doctor who had worked in mental hospitals and observed similar types there and in prisons. It also fitted in with the philosophy of the times.

Garofalo and Ferri, although usually coupled with Lombroso as believing in physical type explanations of crime, each had a somewhat different emphasis and style of explanation. Garofalo was interested in criminal psychology and the anthropological theory of adaptation, deriving from Darwin. He did not identify himself wholly with Lombroso[2]. Ferri was much more sociologically inclined, but even though he called his treatise *Criminal Sociology* he insisted that it should be seen as only part of a larger whole in which criminal biology played a significant part. 'Criminal sociology is inseparable from criminal biology', he maintained, and despite his strong socialist convictions he never believed that social causes were the sole causes of crime[3]. He may be regarded as one of the most colourful and influential figures in criminology[4].

The criticism of the Lombrosian theory of crime remained on a theoretical level until, working independently from one another, a German and an English scholar provided the scientific evidence to refute the theory of the physical criminal type. Adolf Baer's work in 1893 was apparently unknown to Dr. Charles Goring who in 1913 published his book called *The English Convict*[5]. Goring was a prison doctor with links with University College London where the use of statistics had been developed to an advanced level. Using statistical techniques superior to those employed by Lombroso, Goring was able to disprove completely the existence of a criminal type which could be identified solely by head measurements (the cephalic index) and other physical characteristics. This was done by comparing criminals with a control group drawn from the non-criminal population. It was shown that the physical characteristics which Lombroso contended marked out the criminal population were just as common among the non-criminal population. Comparing university staff and students with criminals, he found no appreciable difference, and concluded that 'no

1 G. B. Vold, *Theoretical Criminology* (1958) p. 31. See also p. 50.
2 Ibid., p. 38.
3 S. Schafer, *Theories in Criminology* (1969) p. 132.
4 Sellin, 'The Lombrosian Myth in Criminology' 42 Am Jo Soc 898-899 (May 1937).
5 Published in 1913, the work was republished in an abridged edition in 1919 by HMSO.

evidence has emerged confirming the existence of a physical criminal type'. Adolf Baer[6] had arrived at a similar conclusion.

Goring's work is not immune to criticism, on several different grounds[7]. His handling of statistics was sometimes rather dubious, and led Hooton to doubt his conclusions. Moreover, he was not so much opposed to Lombroso's conclusions as his method, and himself accepted the role of constitutional factors, believing that the criminal was characterised by poor physique and low intelligence. He stressed the importance of these biological factors. One weakness of his work was that the evidence of low intelligence was arrived at in a rather subjective way instead of using the more scientific and objective test already available at this time (the Simon-Binet scale of intelligence). It should be noted that although Goring stressed the role of constitutional factors, he investigated a wide range of social factors, for example, age, social class, occupation, marital status, and what he called the influence of contagion.

After the work of Baer and Goring, one would expect to hear no more about the Lombrosian theory of the physical criminal type. But in Europe the anthropological view of crime continued to have its exponents, as it has done to the present day, and the influence of these ideas continues to prevail.

The neo Lombrosian theories

It also happened that psychiatrists began to interest themselves in the relation between the body and the mind, something which had occurred to scholars since the dawn of science and philosophy. A German psychiatrist Ernst Kretschmer published in 1921 a treatise entitled *Physique and Character*[8], which set out to demonstrate that there was a relationship between body type and certain forms of mental illness. The classification of physical characteristics was achieved by dividing people into one of three physical types (these are known as somatotypes) as follows:

6 A. Baer, *Der Verbrecher in Anthropologischer Beziehung* (1893).
7 See the essay by Edwin D. Driver in *Pioneers in Criminology* (1960), ed. H. Mannheim, p. 335. E. A. Hooton suggests that Goring was biased in his approach to Lombroso, but Hooton may have been biased about Goring; E. A. Hooton, *Crime and the Man* (1939) p. 16.
8 First published in an English translation by W. J. H. Sprott in 1925, the second English edition, revised, with an appendix by Dr. Emanuel Miller, appeared in 1936.

1 Asthenic (Leptosome)	characterised by a deficiency of thickness in the face, neck, trunk, extremities, skin, fat, muscle, bone and vascular system.
2 Athletic	characterised by strong development of the body, and muscles, with wide shoulders, a deep chest and tapering trunk.
3 Pyknic	characterised by medium height, rotund figure with a soft broad face, short, massive neck, soft hands, and generally well rounded appearance.
[Dysplastic	a fourth type was recognised characterised by physical anomalies and disproportions.]

Regarding temperament, Kretschmer saw the tendency towards mental illness, and mental illness itself, in terms of two main kinds of temperament, cycloid or schizoid, according to whether the tendency was towards cyclic mental illness of the manic-depressive type, or was towards schizophrenia. (When the illness itself was present the temperament was described as cyclothyme or schizothyme.) Kretschmer saw a tendency for pyknic types of physique to occur most frequently among cycloids and cyclothymes, and asthenic and athletic types to occur most frequently among schizoid personalities and schizothymes. The work was mainly done on male subjects, since women's physical proportions were less strikingly differentiated according to Kretschmer[9].

Research building on Kretschmer's typology has endeavoured to relate it to crime, and it was said that there was a greater tendency towards crime among schizothymes, and that broadly speaking asthenic and athletic types predominated among persistent criminals. Occasional offenders were predominantly of the pyknic type[10]. Efforts have been made to relate physical type to the kind of crime committed, it being claimed that athletic types tend to commit crimes of violence and robbery, asthenic types petty theft, and pyknics fraud. The better view is that there is no relation between physical endowment and the type of crime committed except that, for example, it takes some physical strength and agility to rob another. Nigel Walker discussed the possibility of natural selection influencing juvenile delinquency but does not suggest any conclusion[11].

9 pp. 20–21.
10 See S. Hurwitz, *Criminology* (1953) p. 130.
11 N. Walker, *Crime and Punishment in Britain* (revsd. edn., 1968) p. 47.

American criminologists have contributed another dimension to the subject, if that is the way to put it, by developing further the study of physical type in relation to human behaviour, and in particular criminal behaviour. There have been two major contributors, both coming from Harvard.

E. A. Hooton's research, which extended over many years, and included over 17,000 subjects, related physique to behaviour among criminals, the mentally ill and non-criminals, differentiating the different American racial groups with some particularity. His conclusion was that the criminals constituted an inferior group in biological terms, and that the biological factor could not be ruled out in the explanation of crime. 'On the whole, the biological superiority of the civilian to the delinquent is quite as certain as his sociological superiority'[12]. He was led to assert that society should protect itself from incorrigible offenders by isolating them in some reservation so that they could not contaminate the rest of the population or prey on them by crime[13].

Not unnaturally, this research came in for severe criticism not only for its conclusions but for its method. The sociologist Sutherland levelled three devastating criticisms directed towards the scientific value of Hooton's work[14]. Reading Hooton today one cannot fail to be astonished and amused at some of his attitudes and value judgments. However, this much is to be said in his favour: he made a powerful case for not regarding crime as a purely sociological phenomenon and reminded us that one must always consider both the organism and its environment and their interaction[15].

Hooton's work also stimulated another Harvard scholar, W. H. Sheldon, to examine the relationship between physique and personality[16]. Unlike Kretschmer, he viewed the physical or physiological component not as being divided into three distinct types but as present in varying degrees among humans so that one could measure the degree of strength of each component and classify people physically in terms of these components, which were measured on a seven point scale. Thus the extremes would be indicated by a score 7–1–1, 1–7–1, 1–1–7, according to the strength of each of the three

---

12 E. A. Hooton, *Crime and the Man* (1939) p. 376.
13 pp. 391–392.
14 E. H. Sutherland and D. R. Cressey, *Principles of Criminology* (1960) p. 104.
15 p. 387.
16 W. H. Sheldon, *The Varieties of Human Physique* (1940), *The Varieties of Temperament* (1942), *Varieties of Delinquent Youth* (1949).

components, and a balanced type would score 4 4 4[17]. The three types of component were differently labelled compared with Kretschmer but otherwise comparable;

1 endomorphic   (soft and well-rounded)

2 mesomorphic   (muscle and bone)

3 ectomorphic   (thin and fragile)

These were related to temperament, as in Kretschmer, but Sheldon, like Hooton, went further and related the types to criminal behaviour. There is no need to describe here in detail the three types of temperament identified by Sheldon after examing 60 different personality traits, nor to discuss the way they related to the physical components in their different combinations. It will suffice to say that the transition from structure to function which is involved in relating body types to temperament remains central to his analysis. In a study of 200 youths who had been referred to a private institution for delinquent and maladjusted youths in Boston between 1939 and 1946 (the Hayden Goodwill Inn), Sheldon found evidence of a hereditary physical type which he claimed could be identified in children at the age of six. Delinquents, he claimed, tended to be mesomorphic or endomorphic rather than ectomorphic[18].

There are problems concerning Sheldon's definition of delinquency in terms of 'disappointing behaviour', and concerning Sheldon's avowed belief in biological determinism. Like Hooton his discussion reads strangely today. His generalisations are mostly rather facile and specious, and he seems almost to be imitating Hooton's garish style[19].

Yet the prevalence of the idea of relating behaviour to physique is witnessed both by some further research carried out in the United States by the Gluecks and Cortes and Gatti, and also by the interest shown by British psychiatrists such as Parnell and Gibbens. The Harvard criminologists Sheldon Glueck and Eleanor Thorold Glueck included an investigation of physiological factors as part of

17 See W. H. Sheldon (1949) pp. 14 15 and P. W. Tappan, *Crime, Justice and Correction* (1960) p. 91. Tappan gives the example that 'a subject with a somatotype of 5 4 2 would be most strongly endomorphic but with a considerable mesomorphic component and a small ectomorphic element in his structure. He would be termed a mesomorphic endomorph'.

18 See D. R. Taft, *Criminology* (3rd edn., 1956) p. 117.

19 Once again Sutherland subjected the study to devastating analysis, criticising Sheldon's methodology on the ground of subjective scoring and overlapping categories.

their comprehensive attempt to unravel juvenile delinquency, published in 1950[20]. Dr. Carl C. Seltzer, who had assisted Sheldon, reported that there was a striking and statistically significant relationship between mesomorphy and crime[1]. This evidence sufficiently impressed the Gluecks to lead them to include a mesomorphic constitution as one of the predisposing factors in relation to crime[2]. In so doing they are careful to point out that they do not wish to imply any Lombrosian hypothesis of a type of born criminal, or any theory about the relative importance of the constitutional factor[3]. Indeed they point out that 'there are instances in which the delinquents are more ectomorphic than mesomorphic in constitution, and cases in which the delinquents are of the introverted, psychoneurotic temperament'. Nevertheless they regarded the question as sufficiently important to devote a whole volume to the re-examination of the evidence, which was published in 1956[4].

Here the Gluecks examine the role of body build in the etiology of crime. The question they set out to answer was what personal traits, out of 67 which were selected, were significantly related to delinquency in the various body types. The assumption tested is that, if body structure is relevant to delinquency, some traits would vary significantly in their association with delinquency between the various body types, showing a greater influence on delinquency in some types as compared with others. Also investigated is the effect of certain socio-cultural factors on delinquency in the different physical types. Forty seven such factors are investigated. The result of all this is the conclusion that while in general individuals of a mesomorphic build are more prone to delinquency, the sensitive ectomorph is more likely to be adversely affected by a variety of social variables. Moreover the mesomorph whose personality does not match his physique and the expectations that this arouses from others may be subject to added stress. Also the absence of suitable environmental facilities, in the way of recreational opportunities, may be more detrimental in the case of mesomorphs. What is here argued is a much more subtle and sophisticated relationship between physical endowment and behaviour involving a careful consideration of character traits or personality factors. But the emphasis on physical endowment being significant remains throughout and has in no way been abandoned.

20 S. and E. T. Glueck, *Unraveling Juvenile Delinquency* (1950).
1 See Gluecks (1950) Appendix C, pp. 307–351.
2 p. 16.
3 p. 282.   **4** S. and E. T. Glueck, *Physique and Delinquency* (1956).

In Britain psychiatrists have continued to pay attention to Sheldon's theory, and measurements of body components still play some part in research concerning behaviour, including delinquent behaviour. Thus in 1958 Parnell produced a practical guide to somatotyping for use by psychiatrists. He discusses why Sheldon's method of somatotyping did not come into general use, and suggests certain improvements, and difficulties encountered in applying the technique. He concludes that 'evidence is steadily collecting that the influence of somatotype on personality is strong'[5].

Trevor Gibbens in his study of borstal youths included an attempt to somatotype his subjects, but only a bare majority of the lads agreed to be photographed in the nude for this purpose. Nevertheless Gibbens claimed that his results confirmed those of Sheldon and the Gluecks[6]. Nigel Walker in his criminology text reproduces a table from the Gluecks' 1956 study, and says this 'appears to confirm' Sheldon's finding[7]. Walker also points out that the Gluecks found that mesomorphs were less sensitive than other physical types and these types predominated among delinquents.

In 1972 Cortes and Gatti added a further dimension to the debate about physique and crime[8]. In their book, the subtitle of which speaks of a biopsychosocial approach, they argue that the constitutional factors and environmental factors should be seen as essentially inter-related, and that the constitutional factors, upon which the study largely concentrates its attention, should be seen 'only as part of a whole, as a pole of the two social continuum'. It is admitted that 'very probably the decisive factors lie on the opposite (or social) pole of this continuum'[9]. The book reports the results of a study of the physique of a sample of 100 adjudicated delinquents compared with a control group, using Parnell's method of somatotyping. The conclusion is that 'there can be little doubt that mesomorphy is a variable in delinquency and crime, and that mesomorphs possess a greater delinquency *potential*'[10]. Mesomorphy is seen as the energetic, masculine component of physique. Contrary to the views of scholars like Lombroso, Goring and Hooton who saw delinquents as physically inferior, if

5 R. W. Parnell, *Behaviour and Physique: An Introduction to Practical and Applied Somatotyping* (1958) p. 101.
6 T. C. N. Gibbens, *Psychiatric Studies of Borstal Lads* (1963).
7 N. Walker, *Crime and Punishment in Britain* (1968) p. 46.
8 J. B. Cortes and F. M. Gatti, *Delinquency and Crime: A Biopsychosocial Approach* (1972).
9 p. 7.
10 p. 346.

anything they are now seen as physically superior. The authors see a link between mesomorphy and extraversion and poor amenability to conditioning, about which we shall speak later.

Problems remain with regard to relating physical type to delinquency. So far only juveniles or young adults have been investigated except for Hooton's extensive studies of the American criminal. The most obvious characteristic of juvenile and adolescent crime is its physical, athletic nature. The activities of delinquent youth frequently involve street violence and misbehaviour, car theft and taking automobiles without consent, and offences connected with drink and drug abuse. These types of behaviour may be expected to occur more frequently among mesomorphic youths. Is one saying more in this connection than describing one further characteristic of youth crime? There may be more to be said about the less direct relationship between physique and crime suggested by the Gluecks' research, where it is seen that sometimes when one's temperament or personality does not match one's physical endowment, this creates problems of adjustment, which, if not satisfactorily resolved, may result in a delinquent outcome. Sheldon suggests something of the kind in discussing the dysplastic type[11].

A very experienced English prison medical officer who had studied the question in connection with various samples, and reached no firm conclusions, suggests that 'the thesis of an association between physique and character should be applied in the field of criminology with extreme caution'[12]. The American sociologist Vold concluded that the physical type theories turn out to be a more or less sophisticated form of shadow-boxing with a much more subtle and difficult to get at problem, namely, that of the constitutional factor in human behaviour. 'There is no present evidence at all of physical type as such, having any consistent relation to legally and sociologically defined crime'[13]. He suggests that improved research may help to show such a relationship in the future. Meanwhile the prudent course would be to suspend judgment about the relation between physical endowment and human behaviour.

Notes. Physique and crime

1 On Lombroso's theory of crime, G. B. Vold (1958) gives a detailed account of the theory and discusses the extent of Lombroso's claims, and his

11 Sheldon (1949) p. 805.
12 Sir Norwood East, *Society and the Criminal* (1949) p. 87.
13 G. B. Vold, *Theoretical Criminology* (1958) p. 74.

modifications introduced in later years: pp. 28 et seq.; pp. 52 et seq. Hooton (1939), discussing Lombroso, 'finds it necessary to agree with much of the adverse criticism which has been directed against previous anthropological studies of the criminal'. He says that both the atavistic and degenerative views of crime are rejected (p. 13). Lombroso is criticised for inadequate sample size, mixing up ethnic and racial strains which are diverse, and lacking a scientific method of statistical analysis (p. 14). Sheldon (1940) says that the principal theoretical conception for which Lombroso is known 'is perhaps a somewhat unfortunate one': p. 306. See also E. A. Hooton, *The American Criminal* (1939) Vol. 1, pp. 11–18. Other European scholars who subscribed to the anthropological view of crime included Louis Vervaeck, *Syllabus du course d'anthropologie criminelle donnée à la prison de Forest* (1926); de Greef, *Introduction à la Criminologie* (1946); Adolf Lenz, *Grundriss der Kriminalbiologie* (1927).

2 On Enrico Ferri's *Criminal Sociology*, the first Italian edition appeared in 1884. An English edition of a portion of the original work edited by Rev. W. Douglas Morrison, appeared in 1897. The 1917 English edition, reprinted in 1967, is a translation from the latest French edition of 1905. The Editorial Preface, by William W. Smithers, says that 'the distinctive contribution of Ferri to the science of criminology has been his insistence that crime is mainly a social phenomenon, though not to be interpreted exclusively as such. He sought to reconcile the physical and anthropological with the social elements in the phenomenon of crime'. ' Ferri may be regarded as Lombroso's most distinguished pupil, and, in a sense, as a continuer of his work, though supplementing it on the sociological side and giving it a greater breadth than Lombroso himself showed': p. xxiii.

3 C. Goring is described by Hooton (1939) as 'a statistical genius' who made 'a more substantial contribution to methods of anthropometric analysis than anyone had made previously'. His book is 'commonly regarded as a final refutation of Lombroso's theories', but he was 'frankly and violently prejudiced against Lombroso and all his theories'. He 'used his statistical genius to distort the results of his investigation to conformity with his bias': p. 16. See also E. A. Hooton, *The American Criminal* (1939) Vol. 1, pp. 18–30. W. H. Sheldon (1940) in the bibliography, describes Goring's work as 'undoubtedly' having 'dealt a lethal blow to the advance of constitutional thought during the generation which followed Goring, for it greatly discouraged the hope of using physical anthropology in social research': p. 304. Vold (1958) gives a detailed discussion of Goring's work: pp. 92 et seq.

4 Hooton is described by Sheldon (1940) as showing by his data 'statistically valid relations between criminal tendency and bodily make-up': p. 305. Hooton's position is summarised by Tappan (1960) pp. 87 et seq., and Vold (1958) pp. 59–63.

5 On phrenology, this is described by Hooton (1939) as a 'pseudo-science': p. 3. Gall and Spurzheim are described by Sheldon (1940) as the founders of the school of phrenology: p. 11. He refers to their joint publication in 1809 in Paris of *Recherches sur le Systeme nerveux*. He goes on to describe how phrenology was replaced following the new scientific spirit generated by Darwin, Huxley and Herbert Spencer. Phrenology 'had neither the calipers nor coefficients of correlation, and so . . . fell upon evil days . . . ': p. 12.

6 On Kretschmer see Vold (1958) pp. 66 et seq.; Sheldon (1940) pp. 25 et seq. Vold is rather critical of attempts to study the Kretschmer types in relation to criminality. Sheldon says that Kretschmer brilliantly described the three physical types 'but the objective data for discrimination between the types are perfunctory and inadequate': p. 306. He says that 'the concept of types had been useful in the study of personality, but, like the poles supporting a clothesline, it provides only end suspensions for distributive classifications': p. 27. 'Although the concept of types had proved inadequate, and although the indiscriminate application of refined mathematics had been futile, there remained reasonable evidence that relations between physical and mental characteristics do exist': p. 28. Taylor, Walton and Young (1973) mention a recent German study by Klaus Conrad, *Der Konstitutionstypus* (1963) concerning the percentage changes in body build as a child grows up (quoted with approval by Eysenck (1965)). Conrad calculated the head to body length against age, and found that on average children were more mesomorphic and adults more ectomorphic. Adult mesomorphs were said to resemble children of a mean age of eight: such mesomorphs were immature psychologically. Taylor, Walton and Young comment that such a finding concerning body type may well have social origins as children of working class parents are more likely to be mesomorphic, and such persons are more likely to be recruited into a delinquent subculture: p. 43.

On the attempts to relate physical types to different kinds of criminal behaviour, see W. A. Willemse, *Constitution-Types in Delinquency* (1932), and O. Kinberg, *Basic Problems in Criminology* (1935). See Reckless (1961) p. 383.

7 On Sheldon, Parnell (1958) gives a useful description of his method and its shortcomings. He suggests that a two dimensional scheme, omitting ectomorphs, would be preferable. The method of measurement on the basis of nude photographs leads to objections and refusals, resulting in unrepresentative samples: pp. 2–5. Vold is critical of Sheldon's criterion of delinquency: Vold (1958) p. 70. Sheldon began his work at Chicago, following the method employed by Naccarati and applying it to American college students. He admits that the results were uniformly negative insofar as they concerned the attempt to relate intellect to physique. 'It had become clear that the missing vital link between psychology and physical anthropology was not to be found in anthropometry and statistical precision alone, however valuable these two aids might later prove to be': Sheldon (1940) p. 20. He was attracted by the

method of clinical observation employed by Kretschmer. He points out that Kretschmer later abandoned the third type (athletic) and fell back on two types, the pyknic and leptosomic. There are difficulties about the description of the types and the handling of the data in the Tables. Sheldon concludes 'The difficulty lies simply in the fact that Kretschmer's conception of polar types implies a bimodality of distribution which is untrue to life. There are not three kinds of people – there is a continuous distribution of people, and of physiques': p. 25. In his chapter entitled 'Some theoretical considerations', Sheldon shows that he is aware of some of the problems concerning his method, and discusses whether the conclusions should be regarded as fatalistic, and whether one's physical type can ever change: pp. 411 et seq. He does not regard the constitutional view as necessarily pessimistic because by selective breeding and other measures one could 'strengthen the mental and spiritual fiber of the race', and hope to eliminate the principal contitutional and degenerative physical scourges of the race: p. 437.

8 Gibbens' (1963) study of borstal youths, based on somatotyping just over half the lads, found a marked preponderance of mesomorphic types, the predominance of persons with a muscular constitution comparing closely with that of students at a physical training college (Loughborough) who were training to be teachers of physical education, and contrasting sharply with undergraduates at Oxford, officer cadets at Sandhurst, and medical students. Of 58 youths examined, 29 had predominantly mesomorphic physique, four predominantly endomorphic, seven predominantly ectomorphic and twelve possessed a balanced physique. Further tests provided some confirmation of the Gluecks' (1956) finding of a relationship between physical endowment and temperament or personality.

9 Sir Norwood East addressed himself to the subject of the relationship between physique and crime in a number of papers. There is a chapter in his *Medical Aspects of Crime* (1936) on 'The Relation of the Skull and Brain to Crime'. He there states his conviction that it is unsound to regard criminals as abnormal by constitutional or psychological criteria. We are all potential criminals, he believes: p. 233. In his book *The Roots of Crime* (1954) he argues persuasively that crime is not a disease although it may sometimes result from a disease: pp. 4–5. His major work was the study entitled *The Adolescent Offender* (1942) in which he reported the results of an examination of 4,000 adolescent offenders, comparing first offenders with persistent offenders. In this study he found no evidence of general physical inferiority among the offenders; but he is prepared to regard hereditary factors as important. 'Behaviour is determined by inherited and environmental factors and one or other may predominate in a given situation': p. 64. On the Kretschmer typology of physique he has this to say: 'Daily medical examination in this country of very large numbers of adult and adolescent offenders over many years . . . lead one to doubt whether the types described are so precise and

definite as to warrant far-reaching conclusions': p. 172, and that 'Kretschmer's hypothesis, in spite of its interest and importance, does not seem to be applicable to the practical problems of adolescent crime at the present time': p. 173. See also p. 201.

The chemistry of crime

Twin studies

One method of testing the question of the possible influence of inherited factors on crime which has been pursued by some scholars is to investigate the criminality of identical twins. One should explain that twins are of two types, identical twins, which result from the fertilisation of a single ovum (sometimes called *monozygotic*) and fraternal twins, which result from the simultaneous fertilisation of two separate ova (sometimes called *dizygotic*). Criminologists have studied and compared the behaviour of each twin in samples of monozygotic and dizygotic twins, and claim that criminal behaviour occurs in both twins more frequently in the former than the latter, thus tending to confirm that there is an inherited factor at work.

In 1929 Johannes Lange wrote a book called *Crime as Destiny*[14] in which he reported the results of a study of 30 pairs of adult male twins: thirteen of these were identical twins, seventeen fraternal twins. One member of each pair was a delinquent. It was found that in the case of 77 per cent of the identical twins both twins were delinquent, compared with only 12 per cent in the case of the fraternal twins. This was claimed to furnish convincing evidence of the inheritance of criminality. Other scholars such as Rosanoff, Stumpfl, Legras and Kranz did similar studies, the result of which were less convincing. It should be noted that Lange's study is based on a very small number of cases. Many criminologists have pointed out the weaknesses and shortcomings of the twin studies, but they still have their supporters[15].

In the last 30 years there has been some revival of interest in the twin studies which have been extended in a number of directions. The principal exponent of this method was K. O. Christiansen of Denmark. He was fortunate to be able to draw on the records kept by

---

14 *Crime as Destiny: A Study of Criminal Twins* was published in an English translation in 1931.
15 For example H. J. Eysenck in *Crime and Personality* (1977) gives considerable weight to the evidence of the twin studies.

the Danish authorities, going back to the end of the nineteenth century, identifying twin births. His main work[16] was a study of 6,000 pairs of twins born on the Danish islands between 1880 and 1910 where both the twins survived to the age of fifteen. 900 of these twins were criminal, judged by police records. The study measured the degree of concordance or agreement, comparing monozygotic and dizygotic twins on the question whether the other twin was also criminal. The term 'conditional frequency' was used to express the degree of concordance, and this was examined in relation to (a) crime proper, (b) minor offences, and (c) no offences. Conditional frequency was highest for (c) no offences, which Christiansen explained by saying that most people are non-violators of the law.

Another concept used was that of the 'twin co-efficient' which expresses the relation of the actual frequency of delinquency with the expected frequency over the whole sample. Nigel Walker explains it thus:

'Amongst *all* his male twins the frequency of those convicted of serious crime was about 9.6 per cent. But if a man's twin had been convicted this percentage (i.e. the concordance rate) was as high as 52.7 per cent. The factor by which it exceeds the general frequency of 9.6 per cent (i.e. x 5.49) is the twin co-efficient; and when these co-efficients are compared for monozygotics and dizygotics they measure more accurately than concordance rates the effect of being the monozygotic twin of a convicted man upon one's own chances of conviction'[17].

The twin co-efficient for monozygotics was found to be much higher than for dizygotics, and this seems to be true for both sexes. Other factors such as whether the twins were brought up in an urban or rural environment seem to be important, the twin co-efficient being higher in rural districts than in towns. An English scholar Dr. J. Shields has studied cases where twins were brought up separately from their natural parents[18]. There is also the study by L. Wheelan[19].

Christiansen's work is characterised by extreme scientific caution and he makes no sweeping claims about the results. He recognises the importance of environmental influences and group pressures on the occurrence and development of delinquency. Others have pointed out

16 See his essays in *The Mentally Abnormal Offender* (1968), ed. de Reuck and in *Crime, Criminology and Public Policy* (1974), ed. R. Hood.
17 N. Walker, *Crime and Punishment in Britain* (2nd edn., 1968) p. 49.
18 J. Shields, *Monozygotic Twins brought up apart and together* (1962).
19 L. Wheelan, 'Aggressive Psychopathy in One of a Pair of Uniovular Twins: A Clinical and Experimental Study' BJD Vol. II, p. 140 (1951–52).

that different rates of crime detection must not be ruled out for monozygotic compared with dizygotic twins. There may also be significant differences in the kinds of offences committed. It has been suggested for example that there is a higher rate of concordance for sexual offences than property crimes. Christiansen recognises the many difficulties which still remain to be resolved in evaluating the twin studies. In 1974 he reviewed the evidence and suggested that twin studies can throw interesting light on the interaction of environment and personality, but that they cannot in themselves solve the problem of nature and nurture[20].

The 1974 study explores the relationship between the most serious manifestations of criminality and inheritance. The method used is once again that of calculating concordance rates and expressing the results in terms of a twin co-efficient. The result is to show a higher level of concordance with monozygotic twins than dizygotic twins, although the picture changed when the twin co-efficient was used, and it became clear that both MZ and DZ twins registered much higher co-efficients for the serious crimes than for minor offences. Professor Christiansen concludes that the more serious the crime and the criminal career the greater the similarities as expressed by the twin co-efficient[1]. Nothing in these results can be interpreted however as indicating a preponderant part being played by heredity in the causation of crime, as suggested by Otto Lange[2].

There are several difficulties about this kind of research. One is that there are so few twins where one partner is criminal. Another is the danger of misclassification between identical and fraternal twins, though modern methods of classification reduce error to a minimum, and Nigel Walker has observed that the direction of any mistake is usually to classify as a fraternal twin one who should be classified as identical, which must only serve to reduce the concordance rate differences thus reinforcing the conclusion in the direction of the inherited factor[3]. A further possibility is that differences have occurred in childhood experience and parental care. Shields' study in 1962 of monozygotic twins brought up together and apart allowed for this factor, but he was mainly concerned with personality dimensions, and the study appears to confirm that there is a marked genetic factor underlying such traits of personality as extraversion, neuroticism and intelligence[4].

20 Op. cit., p. 67, note 3.
 1 Ibid., p. 75.   2 Ibid., p. 77.
 3 N. Walker, op. cit., p. 50.   4 Op. cit., note 5.

Nigel Walker suggests that there may be more room for the genetic factor with regard to adult crime than juvenile delinquency, where environmental factors may have a more pronounced effect[5]. But in any case, Walker thinks that the evidence though it is strong is not conclusive – no-one has found 100 per cent concordance between delinquency and inheritance.

Shah and Roth[6] deprecate any tendency to view these matters in terms of a choice between inheritance and environment. They prefer the view that all human behaviour is a result of a combination of factors and influences some of which are hereditary and some environmental. Nor is it right to limit the debate to hereditary factors which are congenital or innate. Some biological factors may be better described as constitutional factors or conditions existing in the physical and nervous system. 'Recent advances in the biological sciences have led to a veritable explosion of knowledge concerning the variety of biological factors influencing human behaviour'[7]. Moreover there is a continuous interaction between an organism and its environment which natural scientists have come to recognise[8]. From this standpoint one cannot separate the biological factors entirely from the social and environmental factors: it is their interaction which needs to be understood.

A further contribution to the twin studies has come from two Norwegian scholars, Dalgard and Kringlen, who reported in 1976 the results of a Norwegian study[9]. They preface this with a useful review of the previous twin studies, concluding that these gave a consistently higher concordance for MZ compared with DZ twins. However, there are problems of interpretation. Christiansen's 1968 study, like their own, showed only a very small difference in concordance for MZ compared with DZ twins, much smaller than had previously been reported.

Dalgard and Kringlen took 139 male twin pairs where one or both the twins had been convicted, born in the period 1921–1930, and checked for crime in December 1966. Zygosity diagnosis was according to the most rigorous tests. 49 MZ and 89 DZ twins were discovered, and one pair undiagnosed. So far as possible, each twin

5 p. 50.
6 Saleem A. Shah and Loren H. Roth, 'Biological and Psychophysiological Factors in Criminality' in *Handbook of Criminology* (1900), ed. D. Glaser, p. 101.
7 Loc. cit., p. 101.
8 Ibid., p. 106.
9 O. S. Dalgard and E. Kringlen, 'A Norwegian Twin Study of Criminality' BJC Vol. 16, p. 213 (July 1976).

pair was traced and interviewed. There were only four pairs where no interview was obtained with either twin. In 70 per cent of cases both twins were interviewed. Concordance rates were calculated using both a broad concept of crime and a narrower much stricter concept, including only violence, sexual assault, theft and robbery. Differences were observed which were not statistically significant. When allowance was made for differences in environmental influences the differences in the concordance figures disappeared. The writers conclude that the significance of hereditary factors in registered crime is non-existent[10].

They recognise that their findings are at variance with most of the literature on twins and crime, and discuss possible explanations for this, such as the sampling method employed, and tests of zygosity. They believe that sampling errors and unreliable zygosity diagnosis led previous studies to observe too great a difference in concordance rates. They conclude by boldly asserting that when differences in environmental influences are taken into account their findings showed that hereditary factors are of no significance in the etiology of common crime[11].

This study has been severely criticised by Forde[12] for its scientific procedure in measuring the types of crime committed and the testing of environmental influences. Forde believes that 'twin studies cannot provide a final answer to these problems unless they include the study of twins separated shortly after birth and reared apart'. He says that before dismissing the influence of inheritance one should look at certain non-twin studies such as the adoption studies of Hutchings and Mednick[13], and chromosome studies. This we shall now proceed to do.

Chromosome research

In the last two decades considerable interest has been aroused by the suggestion, based on research with mental patients and prisoners, that chromosome imbalance powerfully influences behaviour, including criminal behaviour. To understand the research on which this suggestion is based one must understand something about genetic endowment, in particular in respect of chromosomes.

10 Ibid., p. 226.
11 Ibid., p. 231.
12 R. A. Forde, 'Twin Studies, Inheritance and Criminality' BJC Vol. 18, p. 71 (January 1978).
13 B. Hutchings and S. A. Mednick carried out research on Danish adoptions and crime: see post, p. 35.

Each human cell contains 23 pairs of chromosomes, in 22 of which each member of the pair closely resembles the other, when seen under the microscope. With the twenty-third pair, the two chromosomes look identical in women but different in men. These are the sex chromosomes which determine, among other matters, gender. They are referred to as XX in women and XY in men. Various abnormalities may occur. These have been studied, and in particular the case of males in possession of an extra X chromosome (XXY) or an extra Y chromosome (XYY)[14].

In 1965 Dr. Patricia Jacobs and her colleagues in the mental hospital at Carstairs, Edinburgh, reported the results of an examination of the chromosomes of a sample of mentally subnormal men at various Scottish prisons[15]. They found that a significant proportion of the men possessed chromosome abnormalities, the most frequent being the XYY variety. Later research suggested that the extra Y chromosome was related primarily to the men's aggressive behaviour rather than to mental subnormality. A noticeable feature of this group was that the men were unusually tall.

In 1968 further research by Dr. Mary A. Telfer and others in Pennsylvania appeared to confirm the British observations. They found 'that gross chromosomal errors contribute . . . to the pool of antisocial aggressive males who are mentally ill and who become institutionalized for criminal behaviour'. But it should be observed that only one in eleven of Dr. Telfer's sample (twelve out of 129 patients) had abnormal chromosomes, and seven of these twelve had an extra female chromosome and only five an extra male chromosome. The sample was itself a rather selective one, being drawn from the population of four institutions for offenders by taking only those inmates 71 inches or over in height (5 feet 11 inches and above)[15a]. Further research in the United States by Dr. Richard F. Daly at Wisconsin University appeared to confirm the association between abnormal height and chromosome abnormality[16].

A Norwegian scholar J. Nielsen went so far as to argue that the evidence justified adopting a special defence in law to excuse such persons possessed of an extra Y chromosome from criminal liability[17].

---

14 For a plate showing normal chromosome distribution see H. Prins, *Criminal Behaviour* (1973) following p. 49.

15 P. Jacobs et al., 'Aggressive Behaviour, Mental Subnormality and the XYY Male' Nature Vol. 208, p. 1351 (1965).

15a Richard F. Daly, Nature Vol. 221, p. 472 (1969).

16 M. A. Telfer et al., Science Vol. 159, p. 1249 (March 1968).

17 J. Nielsen, 'XYY Syndrome in a Mental Hospital' BJC Vol. 8, p. 186 (1968).

Not surprisingly the matter attracted considerable attention from the media and received widespread publicity.

Research in Britain continued to investigate the question. Most British scientists have concluded that the evidence so far available is suggestive rather than conclusive and that it is too early to say that any definite relationship has been established between chromosome abnormality and criminality. In Australia, New Zealand, Canada and Israel there have been scientific investigations and discussions, and no doubt elsewhere as well.

The conclusions of the Cambridge symposium in 1969[18] were that too much should not be made of the association between chromosomes and crimes. The matter had been overstated. The fact is that XYY males seem to behave less violently and show less aggression than other inmates of institutions and they commit their crimes more often against property than against persons. The XYY syndrome is less important than had been at first supposed.

Other variations in the chromosome typologies have proved just as interesting, for example, the long Y chromosome has been studied by Dr. J. Kahn of the Maudsley Hospital in London. In 1976 Dr. Kahn reported the results of a careful study of 436 borstal lads compared with 254 controls[19]. He was concerned with the incidence of freak chromosomes generally, and in particular the long Y variant. In fact he only found one XYY subject in the whole study and that was in the control group! The results did suggest that a long Y variant involved a higher risk of delinquency. Dr. Kahn's further work on the same sample has led him to the conclusion that the way a child possessing an extra Y chromosome is brought up may have a great deal to do with the outcome. Such children are often difficult, restless, likely to play truant from school, and generally speaking have a lower threshold of tolerance to a deprived environment than other children. However the incidence of abnormal chromosomes is so rare that one cannot justify any social policy by way of early intervention designed to prevent delinquency. The statistics show that about one in 1,000 male births are affected in this way. It is virtually impossible to predict how such a child will grow up and whether or not there will be behaviour problems. The vast majority of offenders however possess normal chromosomes (i.e. males are XY). Kahn regretted in 1976 that more

---

18 *Criminological Implications of Chromosome Abnormalities* (1969) ed. D. J. West.

19 J. Kahn et al., 'A Survey of Y Chromosome Variants and Personality in 436 Borstal Lads and 254 Controls' BJC Vol. 16, p. 233 (July 1976).

was not known about the biological fathers of the subjects possessing an abnormal chromosome in the form of a Y variant.

The adoption studies

The deficiency referred to by Kahn has now been remedied to some extent by the work of Hutchings and Mednick in Denmark[20]. In what may be described as the adoption studies they used the register of all non-familial adoptions in Denmark between 1924 and 1947, which contained information about the biological and adoptive parents of each child adopted. In one of their studies they took 1,145 male adoptees born in Copenhagen between 1927 and 1941. 16 per cent of these had been convicted of crime (185). Of these they traced the natural fathers of 143, and took a control group of non-adoptive sons matched on age of child and social class of adoptive father. They were then able to make comparisons of adoptive sons and non-adoptive sons with biological (or natural) and adoptive fathers, in regard to registered criminality. The results may be demonstrated thus:

Registered criminality in biological and adoptive fathers of criminal adoptees

	N	Biological Father	Adoptee Father
Criminal adoptive sons	143	70	33
Control non-adoptive sons	143	40	14

The high proportion of sons whose natural or biological father was also criminal suggests that genetic factors do play some role in the etiology of registered crime in Denmark.

The conclusion expressed by Mednick is as follows:

'Evidence has been presented which suggests that biological factors do play some role in the etiology of criminality. It is suggested that longitudinal studies be undertaken in order to help determine the precise mode of action of these biological factors especially with respect to their interactions with milieu factors. The results support an hypothesis of the existence of genetic influence in the etiology of criminality'[1].

20 S. A. Mednick, 'The Biological Model', Proceedings of the II International Symposium on Criminology, CICRIB, Sao Paulo, Brazil, 1975. B. Hutchings and S. A. Mednick, 'Registered criminality in the adoptive and biological parents of registered male adoptees' in S. A. Mednick, *Genetics, Environment and Psychopathology* (1974).
1 Loc. cit., p. 16.

There are problems about the validity of the results of these adoption studies. Hutchings[2] recognises several limitations. The first and most important, he says, is 'the possibility that the adoption procedure results in selective placement, promoting correspondence between the adoptive home and the characteristics of the biological parents'. In terms of social class and cultural background this may well be true, but it hardly explains the difference in the incidence of crime observed between adoptive and natural fathers. More likely to be operating is a second factor, selective influences at work in choosing the adoptive parents. Hutchings admits 'that screening takes place both with regard to the children who are put up for adoption and of the prospective parents'. What is known about adoption procedure suggests that this is indeed a major limitation. Great care would be taken to avoid placing children in homes where one or both the adoptive parents were likely to be criminal. A third limitation concerns the fact that the study concentrated on serious crime, which in Denmark is classified as the concern of the state prosecutor, which crimes are likened to indictable offences in England and Wales. But a vast range of offences are dealt with in Denmark as police offences (politisager) and there is considerable discretion about this. Perhaps this is not such a serious limitation but it does alert one to the fact that the picture of criminality given is by no means the complete picture[3].

Psychopathy and biological factors

Some of the very latest studies to connect biological factors and crime concern psychopathic behaviour, which is an extreme form of misbehaviour characterised by its intractable nature and frequently associated with violence. Here it seems likely that the behaviour of psychopaths corresponds with or resembles that of hyperkinetic children—i.e. hyperactive children who are frequently a serious behaviour problem[4]. Tests have shown that both psychopaths and hyperkinetic children exhibit certain characteristics such as immunity to pain when a shock is administered, perspiration (galvanic skin response), and other characteristics which may well arise from the

---

2 B. Hutchings, 'Genetic factors in criminality' in *Determinants and Origins of Aggressive Behaviour* (1974), eds. J. de Wit and W. W. Hartup, pp. 256 et seq., especially p. 263.

3 For further discussion of Danish prosecution policy, see L. H. Leigh and J. E. Hall Williams, *The Management of Prosecutions in Denmark, Sweden and the Netherlands* (1981).

4 Shah and Roth, op. cit., p. 145 citing the researches of Lykken and Schachter and Latane.

chemistry of their bodies creating abnormalities in their autonomic nervous system. It is perhaps too soon for the criminologist to do more than mention these studies and indicate awareness of the possibility that some links may be found between the chemistry of the body and the working of the mind. If the condition is amenable to treatment this holds out some promise for the future[5]. Meanwhile one is left with the grim reflection that somehow or other the penal system and the hospital service have to accommodate a fair number of psychopaths who can no longer be tolerated in the community. As Conrad and Dinitz observe 'The issue is far from resolved. We are still very much in ignorance of the course, mechanisms, and etiology of the behaviour pattern and mental status currently called antisocial personality . . . the chronically antisocial individual is likely to tax our ingenuity and patience in the foreseeable future to perhaps a greater extent than he has in the past . . . there is considerable room for pessimism, notwithstanding the return of the medical and biological specialists to the field'[6].

Pre-menstrual stress

Another recent development in medicine is the recognition of the significance of pre-mentrual stress on the behaviour of women (known as PMS for pre-menstrual syndrome). This has long been suggested in connection with shoplifting, where there is some evidence in support of its relevance, though it seems likely that shoplifting behaviour occurs over a wide age range and in both sexes[7]. A shortage of progesterone in the period immediately before menstruation has been suggested as significantly influencing the behaviour of certain women, who become disoriented and commit acts which are 'out of character'. They appear to respond well to drug treatment once the condition has been diagnosed[8].

Endocrine abnormalities

There was a time in the 1920s and 30s when endocrine abnormalities were regarded as of great significance in the explanation of crime[9]. The

5 S. Dinitz at p. 35 in J. P. Conrad and S. Dinitz, *In Fear of Each Other* (1977).
6 Ibid., p. 36.
7 T. C. N. Gibbens and J. Prince, *Shoplifting* (1962).
8 Katharina Dalton, cited in BMJ 24 March 1973 (editorial note) 'Premenstrual Symptoms'.
9 M. G. Schlapp and E. H. Smith, *The New Criminology* (1928), M. Molitch, 'Endocrine Disturbance in Behaviour Problems' Am Jo Psychiatry 1179 (March 1937). See the discussion in D. R. Taft (1956) pp. 115–116. P. W. Tappan (1949) pp. 125 et seq., (1960) pp. 98 et seq.

connection between the secretions of the endocrine glands and human behaviour was stressed, and it became fashionable to seek gland treatments to prolong youth and enhance beauty. In some countries the fashion spread to the explanation of criminal behaviour. Italy, Sweden and some countries in South America may be mentioned. The link made is usually with aggression. Though the significance of glandular dysfunction may not yet be fully understood, it seems right to say that the more extravagant claims for this factor as an explanation of crime are not substantiated. With regard to aggressive behaviour, Wolfgang and Ferracuti say that with few exceptions there is no connection[10].

Abnormal EEG

Psychiatry has profited from certain developments in measuring the electrical impulses of the brain by means of an electroencephalograph. These EEG tests, as they are known, chart the electrical impulses made by different sections of the brain, and can be interpreted by skilled practitioners much like the electrocardiograph (ECG) measures heart functioning. A normal EEG can be distinguished from an abnormal one. In connection with criminal behaviour two matters have been noted. The first is a connection between an abnormal EEG and motiveless murder. Stafford Clark and Taylor[11] reported the results of their study of 94 persons awaiting trial for murder, in their evidence to the Royal Commission on Capital Punishment. They found that out of eighteen apparently motiveless murders, no less than fourteen cases had an abnormal EEG, although the prisoner seemed on clinical examination to be sane and normal. They concluded that 'it seems difficult to resist the conclusion that a significant relation exists between apparently motiveless crimes of violence and a defect in the function of the brain as shown by EEG abnormality'. The second way in which abnormal EEG has been related to crime is in connection with certain types of young offender committed to the approved school. Here Sessions Hodge and Grey Walter[12] found a predominance of the slower rhythms (delta rhythm) in the results of EEG testing, which they regarded as a sign of immaturity and a dependent personality.

Wolfgang and Ferracuti refer to certain methodological difficulties

10 M. E. Wolfgang and F. Ferracuti, *The Subculture of Violence* (1900) p. 199.
11 Report of the Royal Commission on Capital Punishment (1949–1953) Cmd. 8932, para. 400, p. 139. Also paras. 389–390, 399 and 415.
12 R. Sessions Hodge and W. Grey Walter, 'Juvenile Delinquency: an Electro-physiological, Psychological and Social Study' BJD Vol. 3, p. 155 (1952).

inherent in EEG research which have never been satisfactorily resolved, and they point out that the significance of environmental factors has been strongly emphasised in the English studies of juvenile delinquents and also epileptic children[13]. It seems that we have yet another example of the chicken and the egg problem. Does the abnormal EEG arise from the background situation or the position at the time of the offence and the subsequent testing or does it explain the behaviour in some causal sense?

Other chemical bodily influences

There remains an area as yet dimly perceived concerning other chemical influences or changes in the body which may affect behaviour, including criminal behaviour. Dietary deficiencies, premature senility (senescence), irregular feeding habits, and not the least, temporary unconsciousness and the influence of drink or drugs. Of these only the latter are recognised in common practice, and they do not necessarily provide a legal defence to a criminal charge. A defence of automatism is sometimes possible, where there is a temporary loss of consciousness or blackout due to some physical or physiological condition or occurrence. The most common is the hypoglycaemic episode suffered when a diabetic who is prescribed insulin fails to heed the warning signs that there is a shortage of sugar in the blood, and take the necessary avoiding action to prevent a loss of consciousness. Lawyers nowadays are familiar with the defence of automatism, and the problems concerning drink or drugs as a legal defence[14]. The future may well hold new developments in relation to the effect of the chemistry of the body on behaviour.

Some scholars in the United States have already claimed far-reaching significance for their findings of a relationship between certain dietary deficiencies and bio-chemical abnormalities of the bodily function and abnormal behaviour, including delinquent behaviour. Thus Dr. Leonard J. Hippshen writes that:

'orthomolecular theory suggests that behaviour associated with delinquency and crime can be caused by chemical deficiencies or imbalances in the body, or by brain toxicity. These problems can originate from genetic factors, or they can be induced, especially

13 Op. cit., p. 198.
14 For further discussion see the author's paper 'Legal Views of Psychiatric Evidence' Medicine, Science and Law (1977) Vol. 20, No. 4, pp. 276 et seq.

during the birth process or in early childhood by improper nutrition of the mother and/or child[15].

Vitamin deficiences, vitamin dependencies, food allergies and the like are listed as known to be linked with schizophrenia and some psychopathic disorders[16]. It is suggested that there may be many other biochemical factors which should be reckoned with in relation to the explanation of criminal behaviour[17].

Clearly, we have moved a long way from the more simplistic attempts to relate crime to physique and inheritance. Knowledge of the physiological correlates of human behaviour, derived from the field of medicine, is likely to extend the area for discussion still further, though the early promise from chromosome research has not been fulfilled with regard to an explanation for certain kinds of criminal behaviour. There may be more to learn about the constitutional factors in psychopathy and certain crimes committed by women under premenstrual stress. Certain types of aggressive behaviour may be committed under the influence of glandular dysfunction. The chapter cannot be regarded as closed concerning chemical influences on the body and human behaviour, including criminal behaviour.

Notes. Twin studies and chromosome research

1 The shortcomings of the twin studies are well described by Sutherland (1960) Mannheim (1955) and Reckless (1940). K. O. Christiansen's studies are reported in a variety of sources; the account in the text draws on his essay in *The Mentally Abnormal Offender* (1968), ed. de Reuck, p. 107 entitled 'Threshold of Tolerance in Various Population Groups Illustrated by Results from Danish Criminological Twin Study', and his essay in *Crime, Criminology and Public Policy* (1974), ed. R. Hood, p. 63, 'Seriousness of Criminality and Concordance among Danish Twins'. T. C. N. Gibbens, in his study of borstal youths, had something to say about twin studies. As he found only seven pairs of twins in his sample he could not draw any firm conclusions. He is inclined to attach considerable importance to the mutual influences at work when twins are brought up together. He regards the leadership factor as very significant, the more delinquent twin frequently leading his brother into trouble: *Psychiatric Studies of Borstal Lads* (1963) Chap. XV.

15 L. J. Hippchen, *Ecologic-Biochemical Approaches to Treatment of Delinquents and Criminals* (1978) p. 13.
16 A. Hoffer, 'Some Theoretical Principles Basic to Orthomolecular Psychiatric Treatment' in L. J. Hippchen (1978) pp. 31 et seq.
17 See C. R. Jeffery, *Biology and Crime* (1979).

2 On chromosome research, the best account of this subject is to be found in the proceedings of the Cropwood Conference held at Cambridge in 1966: see *Criminological Implications of Chromosome Abnormalities* (1969), ed. D. J. West. The author contributed a paper entitled 'Chromosome Abnormality and Legal Accountability' at p. 100. This assesses the relevance of chromosome abnormality to the defences available in criminal law, and discusses various cases decided in different countries. Other useful references are: Richard Fox, 'The XYY Offender: A Modern Myth' 62 Jo Crim L & Crim'ogy & Pol Sci, p. 59 (March 1971); F. Sergovich, 'Chromosome Aberrations and Criminal Behaviour' Criminal Law Quarterly, Vol. 1, p. 303 (May 1969); J. Nielsen 'The XYY Syndrome in a Mental Hospital' BJC Vol. 8 (April 1968). The Institute of Criminology, the Hebrew University of Jerusalem published the Proceedings of a Symposium on *Chromosome Abnormality and Criminal Responsibility* in 1969. Lord Ashby discussed the question in a radio talk on the BBC in 1975, reprinted in *The Listener*, 16 October 1975: 'Does XYY mark the crime frontier?'. Dr. J. Kahn and his colleagues at the Institute of Psychiatry, Maudsley Hospital, London, reported in 1976 the results of 'A Survey of Y Chromosome Variants and Personality in 436 Borstal Lads and 254 Controls' BJC Vol. 16, No. 3, p. 233 (July 1976). They found very few cases of abnormal chromosomes in the whole study sample, and of these five were XXY rather than XYY, and there was only one XYY and he was in the control group. Dr. Kahn has pointed out that there are also very few XYY cases in the normal population. Lubs found only seventeen XYY cases out of a total of 11,039 new born babies, which is 0.15 per cent. Walzer and Gerald found three out of 11,154, which is 0.027 per cent: see H. A. Lubs, 'Neonatal Cytogenetic survey' in *Perspectives in Cytogenetics: The Next Decade*, (1972), eds. S. W. Wright, B. F. Crandall and L. Boyes; S. Walzer and P. S. Gerald, 'Chromosome Abnormalities in 11,154 newborn infants' Amer J Hum Genet Vol. 24, 38a (abstr.) (1972). Kahn and his colleagues were more concerned with freak chromosome constitutions generally, and in particular the long Y variant, rather than in studying simply the XYY chromosome. Marginally long Y variants were also included in the study, because of the difficulty in deciding whether a Y chromosome was truly a long Y variant. The controls came from factories in Rochester and Maidstone, and were all volunteers. Half the borstal lads were interviewed, and all were tested for various personality characteristics. There were 23 long Ys and 21 marginally long Ys in the borstal sample: see p. 238. Among the controls there were twelve long Ys (including two who were brothers) and eight marginally long Ys. The results suggest that carriers of the long Y variant have a higher incidence of delinquency. Dr. Kahn recently commented that in the last few years there has been a falling off of interest in the relationship between chromosome abnormalities and crime. This is because, in his view, the subject is very near to being concluded. He also thinks that a great deal depends in the case of an abnormal chromosome carrier upon the environment in which he is brought up. A favourable environment enhances the chance of

survival without being involved in delinquency. The converse is also true.

The question of the legal relevance of chromosome abnormality has been discussed in the author's contribution to the Cropwood Conference papers in 1969, already referred to. Extravagant claims were made at first regarding the possibility of elevating possession of an extra Y chromosome into a new form of defence to crime. Its relevance to defences based on mental disorder, such as the insanity defence or diminished responsibility, is clearly minimal or non-existent, since the evidence concerning such an extra Y is so weak or contradictory regarding its effect on behaviour. At most it can be regarded as an additional element in making out such a defence which is based on other grounds such as clear evidence of mental disorder. It can be mentioned in mitigation and might be relevant to the use of the prerogative power of mercy, but since the abolition of capital punishment in the United Kingdom this consideration seems unlikely to be of much use. In regard to sentencing the possession of an extra Y chromosome seems unlikely to carry much weight. Unless and until more firm evidence is forthcoming of the relevance of such a chromosome abnormality, there is little scope for its use in the courts by the defence lawyer.

3 Professor Mednick has written extensively about the possibility of using the results of the adoption research as a means of early detection of crime-prone individuals, with a view to crime prevention. He does not specify what methods would then be used on the subjects to correct their criminal tendencies, and seems blithely unaware of the implications of this procedure and the problems this would raise: see S. A. Mednick and S. G. Shoham, *New Paths in Criminology: Interdisciplinary and Intercultural Explorations* (1979) Chap. 4, Sarnoff A. Mednick, 'Bio social Factors and Primary Prevention of Anti-social Behaviour' p. 45. Also S. A. Mednick 'A Biosocial Theory of the Learning of Law-Abiding Behaviour' in *Criminology Review Yearbook* (1980).

Chapter 3

Mental factors and crime

Having examined the evidence concerning the relationship between physical factors and criminal behaviour, it seems logical to turn to the examination of mental factors. We start with a discussion of the relation between mental disorder and crime. There follows an account of the psychoanalytical explanations of criminal behaviour, then we shall deal with psychological theories.

Mental disorder

Mental disorder is a general descriptive term which covers a wide variety of different types of mental conditions the only connecting link between which is that they are commonly regarded as abnormal, and may be treated as such by doctors and sometimes by criminal courts. The concept of mental illness is itself a difficult one since it presupposes some standard or criterion of mental health or normality. Lady Wootton[1] pointed out this difficulty in her trenchant examination of the subject in 1959, and Marie Jahoda[2] has reviewed the matter as seen by various authors. Simply because there are cultural and social influences at work in defining mental health does not mean that there is not a consensus of medical opinion about the more serious kinds of mental illness, schizophrenia for example. Wing[3] has shown how far doctors were able to agree on the diagnosis of this condition using standard tests and criteria. The fact that the definition of schizophrenia was shown to be much broader in the United States and the Soviet Union does not render the description of this disease useless by any means. It has great practical utility in psychiatry both for diagnosis and for treatment.

Alternative views about mental illness, its diagnosis and treatment,

1 B. Wootton, *Social Science and Social Pathology* (1959) pp. 227 et seq.
2 M. Jahoda, *Current Concepts of Positive Mental Health* (1958).
3 J. K. Wing, *Reasoning about Madness* (1978) pp. 103 et seq.

have been propounded and developed in recent years by Thomas Szasz[4], R. D. Laing[5] and others. They claim that there is no reliable means of separating the mentally normal from the abnormal, and that the definitions and distinctions made by psychiatrists are governed by social need and are not in the patient's interest, that drug treatment and other psychiatric treatments are unacceptable means of providing social control, and that treatment should follow different lines altogether. This is not the place to examine these ideas in detail. We may simply mention that they have not gained much support from psychiatrists, and that those who, like Wing[6], have made the most strenuous efforts to explore the concept of mental disease and disorder, find no scientific basis on which these ideas can rest, and reject them as unscientific and specious.

The classification of mental disorders

There are several different ways in which mental disorders may be classified. Traditionally a distinction has been drawn between the psychotic disorders, stemming from some organic condition or some functional disorder which has no organic origin or explanation, or none that is yet known, on the one hand, and the neurotic disorders, which occur when a person's personality is seriously disturbed by some non-organic non-functional condition which seriously affects the patient's performance and behaviour. The terms 'psychosis' and 'neurosis' have fallen out of favour in modern psychiatry, being regarded as useless or redundant[7]. It is better to concentrate on the different ways in which the mental disorder affects the personality, and the particular aspect of behaviour or the particular faculty which is affected. The traditional classification does have the merit of assigning a separate heading to the so-called psychopathic personality, separate from the psychotic and neurotic disorders, but this is highly controversial, as we shall see, and this type of behaviour may be better regarded as a personality disorder, which is preferred in modern usage[8].

The classification of mental disorders by faculty or function

4 T. Szasz, *The Myth of Mental Illness* (1961); *The Manufacture of Madness* (1973).
5 R. D. Laing, *The Divided Self* (1959), *The Politics of Experience* (1967).
6 Op. cit., pp. 161–162.
7 Wing, pp. 47–48.
8 See the World Health Organisation's *Glossary of Mental Disorders and Guide to their Classification* (1974).

proceeds along the following lines[9]. The disorder may affect the personality in one of the following ways:

1 *The consciousness* may be affected, as in delirium, and certain confused states of clouded consciousness, and illusion or hallucination. The result is that stimuli are misinterpreted and behaviour is seriously affected.

2 *The memory* may be affected, including loss of memory of recent events and the consequent disorientation. This occurs in dementia.

3 *The thinking* process may be disordered, as it is in schizophrenia, delusional and paranoid states.

4 *The intelligence* may be impaired, as in the case of subnormality.

5 *The emotions* may be affected – what is sometimes termed 'affect'. This occurs in depression, hypomania and mania; also in the case of hysteria, various neurotic and obsessional states, and phobia.

6 *The whole personality* may be impaired, as in the case of psychopathic disorder.

This way of approaching the classification of mental disorders appears to have influenced the Butler Committee on Mentally Abnormal Offenders, in their report of 1975[10]. They adopted a definition of *severe* mental illness as follows:

1 lasting impairment of intellectual faculties,

2 lasting change of mood,

3 delusional beliefs,

4 abnormal perceptions,

5 disordered thinking.

It will be seen that they classify according to the function of the personality which is impaired, whether it is the thinking, the perception, the belief, the mood or the intelligence. Severe subnormality however was to be separately provided for in their scheme of legal defences to crime, and the term 'psychopathic disorder' is avoided altogether, though they found room for 'personality disorder'

---

9 This analysis follows that of W. L. Linford Rees, *A Short Textbook of Psychiatry* (1967) pp. 105 et seq.

10 Cmnd. 6244, October 1975, para 18.35, p. 229 and Appendix 10, p. 317.

to take its place in the definition of mental illness for the purpose of the Mental Health Act. We shall come back to the subject of psychopathy later. First we must consider the relevance of mental disorder to crime and what is known about the connection between them.

Mental disorders and crime

We should start by making it quite clear that the criminologist does not attribute crime to mental disease or illness and seek to excuse criminal behaviour accordingly. The 'disease' theory may appeal to some rather non-scientific souls just as the 'social disease' or 'deprivation' theory does to others. We must leave them with their illusions. For our purpose it is clear that the connection between mental disorder and crime, except in certain instances and in connection with some kinds of crime, is minimal. Reckless said in 1940 that 'there is no clear indication at present that mental disorders . . . play a very important part in the etiology of crime. It cannot be shown that the general run of adult offenders are alarmingly more psychotic than the non-delinquent population'[11]. It is also doubtful how far neurotic disorders are significantly related to crime[12]. All that can be said with any degree of certainty is that some types of mental disorder are related to certain types of offence. Thus it is clear that epileptics sometimes are prone to violent outbursts, that homicide is frequently the result of mental disorder, and that certain sexual offences are often committed by persons of low intelligence[13].

The Butler Committee Report provides some useful evidence on this question[14]. Of all admissions to hospital on mental grounds less than 1 per cent came from the courts or penal establishments. In the criminal courts, taking convictions for non-motoring offences, less than $\frac{1}{2}$ per cent resulted in psychiatric disposals. In the prisons, as might be expected, the proportion of prisoners showing signs of mental disorder is considerably higher. Estimates vary from 10 per cent of the population to as high as one-quarter or one-third of all prisoners either possessing a mental history or showing signs of mental disorder or mental handicap. The proportion is much higher for female prisoners. Yet surveys of prison populations designed to assess

11 W. C. Reckless, *Criminal Behaviour* (1940) p. 205.
12 Reckless (1955) p. 104. P. W. Tappan (1960) pp. 150–151.
13 Butler Committee Report (1975) p. 11. N. D. Walker (1968) p. 59.
14 Op. cit., pp.7, 11, 35–36, 57.

the number of prisoners suffering from clearly identifiable mental disorder come up with surprisingly small numbers. Proposals are frequently made for the transfer of such prisoners out of the penal system, since even the presence of a very small number can be extremely disturbing[15]. The real problem is to get them accepted by the hospitals, who for a variety of reasons find such patients unacceptable[16].

For the purpose of this discussion, the conclusion must surely be that the vast majority of offenders are surprisingly normal, in mental health terms. Support for this view may be derived from the surveys of the general population which have shown how widespread is the distribution of neurotic disorders and how many patients seen by general practitioners exhibit such symptoms[17]. Indeed, many offenders are only too well-adjusted and composed: the problem is that their adjustment is to a life of crime[18].

General emotional lability

Short of mental disorder there remains the possibility of there being an association between the general level of emotional stability of a person and the tendency towards criminal behaviour. A person whose emotions are subject to rapid swings or changes of mood but who is not so seriously disturbed as to be regarded as suffering from mental disorder is frequently described as 'emotionally labile'. Some criminologists have connected this state with criminal behaviour. As we shall see, in modern times Hans Eysenck has explored the connection between the level of emotionality and the degree of extraversion or introversion, and neuroticism. In 1925 Cyril Burt[19] in his classic English study of young offenders contended that the general level of emotionality was significantly connected with criminal behaviour. In a multi-factor study which, following the approach of the American

15 House of Commons, Fifteenth Report from the Expenditure Committee, *The Reduction of Pressure on the Prison System* HC 622–I Session 1977–78. Parliamentary All-Party Penal Affairs Group, *Too Many Prisoners* (1980).
16 Report of Proceedings of Day Conference, July 1980, NACRO on *The Reduction of Pressure on the Prison System*, especially at pp. 4–5.
17 J. K. Wing (1978) pp. 82 et seq.
18 J. K. Wing speaks of the well-integrated burglar who would come out quite high on all the recognised general characteristics of mental health: op. cit., p. 33.
19 Sir Cyril Burt, *The Young Delinquent* (1925). This was re-published in a Fourth Edition in 1944, from which the references are taken.

William Healy, analysed a wide range of different conditions, no less than 170 factors, Burt found on average 9.5 factors associated with each case (Healy found only 3.5). Some thought that this was carrying multiple causation too far[20]. Vice and crime were present already in the homes of delinquents, five times more often than in the controls. Defective discipline was found there nearly seven times more frequently. A disproportionate amount of crime was committed by 'only children'. The most important finding was that the majority of the young delinquents had some instinct defectively developed. (This was written at a time when psychology relied heavily on the notion of instincts in relation to behaviour.) Burt claims that 'every member of the human race inherits a number of innate emotional tendencies, more or less specific' from which he infers that differences occur in the degree to which such instincts are inherited, and such differences may account for differences in conduct . . . 'it becomes conceivable that the inheritance of an ordinary emotion in an extraordinary degree may be sufficient to drive a young person to misconduct'. Thus the violent-tempered child will tend to commit assaults, the over-sexed child to commit sex offences, and so on. This approach is nowadays regarded as naive and discredited[1]. But there may be something to be said in favour of Burt's theory that there is a general level of emotionality lying behind all these specific instincts, which may be unstable or defective and not well-balanced[2]. This may amount to no more than a statement that most offenders are temperamentally unstable or defective. Some appear to have an abnormal excess of their instinctual drives, others may suffer a deficiency[2]. Burt concluded that among all the innate psychological characteristics a marked degree of emotionality was the one most frequently found in the case of delinquents. It was the most influential factor. In addition, according to Burt, a principal personal cause of juvenile delinquency was dullness not amounting to mental deficiency[3]. We shall now examine the evidence concerning low intelligence and crime, but before leaving Burt one might observe that his view of how this emotional imbalance arises (that it is innate) does not square with the view of psychoanalysts or indeed of modern child psychologists, who see in the family pathology more likely sources of emotional instability.

20　W. C. Reckless (1955) p. 67.
1　Taft (1956) p. 94.
2　H. Jones, *Crime and the Penal System* (1962) p. 43.
3　See M. Grünhüt, *Penal Reform* (1948) p. 428.

The role of low intelligence

Burt was not the first to see a connection between low intelligence and crime. It will be recalled that Goring in 1913 had found something similar[4]. In the United States in the early 1920s it was the vogue to see a strong connection. H. H. Goddard[5] argued that nearly all criminals were feeble-minded and produced evidence to support this view. There can be no doubt, however, that he over-stated the case, and the researches of other American scholars, like Sutherland[6], Zeleny[7] and Chassell[8], showed that the relationship was in fact slight. The extreme position argued by Goddard could not be sustained.

In Britain too the same conclusion has been reached by Woodward[9]. Reviewing all the available evidence, Woodward concludes that 'low intelligence plays little or no part in delinquency' but it may provide additional stress to a person who is already predisposed towards crime. The stress engendered may be even greater for the mental defective than for the simply dull child, but even there 'intellectual defect is by no means the sole factor in delinquency'[10]. This conclusion closely corresponds with that expressed by Paul Tappan that mental defect may be associated with misconduct in several ways because of the obstacles to healthy adjustment that it erects[11].

D. H. Stott in 1952 provided an interesting note on the relationship of mental dullness to delinquency in which he asserts, quite categorically, that he does not believe that dullness is 'even a contributory factor' in delinquency[12]. He claims that the assumption that dullness is a cause of delinquency rests upon our failure to understand the mental processes and habits of delinquents and to study their level of intelligence. The ingenuity or stupidity of the offence is no guide, since in Stott's view the commission of the offence

---

4 See Chapter 2, ante.
5 H. H. Goddard, *Human Efficiency and Levels of Intelligence* (1920); *Juvenile Delinquency* (1921); *Feeble-mindedness: Its Causes and Consequences* (1926).
6 E. H. Sutherland, 'Mental Deficiency and Crime' in *Social Attitudes* (1931), ed. Kimball Young, Chapt. XV.
7 L. D. Zeleny, 'Feeble-mindedness and Criminal Conduct' 38 Am Jo Soc 564 (1933).
8 Clara F. Chassell, *The Relation between Morality and Intellect* (1935).
9 Mary Woodward, *Low Intelligence and Delinquency* I.S.T.D. pamphlet (1955) reprinted from B J D Vol. 5, p. 281 (April 1955).
10 BJ D Vol. 5, p. 281 (April 1955) at 300.
11 P. W. Tappan, *Juvenile Delinquency* (1949) p. 122.
12 D. H. Stott, *Saving Children From Delinquency* (1952) Appendix II, 'Delinquency and Dullness' p. 240.

is determined more by the emotional state of the offender than by his mental ability.

It seems likely that there is a positive connection between the more marked degrees of low intelligence and certain forms of sexual offence, but this is not the case for violent crime[13]. Thus paedophiles are frequently persons whose mental age (eleven or twelve) corresponds with that of their victims. Such sexual offenders find it more comfortable to relate to children than adults, with whom they find making relationships (including sexual relationships) difficult[14].

The Cambridge Study in Delinquent Development which involved a longitudinal study of boys drawn from an area of north-east London, found a much stronger association between low intelligence and delinquency, reaching the conclusion that 'low IQ was a significant precursor of delinquency to much the same extent as other major factors'[15]. These were factors relating to troublesomeness at school, and patterns of parental pathology such as discipline, neglect or cruelty, poor supervision, parental conflict or separation, and parental instability. They remark that 'the association between low IQ and delinquency surprised the investigators, since recent criminological writings tend to under-play the factor of intelligence'[16]. Further analysis led them to conclude that two factors were strongly related to low intelligence, viz., recidivism and the fact of being convicted at an early age. There is some discussion of the meaning of these unexpected findings, which appear to remain unique so far.

A different view of the relationship between low intelligence and delinquency is advanced by Hirschi and Hindelang[17]. They claim that recent research suggests that the relation between intelligence and crime as measured by official delinquency records and self-report studies is at least as strong as the relation of class or race, and that it has an effect independent of race and class. This finding they believe has important implications for sociological theorising and research, most of which has taken place within the context of a denial of such differences[18]. Another American criminologist, Robert A. Gordon,

13 N. D. Walker (1968) pp. 59–60.

14 The author's study of 'Serious Heterosexual Attack' Medicine Science & Law (1977) Vol. 17, No. 2, pp. 140 et seq. included a study of this factor of low intelligence, and the sample included paedophilic offences.

15 D. J. West and D. P. Farrington, *Who Becomes Delinquent?* (1973) p. 85.

16 Ibid.

17 T. Hirschi and M. J. Hindelang, 'Intelligence and Delinquency: A Revisionist Review' 42 Am Soc Rev 571 (August 1977).

18 p. 572.

independently reached similar conclusions[19]. Hirschi and Hindelang cite half a dozen recent studies conducted in diverse settings which all show IQ to be an important predictor of official delinquency. Among these are Hirschi's own study of boys in California and Wolfgang's Philadelphia cohort study[20], as well as West's 1973 volume[1].

It may well be that the time has come for a re-evaluation of the evidence concerning a relationship between low intelligence and crime. One difficulty encountered here is that intelligence is tested by measuring the IQ. There is some evidence to suggest that such measurements are culturally loaded. Albert K. Cohen refers to the middle class values and expectations which are measured by these tests[2]. An alternative view is that educational and cultural deprivation is reflected in the findings. The same kind of argument is used to refute current suggestions about a relationship between race and intelligence[3]. Clearly more work requires to be done on these matters.

High intelligence and crime

An interesting variant on the argument about the relation between intelligence and crime is the suggestion that high intelligence may in some cases be related to criminal behaviour. So far this has been tested only in relation to juvenile delinquents, but one might suppose that, as in other careers, it takes quite a bit of intelligence to become successful, and there is no reason to think that a criminal career is different in this respect. Tennent and Gath[4] studied what they described as 'bright delinquents' or intellectually gifted children who became delinquent. Their findings are presented in two stages, representing the basic study, reported in 1970 and 1971, and a follow-up study, reported in 1975. The sample was drawn from London by taking boys remanded for assessment during the period May–November 1967. 50 boys of

---

19 Robert A. Gordon, 'Prevalence: the rare datum in delinquency measurement and its implications for the theory of delinquency' in *The Juvenile Justice System* (1976), ed. M. W. Klein, p. 201.
20 M. E. Wolfgang, *Delinquency in a Birth Cohort* (1972).
1 D. J. West, *Who Becomes Delinquent?* (1973).
2 Hirschi and Hindelang, p. 578 quoting Cohen (1955) pp. 102–103.
3 See Robert A. Gordon, 'Research on IQ, Race and Delinquency' in *Taboos in Criminology* (1980), ed. E. Sagarin, p. 37.
4 Gavin Tennent and Dennis Gath, 'Bright Delinquents' BJC Vol. 15, No. 4, p.386 (1975).

superior intelligence were compared with 50 boys of average intelligence (the measure of superior intelligence being a full scale IQ score of 115 or over and average intelligence being a full scale IQ score within the range 90–105). The boys were matched for age, ethnic origin and court referral. Information was compiled about each boy's delinquency characteristics from reports prepared by probation officers, children's officers and the schools, and from interviews with each boy and his parents.

The basic study[5] found that the social characteristics of the two groups of boys were largely similar, though the bright delinquents came from smaller families and were significantly higher in birth order. A greater degree of psychological disturbance was found among the bright boys and there was a tendency for their offences to have had psychological determinants. Moreover the bright boys tended to make their first appearance in court significantly later, and there was a distinct tendency to treat them more leniently. The follow-up study looked at their reconvictions after three years (or 36 months from the time of the original interview, which took place after conviction but before sentence). It was found that there was no significant difference in the frequency of re-offending between the two groups of boys. Nor was there any great difference in the nature of the offences committed. A very high proportion of those boys who were 'at risk' (in that they remained in the community following the first offence) re-offended in each of the three years of the follow-up period, taking each year separately. Tennent and Gath could find no difference in the degree of recidivism between the two groups. The conclusion drawn is that 'high intelligence makes no difference to prognosis, at least over the three-year follow-up period'[6].

Thus we find that another promising lead ends with no positive conclusion. The study does alert one, however, to the fact that delinquency is by no means confined to those of normal or average intelligence and may well occur among persons of superior intelligence. This is a well-known feature of some kinds of crime, psychopathy for example, as we shall see.

---

5 D. H. Gath, T. G. Tennent and R. Pidduck, 'Criminological Characteristics of Bright Delinquents' BJC Vol. 11, p. 275 (1971); see also by the same authors 'Psychiatric and Social Characteristics of Bright Delinquents' BJ Psychiat Vol. 116, p. 151 (1970); 'Educational Characteristics of Bright Delinquents' BJ Educ Psychol Vol. 40, p. 1 (1970).

6 p. 390.

Notes. Mental disorder and crime

1 One of the best discussions is to be found in the CIBA symposium papers, *The Mentally Abnormal Offender* (1969), ed. de Reuck. See also *Mental Abnormality and Crime* (1944) eds. L. Radzinowicz and J. W. C. Turner; Manfred S. Guttmacher and H. Weihofen, *Psychiatry and the Law* (1952).

2 On the relation between schizophrenia and crime, the CIBA report contains some useful comments. Professor J. Kloek in a paper on 'Schizophrenia and Delinquency' asserts that 'the number of schizophrenics among delinquents is extremely small' (p. 19). According to Professor Wyrsch, *Gerichtliche Psychiatrie* (1955) schizophrenics on rare occasions have been known to commit a violent crime, but as a rule their delinquency concerns petty acts, sometimes rather bizarre, and hardly worth prosecution. Professor B. L. Diamond says that 'many studies throughout the world confirm . . . that obvious schizophrenia is uncommon in criminals' (p. 30). N. Walker (1968) points out that, as with the subnormal offender, the majority of the crimes of the mentally ill are property offences (p. 65). G. M. Woddis, in 1964 in an article on 'Clinical Psychiatry and Crime' BJC Vol 4, No. 5, p. 443 (1964), discusses the relation between mental disorder and crime. He notes the conclusion of Dr. Peter Scott that belief in a correlation between crime and mental disorder is diminishing. Woddis reports the results of a study of 91 cases referred to him because it was thought there were signs of mental abnormality. He suggests that almost any type of mental disorder may be associated with almost any type of crime.

3 A commonly held view is that there is frequently a connection between epilepsy and crime, especially in the twilight state which follows an epileptic seizure: see N. Walker (1968) p. 61. J. Gunn in his book, *Epileptics in Prison* (1977), examines the evidence from a dozen studies, and draws the conclusion that 'the prevalence of criminals attending epilepsy clinics seems to be no greater than the prevalence of criminals in the general population' (p. 9). However, in institutions, among male offenders there is evidence suggesting a higher prevalence of epilepsy than in the normal population, and the prevalence of epilepsy is specially high in young offenders and in violent offenders (p. 10). The study of the patterns of crime suggests that epileptic offenders like other offenders are usually sent to prison because of property crimes (p. 29). Gunn discusses the implications of his findings, and emphasises most strongly that his study cannot be regarded as giving definite answers to any questions about a possible association between epilepsy and crime (pp. 86–98 specially at p. 87). He discusses five possible ways in which epileptics may be found more frequently in prison than elsewhere. These include social and environmental factors as well as selective influences on the part of the courts.

4 On the question how many psychiatric cases there are in the prison population, see J. Gunn et al., *Psychiatric Aspects of Imprisonment* (1978).

5 On 'bright' delinquents, it may be of interest to note that Tennent and Gath found that they were under-functioning educationally. Their ages are given as between twelve and seventeen, with a mean age of fifteen and a half years. The cases where the offence was thought to be predominantly determined by psychological factors (26 per cent) were separated off from those which were judged to be predominantly subcultural in nature. Of these eighteen cases were found to occur among the 'bright' boys and only eight cases among the average boys (n 26 out of 100 = 26 per cent). In the remand home where these cases were collected bright delinquents were found to be comparatively rare. Whereas 16.5 per cent of the general population would be expected to possess an IQ of 115+, only 7.8 per cent of the remand population tested (639 in all) had IQs of 115+ (i.e. less than half the proportion expected). That there is a problem with bright delinquents who are under-achievers is confirmed from the author's experience as a member of the Parole Board for England and Wales.

Chapter 4

Psychoanalytical explanations of crime

The development of psychoanalytical explanations for human behaviour led not unnaturally to attempts to explain criminal behaviour
in these terms. Most of these relied on the Freudian approach[1] though
it should be appreciated that there are other schools of thought in
psychoanalysis. The results of these attempts appear in many ways to
be rather convincing though it is fair to say that many including most
sociologists remain unconvinced. These studies appear to lay much
emphasis on making satisfactory emotional adjustment, and in their
stress on emotional stability it seems they bear some resemblance to
the ideas already mentioned concerning the level of emotional
endowment, expressed by Sir Cyril Burt.

Aichhorn

August Aichhorn was possibly the first to develop a full-scale
psychoanalytical approach to the problem of juvenile delinquency. In
1925 he published his book *Wayward Youth*, which described the
way in which, as a teacher concerned with disturbed and delinquent
children, he had probed the meaning of their behaviour with the
children and their parents, and had achieved remarkable success by his
methods. He introduced the concept of 'latent delinquency' into
psychoanalytical literature[2], which he maintained it was essential to

1 This is not the place to give an exhaustive account of Freudian theory and it must be
assumed that the reader is familiar with the broad outlines. For a popular
exposition, see Calvin S. Hall, *A Primer of Freudian Psychology* (1954).
H. Mannheim, *Comparative Criminology* (1965) Vol. 1, pp. 312 et seq. provides a
useful summary.
2 Kate Friedlander, 'Latent Delinquency and Ego Development' in *Searchlights on
Delinquency* (1949), ed. Kurt R. Eissler, p. 205, at p. 207, cited by W. C. Reckless
(1955) p. 101. See also A. Aichhorn *Delinquency and Child Guidance: Selected
Papers* (1964). The idea of a condition of 'latent delinquency' should not be
confused with the Freudian concept of latency which occurs in the pre-pubertal
period.

understand before progress could be made in understanding the delinquent behaviour itself.

He believed that 'to find the causes of delinquency we must not only seek the provocation which made the latent delinquency manifest, but we must also determine what created the latent delinquency'[3]. 'The predisposition to delinquency is not a finished product at birth', he maintained, 'but is determined by the emotional relationships, that is, by the first experiences which the environment forces upon the child'[4]. 'Every child is at first an asocial being in that he demands direct primitive instinctual satisfaction without regard for the world around him. This behaviour, normal for the young child, is considered asocial or dissocial in the adult. The task of upbringing is to lead the child from this asocial to a social state'[5]. But the development of some children does not pursue the normal course, so that the child remains asocial or simulates social adjustment by suppressing his instinctual wishes so that a state of 'latent delinquency' arises. Aichhorn uses the term 'dissocial' to describe this state. There is also much discussion of the need to achieve a balance between the 'pleasure' principle and the 'reality' principle – broadly the difference between indulging one's every whim or modifying one's behaviour by having some regard for the surroundings and consequences both to oneself and to others. There is also some discussion of the role of the therapist in achieving a 'transference' in order to help establish in the subject a super-ego or 'ego-ideal' or conscience by which behaviour may be controlled.

While Aichhorn has this heavy psychoanalytic approach he does not wish to suggest that every delinquent is an interesting psychoanalytic or neurotic problem, and regards the neurotic delinquent as only one type, resisting the temptation to propound a global theory of delinquency[6]. Not every delinquent is neurotic but the neurotic delinquent is one who suffers from his misconduct, whereas there are those who experience no such guilt feelings about their delinquent behaviour, and may not only benefit from it but actually enjoy it.

Healy and Bronner

The possibility that delinquency might be the result of sublimation, or the substitution for one's thwarted instinctual urges which are

3 p. 41.
4 p. 40.
5 p. 4.
6 pp. 9, 37 and 63.

deflected into other channels, was not allowed for by Aichhorn but constituted one of the main themes of the book by Healy and Bronner published in 1936 entitled *New Light on Delinquency and its Treatment*. This reported the results of research carried out in three American cities, centred on the family life of a sample of delinquents, compared with non-delinquents taken from the same family[7]. All the delinquent children were juvenile court cases referred to a child guidance clinic. The view of delinquency adopted by these authors is that it represents a deviation from the stream of socially acceptable behaviour as a result of thwarted desires and deprivations which have caused deep dissatisfactions. Delinquency is seen as rooted in unsatisfied desires and urges and representing a response to inner drives as well as outer stimuli[8]. They were interested in comparing the delinquents with their non-delinquent siblings, and found that the latter felt the same frustrations less keenly, and those few who had felt just as badly 'found in channels other than delinquency some modes of compensatory satisfactions'. Moreover the non-delinquents had experienced 'distinctly more satisfactory human relationships than had the delinquents'[9]. Delinquents, on the other hand, had no strong emotional ties to anyone: 'the child had never had an affectual identification with one who seemed to him a good parent'[10]. The result was the failure to develop a super ego to provide a barrier against socially unacceptable behaviour. The vast majority of the delinquents suffered from major emotional disturbance.

The distinguishing feature of the Healy and Bronner study was the technique adopted of studying the non-delinquent siblings. In the case of 105 of their 143 delinquents it was possible to make this comparison. They were interested to discover that within the same family inimical situations which existed were experienced differently or responded to in a different way. The Table below shows that 86 of the delinquents

	Delinquents	Controls
Apparently inimical	86	75
Apparently favourable	19	30
	105	105

7 Chapter 2 gives an account of the project, which developed under the auspices of the Institute of Human Relations at Yale University and involved the cities of New Haven, Boston and Detroit.

8 Chapter 1 gives a general orientation, see especially pp. 2 and 7.

9 pp. 7 and 9.   10 p. 10.

lived in apparently inimical family situations, leaving nineteen in apparently favourable situations. Of the non-delinquents, 75 lived in apparently inimical family situations and 30 in apparently favourable situations. It should be obvious from these figures that some family situations may be inimical to one child and not to the other, but it should be equally obvious that not all children who experience an apparently inimical family situation react towards it by delinquent behaviour. Healy and Bronner inquired into the reason for this and concluded that the delinquents were more often thwarted, rejected and disturbed, and found substitutive satisfaction for their psychological needs in channels leading to delinquency. The non-delinquents were less often disturbed emotionally and expressed their disturbed needs in socially acceptable ways without excessive aggressive or escape techniques[11]. This study, though well planned and brilliantly executed, came in for some criticism[12]. The sample was on the authors' own admission a rather selective one, in that the subjects were drawn from the juvenile courts, and there had already been some selection of which cases to bring before the courts. Also they deliberately excluded sub-normal children and those who were not fluent in English or whose parents had language difficulties, also those who had no comparable sibling. They looked only at those recognisable as potentially serious offenders, i.e. recidivists. Despite these limitations the study deserves an honoured place in the history of criminology, for, as Tappan suggests, there is a danger in looking only for exactly quantifiable data, and disregarding 'the subtle and complex variables that motivate conduct'[13].

Psychoanalytical explanations of criminal behaviour have been quite common, both in America and Europe. In some cases between the wars, scholars from central Europe took these ideas with them to America, and popularised them. Thus Franz Alexander who later collaborated with William Healy[14], had earlier written a book with Hugo Staub in which an attempt was made to provide a serviceable classification of criminals which reflects psychoanalytical thinking, and which has proved rather influential. Alexander and Staub differentiate between chronic criminals (persistent offenders) and acute criminals (whose crimes are explained in situational terms and

---

11 This summary derives from P. W. Tappan (1949) p. 112.
12 See the account in P. W. Tappan (1949) pp. 108 and 116–117.
13 Op. cit. pp. 116–117.
14 F. Alexander and W. Healy, *Roots of Crime* (1935).

are unlikely to recur). There is a further subdivision of chronic criminals into three categories[15]:

1 *the neurotic criminal* whose behaviour is conditioned by a neurosis. Many such offenders 'act out' in their criminal behaviour by finding in it some substitute satisfaction for their unsatisfied emotional needs and desires.

2 *the normal criminal* who is well-adjusted to a delinquent culture and way of life, and feels no anxiety or guilt on account of his behaviour.

3 *the pathological criminal* who is in some way psychologically damaged to such a degree that his behaviour must be regarded as pathological in origin. Such persons would include the mentally abnormal offender and the psychopath.

It has been suggested by Howard Jones that Alexander's view of the criminal as either well-adjusted or neurotic and the view of Healy and Bronner that delinquency is often misdirected sublimation together had an enormous influence on criminological thought[16]. This may be observed in the way prison staff view their prisoners, and probation and social workers view their subjects.

Space does not permit any further exploration of the American literature which follows along psychoanalytical lines[17]. It is time to turn to the English literature and in particular to the developments which occurred since 1945. This too sometimes had its central European connection[18] but has developed along its own particular lines. These are generally associated with the work of Dr. John Bowlby and his colleagues at the Tavistock Clinic.

Bowlby's theory of maternal deprivation

In 1944 Bowlby published the results of his study of 44 juvenile thieves who had been referred to his child guidance clinic in London[19]. These

---

15 F. Alexander and H. Staub, *The Criminal, The Judge and the Public* (1931). A revised edition was published in 1956. The present summary is taken from P. W. Tappan (1949) pp. 89–90 and is a gloss on the original. See also W. Reckless (1955) pp. 99–100.

16 H. Jones, *Crime and the Penal System* (1956) p. 47.

17 For example, see D. Abrahamsen, *Crime and the Human Mind* (1944); *Searchlights on Delinquency* (1949), ed. K. R. Eissler; F. Redl and D. Wineman, *Children Who Hate* (1951).

18 See for example, Kate Friedlander, *The Psychoanalytical Approach to Juvenile Delinquency* (1947).

19 Later republished in book form as *Forty-Four Juvenile Thieves: Their Characters and Home-Life* (1946).

were compared with a control group of 44 similar children who had been seen at the clinic, matched for age and intelligence. It is admitted that these thieves were by no means typical of delinquents coming before the courts: they had all been selected because their conduct appeared to be disturbed. Only a minority had actually been charged in court. Many were chronic delinquents, but by no means all.

Bowlby found, comparing the thieves and the controls, that seventeen out of the 44 thieves had been separated completely from their mothers for six months or more during the first five years of their lives – but only two of the control group had experienced such a separation. From this Bowlby concluded that maternal deprivation involving a prolonged separation is a principal cause of delinquency. Bowlby focused particularly on the so-called 'affectionless character'. Fourteen out of the seventeen thieves who had suffered maternal deprivation exhibited a serious and distinctive personality characterised by showing a marked disability to form close personal relationships with others, which merited the label 'affectionless character'. Such a character could be diagnosed at the age of three years and possibly earlier, and Bowlby made a strong plea for early diagnosis and above all that attention should be given to prevention. In particular he thought that many prolonged separations could be avoided.

In 1951 Bowlby prepared a report for the World Health Organisation, in which the evidence was reviewed[20]. He found that scholars working independently had reached substantially similar conclusions about the effects of maternal deprivation. This report and the other studies undoubtedly had a profound influence on standards of care of children and attitudes of social workers and hospital staff and those working in other institutions for children, in the direction of improving the prevalence of caring attitudes and preventing harmful deprivation experiences. But the thesis soon came under severe criticism from both sociologists like Lady Wootton and psychologists like the Clarkes, Andry and Grygier. We shall now review some of the criticisms. A reply to some of these together with some restatement of the criticisms appeared in 1962[1]. A further re-assessment, by Rutter, appeared in 1972[2].

20 J. Bowlby, *Maternal Care and Mental Health* (2nd edn., 1952) (W.H.O.).
 1 Mary D. Ainsworth et al., *Deprivation of Maternal Care: A Reassessment of its Effects* (1962) (W.H.O.).
 2 M. Rutter *Maternal Deprivation Reassessed* (1972) (2nd edn. was published in 1981).

Research tending to contradict Bowlby

Andry in 1957[3], in his study of parental pathology and delinquency, pointed out that one should not overlook the importance of the paternal influence in moulding character development. This may be more significant at a later stage. He was able to show that to concentrate entirely on the mother's role, and the importance of avoiding maternal deprivation through separation experiences, was to take too narrow a view. Faulty child-parent relationships in general should be considered and the role of each parent or both together should be examined, a point later borne out by Grygier's research[4].

Andry points out also that Bowlby found only about one-quarter of his delinquents had suffered separation from their mothers to the extent that it appeared to have given rise to the maternal-deprivation syndrome. He observes that Bowlby was really confining his attention to a specialised sub-group of delinquents who had suffered maternal deprivation – the affectionless character. He believes that recent research has tended if anything to prove the opposite to Bowlby – that maternal deprivation is relatively unimportant in the majority of cases of deviant behaviour.

Little in 1965[5] reported the results of research on a sample of borstal youths with for the most part long criminal records. His aim was to study the effect of a separation experience, involving separation from either parent, with regard to subsequent behaviour, and in particular he took 500 boys more or less at random out of over 3,000 receptions into borstal institutions in 1958. Four out of five of this sample had experienced several separations at different periods of time. Father-separations were more common than mother-separations, mostly because of the war years 1939-45. Little observes that the incidence of separation experiences in the general population being unknown, this cannot be used for comparison. The best one can do, he believes, is to examine the relationship of separation to certain other factors such as date of first court appearance, length of criminal record, reconviction rate, and types of crime committed. He examines these matters in relation to three groups of offenders:

3 R. G. Andry, *Delinquency and Parental Pathology* (1960) and article in BJD Vol. VIII, p. 34 (1957-1958) 'Faulty Paternal and Maternal Child Relationships Affection and Delinquency'. See also his essay 'Paternal and Maternal Roles and Delinquency' in M. D. Ainsworth et al. (1962).
4 See his essay in M. D. Ainsworth et al. (1962) pp. 32-34.
5 Alan Little, 'Parental Deprivation, Separation and Crime: A Test on Adolescent Recidivists' BJC Vol. 5, No. 4, p. 419 (October 1965).

1 the non-deprived (in terms of separation experience);

2 those separated once or twice;

3 those experiencing multiple separations (three or more).

It was discovered that 'when the population is divided into (these) three groups . . . no large or consistent differences can be found in age of first conviction, numbers of previous convictions, and frequency of recidivism after discharge from Borstal. Nor does this seem to influence the types of crime committed, though there is some evidence to suggest a higher incidence of sex crimes and malicious damage amongst the non-deprived'[6]. Maternal deprivation did, however, seem to be related to early appearance in court.

Hilda Lewis in her study of *Deprived Children* in 1954, a study of 500 children in a reception centre, was unable to find a clear connection between a child's separation from his mother and any particular pattern of disturbed child behaviour. 'Neither delinquency nor incapacity for affectionate relationships was significantly more frequent in the separated children'[7].

Neither was O'Connor in 1956 able to demonstrate any permanently disturbing effects of mother-child separation[8].

Siri Naess[9] found that in Norway, comparing a matched group of delinquents and non-delinquents, separation had occurred more frequently among the non-delinquents, a finding later qualified because further study of the sample had revealed that early mother-child separations had occurred more frequently among the delinquents than had been thought at first[10]. She still concluded that separation as an isolated factor was not strongly criminogenic, but was a minor factor to be conceived as part of the picture of an unstable family life[11].

Grygier's Canadian study led to much the same conclusion: 'Separation from either parent does not seem to be a single factor in delinquency, rather it is part of the entire family situation, of the pathology inherent in unstable families'[12].

6 p. 429.   7 H. Lewis, *Deprived Children* (1954) p. 83.
8 N. O'Connor, 'The evidence for the permanently disturbing effects of mother–child separation' Acta Psychol Vol. 12, p. 174 (1956).
9 S. Naess, 'Mother–child Separation and Delinquency' BJD Vol. 10, p. 22.
10 S. Naess, 'Mother–child Separation and Delinquency: Further Evidence' BJC Vol. 2, No. 4, p. 361 (April 1962).
11 p. 373.
12 T. Grygier, 'Parental Deprivation: A Study of Delinquent Children' BJC Vol. 9, No. 3, p. 209 (July 1969).

Criticism and reassessment of Bowlby's thesis

The sociologist Barbara Wootton subjected the Bowlby thesis to a most devastating examination in 1959[13], criticism which she repeated in 1962[14]. It may be helpful to summarise her arguments as follows:

1 Bowlby paid too little attention to contradictory evidence, to the findings of research running counter to his thesis about the damaging effects of maternal deprivation.

But the weight of the evidence appears to be rather on Bowlby's side, and he has suffered from some misinterpretation of his position, which was that he never claimed to explain all delinquency and himself modified his case in later years[15].

2 The interpretation of the evidence is open to criticism on the ground that there are dangers in relying on evidence from institutions (and, one might add, on cases referred to psychiatric clinics).

3 There is no proof that the damage done by a mother-separation experience is irreversible.

4 There is no warrant for the conclusion that a separation experience is strongly related to delinquency. 'No evidence has been produced' says Lady Wootton, 'to support the view that this type (the affection-less character) constitutes anything but a small minority of the delinquent population'[16].

5 Insufficient evidence is available relating to the population at large concerning the incidence of maternal separation experiences. But we do have some idea that it occurs much more frequently than might be supposed, though Lady Wootton regards the evidence as inconclusive.

Douglas and Blomfield[17] and Rowntree[18] have examined the incidence of maternal deprivation in their cohort studies. The former study showed that over 50 per cent of children had been separated by the age of six.

13 Barbara Lady Wootton, *Social Science and Social Pathology* (1959).
14 M. D. Ainsworth et al., 'A Social Scientist's Approach to Maternal Deprivation' (1962) p. 62.
15 Andry, loc. cit. in M. D. Ainsworth et al. (1962).
16 M. D. Ainsworth et al. (1962) p. 69.
17 J. W. B. Douglas and J. M. Blomfield, *Children under Five* (1958).
18 G. Rowntree 'Early childhood in broken families' Populat Stud, Vol. 8, p. 247.

6 There remains the problem of distinguishing between deprivation and separation. Nowadays there is a growing realisation that it is not necessarily the separation experience which matters so much as the overall quality of the family relationships, what is sometimes described as 'the under-the-roof culture'. Prugh and Harlow have discussed what they describe as the 'masked deprivation' which occurs where relationships with the mother are either insufficient or distorted[19].

Michael Rutter's review of the situation in 1972 represents a major contribution towards clarifying the concept of maternal deprivation and assessing its true significance[20]. Rutter says that it is necessary to distinguish between a failure to make bonds of affection on the part of a child, and deprivation after such bonds have been made. It is also essential to distinguish between the various kinds of deprivation. It must be recognised that the experiences subsumed under the notion of 'maternal deprivation' are complex and there is a danger of making it into a unitary concept which can be discussed as a whole. This was a criticism forcefully expressed by Yarrow and others in the 1960's[1]. There is also the danger of interpreting the Bowlby thesis too strictly and on this he says: 'Bowlby's writings have often been misinterpreted and wrongly used to support the notion that only twenty-four hours care day in and day out, by the same person, is good enough'[2]. This would preclude the use of fostering, day nurseries and creches.

Rutter identifies six characteristics of adequate mothering and relates the research findings relevant to each. These are as follows:

1 a loving relationship

2 attachment

3 an unbroken relationship

4 a stimulating interaction

5 the relationship being with one person

6 in the child's own home[3].

Space does not permit us to discuss all the details here relevant to each characteristic, but a few observations may be mentioned to give the

19 Mary D. Ainsworth et al. (1962) p. 9 et seq.
20 Michael Rutter, *Maternal Deprivation Reassessed* (2nd edn., 1981).
  1 pp. 14–15.
  2 p. 16
  3 p. 18

flavour of the discussion. Thus on 2 'attachment', Rutter says there are few facts in spite of an abundance of theories[4]. He discusses the importance of the intensity of the relationship as compared to its duration and examines the relevance of animal studies of imprinting. On the subject of 3 'an unbroken relationship', like Lady Wootton, he refers to the evidence concerning the frequency of separation experiences in the normal population. Douglas, Ross and Simpson, in a national sample of some 5,000 children, showed that by four and a half years of age a third of children had been separated from their mother for at least one week. They also showed that only a weak association existed between brief separations and delinquency[5]. On 5, the relationship with one person, described by Rutter as monotropy, he says that this suggested requirement is not established: 'the very limited available evidence suggests that, if the mothering is of high quality and is provided by figures who remain the same during the child's early life, then (at least up to four or five mother-figures) multiple mothering need have no adverse effects'[6]. Thus the use of the children's nanny stands exonerated, not that this is likely to have much relevance to delinquency. On 6, the significance of the relationship being established and maintained in the child's own home, Rutter maintains that there is no satisfactory evidence in support of the dictum 'better a bad family than a good institution'. Views have changed concerning the wisdom of keeping the home intact particularly with the increased awareness of the baby battering syndrome, and there is less reluctance to disrupt the family unit in the worst cases[7]. Rutter discusses the importance of other features in the child's home, such as the provision of adequate food, opportunities for play, and discipline. He concludes that 'love, the development of enduring bonds, a stable but not necessarily unbroken relationship, and a "stimulating" interaction are all necessary qualities, but there are many more. Children also need food, care and protection, discipline, models of behaviour, play and conversation'[8].

One of the distinctions which is essential to an understanding of this subject is that between *privation* or lack of some vital ingredient in the parental relationship and *deprivation* through separation experience. Also one must distinguish between the short-term effects of maternal

4 p. 20.
5 p. 25.
6 p. 27.
7 p. 28.
8 p. 30.

deprivation and the long-term consequences. These vary according to the age, sex, temperament and the previous mother-child relationship and whether the separation occurs in a familiar or in a strange environment[9]. Rutter's final conclusion is that 'the evidence strongly suggests that most of the long-term consequences are due to privation or lack of some kind, rather than to any type of loss'. Accordingly, the 'deprivation' half of the concept is somewhat misleading. The 'maternal' half of the concept is also inaccurate in that, with but few exceptions, the deleterious influences concern the care of the child or relationships with people rather than any specific defect of the mother'[10]. Bowlby's thesis is now better understood but the idea of one specific syndrome is no longer acceptable[11].

Another comprehensive review of the evidence by Clarke and Clarke[12] leads to very similar conclusions. They show how recent studies have tended to take a much more rounded view of the whole subject of child development and parental pathology. The trend of earlier studies to be preoccupied with the role of the mother in early childhood has been reversed. It is now clear that a disproportionate amount of time and effort has been devoted to studying the earliest years of child development. What is called the myth of maternal deprivation has been exploded.

Clarke and Clarke is particularly helpful on two aspects of the question. First, there is the growing recognition of the different dimensions of learning and the different ways in which learning takes place and the different stages. They refer to the significant work of Hebb in this connection, whose work in 1949 'initiated a different approach to the problem of early learning'[13]. The point here being made is that much learning takes place in later periods of life; especially in man, as he approaches and reaches maturity. 'The effects of social learning through modelling, identification with selected adults and peers and feedback from the environment operate on the maturing organism in ways as yet little understood'[14]. A sociologist might well have written that. The second point where Clarke and Clarke seems helpful concerns the relevance of animal studies. They show that extrapolating from the results of animal studies to humans

9 Chapter 3 of Rutter discusses the short-term effects of 'maternal deprivation' and Chapter 4 the long-term consequences, and modifying factors.
10 p. 121.
11 p. 124.
12 Ann M. Clarke and A. D. B. Clarke, *Early Experience: Myth and Evidence* (1976).
13 p. 11. See also p. 8. D. O. Hebb, *The Organization of Behaviour* (1949).
14 p. 13.

'must for a number of reasons be regarded with caution'[15]. They are extremely sceptical of the use of such animal studies to support theories about early learning experiences with children. It is accepted that the basic personality of an individual is 'laid down' in early life, as a result of genetic/environmental interactions, but this by itself is not the end of the story by any means.

'Our main general conclusion is that, in man, early learning is mainly important for its foundational character. By itself, and when unrepeated over time, it serves as no more than a link in the developmental chain, shaping proximate behaviour less powerfully as age increases'[16], 'a child's future is far from wholly shaped in the "formative years" of early childhood'[17], 'the whole of development is important, not merely the early years'[18].

Child psychologists and psychiatrists appear nowadays to agree that one needs to take a broader view of the factors which influence child development. There is no longer any need to over-emphasise the significance of one phase and one relationship. Thus Dr. Kenneth Soddy[19] lists the following factors (among others) as important for the clinician to consider in dealing with child and adolescent behaviour problems:

instinctual forces and their modification
the pain-pleasure cycle
failure to form object-relationships
separation of infant from mother
general insecurity, tension and anxiety
poverty of relationship formation
sexual difficulties
over-identification with father or mother
overwhelmed parents
father desertion
reactive states, either of aggression or withdrawal

While Dr. Soddy freely acknowledges his great debt to psychoanalytical thinking, he himself does not adhere strictly to orthodox psychoanalytical theory, and suggests that a certain rigidity in later analytical thinking may have obscured the truth[20].

15 p. 12 and pp. 14-15.
16 p. 18.
17 p. 24.
18 p. 272.
19 K. Soddy, *Clinical Child Psychiatry* (1960).
20 p. 86.

John Bowlby has gone so far as to admit that there has been a tendency for some scholars to overstate their case[1], and yet he has never waivered in his view of the vital importance of the earliest experiences of the child, which is no more than one would expect from someone whose whole life has been devoted to research based on psychoanalytical assumptions. Three volumes published in 1969, 1973 and 1980 on *Attachment and Loss* give an overview of the evidence as seen from his point of view. Nor does one wish to deny that the thesis concerning maternal deprivation had an enormous practical effect in improving child-rearing practice both in and out of hospitals and other institutions, an effect which Wootton, Rutter and Clarke and Clarke freely acknowledge. What one concludes in this matter will depend very largely on the extent to which one is embracing psychoanalytical modes of thought. To those who have received the faith the conclusions seem self evident: to the rest a healthy scepticism seems a more suitable response.

Notes. The psychoanalytical approach to crime

1 American books adopting the psychoanalytical approach to the explanation of crime abound. Among the best known are D. Abrahamsen, *Crime and the Human Mind* (1944); F. Redl and D. Wineman, *Children who Hate* (1951); F. Alexander and W. Healy, *Roots of Crime: Psychoanalytic Studies* (1935); R. M. Lindner, *Rebel Without a Cause* (1944); F. Wertham, *Show of Violence* (1949); B. Karpman, *Case Studies in the Psychopathology of Crime* (1944).

2 The English literature adopting the psychoanalytical approach to crime includes Kate Friedlander, *The Psycho-Analytical Approach to Juvenile Delinquency* (1947); E. Glover, *The Roots of Crime* (1960); S. H. Foulkes, *Psycho-Analysis and Crime* (1944).

A more eclectic view is presented by J. D. W. Pearce, *Juvenile Delinquency* (1952).

3 Lawyers may be particularly interested in the book by Paul Reiwald, *Society and its Criminals* (1949) which is an attempt by a Swiss scholar to apply the psychoanalytical approach to the role of the judge as father-figure. For a more balanced assessment of the European literature, see Lucien Bovet, *Psychiatric Aspects of Juvenile Delinquency* (1951).

4 The psychologist D. H. Stott carried out a number of studies of delinquents and school populations, developing an instrument, known as the Bristol Social

---

1 J. Bowlby, M. D. Ainsworth, M. Boston and D. Rosenbluth 'The effects of mother–child separation: a follow-up study' B J Med Psychol Vol. 29, p. 211 (1956).

Adjustment Guides, by which to measure the predisposition to delinquency. Stott's study of an approved school population *Delinquency and Human Nature* (1950, 2nd edn., 1980) used a classification of delinquent behaviour which viewed it as a symbolic expression of deep-seated tensions anxieties and frustrations. The following modes of behaviour were seen as typical:

1 avoidance–excitement;

2 inferiority–compensation;

3 delinquency–attention;

4 resentment directed against parents;

5 removal from the home.

See also D. H. Stott, *Saving Children from Delinquency* (1952); *Unsettled Children and Their Families* (1956), *Studies of Troublesome Children* (1966). The latter derived from his research on a population of Glasgow school children. For the Bristol Social Adjustment Guides, see D. H. Stott, 'Delinquency Proneness and Court Disposal of Young Offenders' BJC Vol. 4, No. 1, p. 37 (July 1963).

The idea of delinquency as a form of 'acting out' by deviant behaviour one's frustrated desires and expressing one's needs symbolically has received considerable support. Thus shoplifters are frequently seen as having wished not to make any material gain so much as to obtain some excitement, to relieve boredom, to call attention to their problem so that something is done about it (a cry for help) and a host of other explanations mostly of a psychoanalytical nature. The same may well be true of some other instances of criminal behaviour, e.g. arson and criminal damage will frequently be best viewed in these terms.

5 Kate Friedlander's statement of the analytic theory of anti-social character formation is unusually forthright and lucid. She classifies as secondary causes all those environmental factors which affect the child from the age of seven onwards, including the influence of companions, the use of leisure, the type of school and neighbourhood, and the experience of frustration or satisfaction in employment. The important primary causes operate during infancy, largely through the mother's handling of the child. These primary factors may lead to the development of an anti-social character formation, without which, it is maintained, later environmental influences will not lead to the manifestation of antisocial behaviour: K. Friedlander, *The Psycho-Analytical Approach to Juvenile Delinquency* (1947) p. 104.

6 The unscientific nature of the claims made by proponents of the psychoanalytical approach to the explanation of crime is given by the American sociologist George Vold as a sufficient ground for rejecting them. This 'closed' system of concepts, he believes, is inherently untestable by scientific

standards: G. B. Vold, *Theoretical Criminology* (1956) pp. 125–126. This may seem a somewhat harsh judgment, particularly since Bowlby himself admits the difficulties involved in scientifically testing analytical claims, and for that reason prefers observations and measurement conducted along rigorous lines: see J. Bowlby, *Attachment and Loss* Vol. 1 (1969) pp. 41–42.

7 Bowlby gives a useful discussion of the role of instincts in Freudian theory: op. cit., pp. 61 et seq. In this he rejects the dichotomy between innate and acquired instincts, in favour of the view adopted by Hinde that one should distinguish traits that are environmentally stable as opposed to those that are environmentally labile: R. A. Hinde, 'Behaviour and Speciation in Birds and Lower Vertebrates' Biol Rev Vol. 34, p. 85 (1959). Bowlby couples this with the notion of a control system and the concept of adaptation. These ideas draw heavily upon research in animal ethology, which as has already been pointed out is of doubtful relevance to man. Bowlby's debt to the ethologists is acknowledged at p. 18 in his list of acknowledgements. His position is expressed thus: 'until the concepts of ethology have been tried out in the field of human behaviour we shall be in no position to determine how useful they are': pp. 27–28.

For further reading see R. E. Hinde, *Animal Behaviour* (1970), and the references in Bowlby (1971) pp. 83–84. Bowlby devotes over 150 pages to a discussion of animal and bird behaviour related where possible to man: pp. 61–218. Volume I of his book *Attachment and Loss* is devoted to attachment, by which he means the ways by which a child and its mother form ties and the child's primitive learning grows from this experience. The volume ends with a review of the psychoanalytical literature relating to the child's tie to his mother: pp. 424 et seq.

The volume *Child Care and the Growth of Love* by John Bowlby, 2nd ed., (1965) contains some additional material discussing what are described as the 'controversial issues' and the conclusions from recent research, contributed by Dr. Mary Ainsworth. He.·e despite recognition of the various criticisms, most of the previous claims are seen as justified:

'An examination of the evidence that has accumulated during the last thirteen years leaves no doubt that maternal deprivation in infancy and early childhood has indeed an adverse effect on development both during the deprivation experience and for a longer or shorter time after deprivation is relieved, and that severe deprivation experience *can* lead in some cases to grave effects that resist reversal. This conclusion is essentially the same as Bowlby's in 1951'.

The interpretation of some of the evidence is, to say the least, rather partial. Thus even Yarrow and the Clarkes are seen as providing some support, as well as Siri Naess: pp. 229, 231, 232. There is a messianic air about the whole business.

Chapter 5

Personality theories about crime

Personality traits have been developed by psychologists by measuring various human characteristics, in terms of what one might broadly term personality. The feature which distinguishes a *trait* is its persistence or stability or predictability. Given a certain stimulus the expected response is likely to follow. When these traits are grouped because they tend in the same direction, they can be regarded as forming a type or *personality dimension*. What lay persons may appropriately identify as part of a person's character thus becomes more than a lay observation, it is a scientific fact[1].

Psychologists claim to be able to measure a person's traits by a variety of tests such as measurements of the speed of response of the autonomic nervous system to some external stimulus, e.g. the response of an eye blinking when a light flashes. The speed of responses can be related to a person's temperament, so that different personalities will score differently. Questionnaire techniques and self-rating procedures may also be used to build up a picture of the characteristics of the person is to suggestion will often reflect such factors. Various dimensions of human personality have been identified, including the introvert/extravert dimension, neuroticism, and psychoticism. The amenability of these different personality types to 'conditioning' will vary greatly, i.e. the extent to which they can learn to alter their response to different stimuli.

The Eysenck theory of personality

One of the best known theories of human personality is that linked with the name of Hans J. Eysenck, who, in a series of texts and popular

---

1 For a general introduction to this subject, see H. J. Eysenck, *Crime and Personality* (1977) and his *Sense and Nonsense in Psychology* (1957), in particular Eysenck (1977) Chaps. 1 and 2.

books[2], has demonstrated the way in which traits are measured and has shown how the different types of personality, identified as neurotic, extravert, and more recently, psychotic, relate to behaviour. This has been applied to the explanation of criminal behaviour in general, though it seems clear that Eysenck is particularly interested in that form of criminal behaviour which is neurotic or psychopathic, where his theory fits most closely, and he recognises that not all crime is of that nature[3].

The background to this development may be traced to the writings of nineteenth century scholars like Wilhelm Wundt and to Mowrer who built on the work of the Russian Pavlov. The recognition of moods and temperaments as emotionally strong and stable or weak and changeable, and the emphasis on neuroticism and extraversion which is central to Eysenck's theory, derives from these sources, together with the contribution made by the psychoanalyst Jung, who popularised the notions of extraversion and introversion[4]. With the development of improved techniques for observation and measurement and their application to a wide range of populations, it has become possible to hypothesise ideal types such as the extravert and the neurotic, and to measure on a scale the degree of extraversion or neuroticism present in each particular person[5]. Dimensions of the personality are thus measured and compared.

To quote West[6], it may be said that:

'certain attitudes, collectively suggesting a sensitive, imaginative, reflective and somewhat inhibited temperament, tend to cluster together in the same individual: while another cluster, suggesting a cheerful, matter-of-fact person who adapts himself readily without much need for thought, occur together in individuals of opposite temperament. These clusters represent the opposite extreme of a continuous variation from the predominantly introverted to predominantly extraverted individuals, with the majority falling somewhere between'.

---

2 H. J. Eysenck, *The Scientific Study of Personality* (1952); *The Structure of Human Personality* (1960); *Dimensions of Personality* (1947) and the books referred to in note 1, above.
3 (1977) p. 55 and p. 131.
4 (1977) pp. 49–51.
5 Ibid., pp. 48 and 50.
6 D. J. West, *The Young Offender* (1967) p. 143.

Relating these personality types to crime, Eysenck maintains that persistent criminal behaviour, especially of the psychopathic variety, is closely related to extraversion and that socially conforming individuals are more likely to be introverted personalities. He cites the evidence of several English studies in support of this view[7].

To quote West[8] again: 'another important dimension upon which individuals vary is in neurotic tendency or emotional instability'. Eysenck and others have developed tests for measuring people on this trait, and have found that 'those who are prone, when under stress, to produce neurotic symptoms have high scores on these tests'. Moreover 'the quality of neurotic reactions varies according to one's position on the extraversion introversion continuum'.

Neurotic extraverts such as hysterical personalities and psychopaths are mentioned as the extreme cases. West believes that common experience tends to support this conclusion, which is also supported by scientific studies. Thus Hathaway and Monachesi[9] found it to be true of young delinquents and Eysenck mentions that unmarried mothers in public or private homes were also high on emotionality or neuroticism as well as extraversion[10]. So were female prisoners, samples of American and Australian prisoners, and psychopathic patients. The Table overleaf shows their position on the extraversion-introversion/neuroticism scale.

For the criminologist the significance of these personality traits lies in their relevance to the prevention of crime and the treatment of offenders. It is not suggested by Eysenck that physical methods should be employed to alter personality, though it is admitted that psychiatrists do frequently use drug therapy and electro-convulsive treatment. What is preferred is some form of behaviour therapy 'which attempts to use psychological methods derived from learning theory and conditioning in a therapeutic manner'[11]. The response of introverts is likely to be better than criminals who being extravert are seen as rather difficult to condition, while neurotics will condition too quickly and

7 (1977) pp. 130 et seq.
8 Op. cit., p. 144.
9 S. R. Hathaway and E. P. Monachesi, 'The Personality of Pre-Delinquent Boys' 48 Jo Crim L & Crim'ogy & Pol Sci p. 149 (1957).
10 (1977) p. 134 quoting Sybil B. G. Eysenck, 'Personality and Pain Assessment in Childbirth of Married and Unmarried Mothers' J Ment Sci Vol. 107, p. 417 (1961).
11 (1977) p. 14.

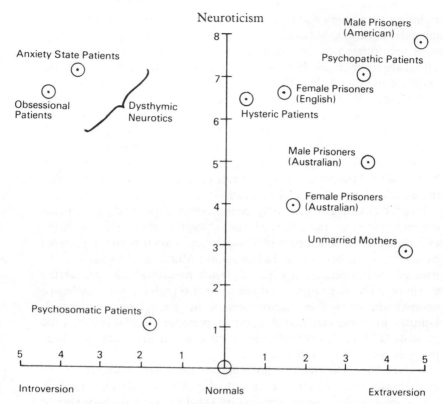

Neuroticism and extraversion-introversion scores of various neurotic and criminal groups. Note the high degree of introversion of neurotic groups and the high degree of extraversion of criminal and psychopathic groups. Note also the high degree of neuroticism of both neurotics and criminals.

Source: H. J. Eysenck, Crime and Personality (1970) (Paladin Books) p.56.

too strongly. Moreover, insofar as these traits are of genetic origin, there may not be much hope of achieving significant alterations. The need to develop treatment programmes geared to the personalities of offenders is emphasised. Resources should be devoted to exploit the potentialities of this 'conditioning' approach, for example, using such techniques as token economies, without going so far as any form of brain-washing. More research and experiment must no doubt precede such a development. Eysenck concludes that 'modern psychology holds out to society an altogether different approach to criminality, an approach geared only to practical ends, such as the elimination of antisocial conduct, and not cluttered with irrelevant, philosophical, retributory and ethico-religious beliefs'[12]. What he propounds is essentially a learning theory and an explanation why there are differences in the rate of response to conditioning. For another quite different approach towards a psychologically based learning theory, one should refer to the work of Bandura and his American colleagues.

Criticism of Eysenck's theory

Like Bowlby, Eysenck's theory about crime has not gone without severe criticism. These criticisms turn on the apparently deterministic nature of his conclusions, his biological positivism, and the results of further research. While there may be a great deal to be said in support of these criticisms so far as the first two points are concerned, the results of recent research go some way towards supporting Eysenck's position, with some qualifications.

Determinism and biological positivism

By this we mean that Eysenck sees a criminal personality or a disposition towards committing crime as largely an inherited characteristic rather than something acquired later on. He relies heavily on the evidence of the twin studies particularly that of Johannes Lange. He does not refer to more recent studies such as those of Christiansen and others. He appears to regard the evidence as conclusive and this leads him to speculate why it should be rejected. He views criminality as a continuous trait like the other traits which means that the degree of criminality can be measured on a scale. The more seriously criminal are seen as likely to have inherited certain traits such as extraversion and neuroticism[13]. The evidence for this is suspect. Not content with relying so heavily on twin studies, Eysenck also cites the various studies concerning the relation of physical type to crime, such as Kretschmer, Hooton and Sheldon, which he regards as supporting his general hypothesis.

He cites some English studies such as that of Gibbens in support

---

12 (1977) p. 213.
13 Figure 6, p. 56 of an earlier edition of Eysenck (1970), reproduced below.

though as we have observed Gibbens was able to somatotype barely half his sample[14]. He regards all the data both from America and from England as being in agreement:

'that criminals, on the whole, tend to be athletic in body build, that is stocky and muscular rather than fat, and that they tend to show a temperamental tendency towards extraversion, particularly towards impulsiveness[15].

It is very questionable whether Eysenck's claims are borne out regarding the relevance of mesomorphy to crime and the possible influence of inherited factors. His claims concerning the relevance of extraversion and neuroticism must now be examined.

Research on personality dimensions and crime

West[16] cites a recent investigation in which he was concerned, using a sample of schoolboys, which showed that those graded unstable extraverts on psychological tests were significantly more often graded badly behaved by teachers, compared with the rest. He suggests that it is the combination of the neurotic tendency with extraversion which seems to be closely related to delinquency. Little[17] tested the two basic dimensions of personality outlined by Eysenck, introversion – extraversion and neuroticism–normality, on a population of young offenders detained in three different borstal institutions in England and Wales. Their scores were compared with those of a non-delinquent population measured by Eysenck. The results were to show that the delinquent population did not differ from the normal population with regard to extraversion, and differed only slightly with regard to neuroticism (though the difference here was significant). Little explains the latter finding as no more than might be expected from such a population of young offenders, where emotional instability is likely to be high[18]. What is interesting is the evidence showing no high degree of extraversion among these young offenders. Little also tested whether there was any relationship between the two dimensions (extraversion and neuroticism) and recidivism, taking as his test the probability of reconviction established according to the

14 See p. 23, ante.
15 (1977) pp. 146–147.
16 West (1967) p. 144.
17 A. Little, 'Professor Eysenck's Theory of Crime: An Empirical Test on Adolescent Offenders' BJC Vol. 4, No. 2, p. 152 (October 1963).
18 p. 155.

Mannheim/Wilkins prediction tables[19]. Again no connection between extraversion and the probability of reconviction (or recidivist tendencies) could be discovered[20]. Nor was any relationship shown between neuroticism and the probability of reconviction. Little claims that his study shows that 'the Eysenck theory is of little use for explaining adolescent delinquency and recidivism'[1]. This does not mean, he points out, that it might not still be useful for explaining and categorizing types of adult offenders and recidivists.

Eysenck in a comment points out that the borstal population tested may not be typical of the whole population of offenders, and that he regards his theory as a theory concerning psychopathic behaviour, and he recognises that not all criminals are psychopaths. He denies having suggested a global theory designed to explain all crime, and thinks it likely that a more limited approach which concentrates on certain groups of offenders will prove to be more successful[2].

Little's conclusions concerning the relevance of the Eysenck personality dimensions to recidivism are contradicted by the 1974 study by Eysenck and his wife, which also related to borstal boys[3]. Instead of using the prediction scores to measure the likelihood of recidivism, the Eysencks were able to follow up a group of borstal boys three years and nine months after they had been originally tested while in the borstal institution. This was taken to provide evidence of their conduct three years after release. One hundred and twenty two boys out of the sample of 178 had been reconvicted and only 56 were non-recidivist according to this criterion. The scores on the three personality inventories showed a significant difference existed regarding the factor of extraversion among the recidivists and a slight but non-significant difference for the factors neuroticism and psychoticism. They claim that these results lend support to Eysenck's theory, particularly over the factor of extraversion.

An attempt by Hoghughi and Forrest[4] to measure an approved school population in order to test Eysenck's theories proved unsuccessful. It was shown that these youths, committed to an

19 H. Mannheim and L. T. Wilkins, *Prediction Methods in Relation to Borstal Training* (1955).
20 p. 158.
1 p. 160.
2 p. 161.
3 S. B. G. Eysenck and H. J. Eysenck, 'Personality and Recidivism in Borstal Boys' BJC Vol. 14, No. 4, p. 385 (October 1974).
4 M. S. Hoghughi and A. R. Forrest, 'Eysenck's Theory of Criminality: An Examination with Approved School Boys' BJC Vol. 10, No. 3, p. 240 (July 1970).

institutional environment on account of their criminal behaviour, were not more extravert than normal, though they were significantly more introverted, which is quite contrary to the prediction from Eysenck's theory. It is pointed out that if selection is a factor to bear in mind, these selected offenders are more criminal than those dealt with in other ways or still at large, and might be expected to be more often scoring high in terms of the extraversion dimension. They were not. On the neuroticism dimension there was evidence to show the boys were more neurotic but there are several factors which may help to explain this apart from some innate tendency, and there are limitations in the measuring instruments used to test this dimension[5]. Hoghughi and Forrest conclude 'from the evidence presented that Eysenck's theory of criminality as applied to the juvenile end of the criminal population is at present untenable'[6]. The results showed that 'contrary to Eysenck's hypothesis, approved school boys in general are not more extraverted than the normals and would in fact be very amenable to social conditioning' (p. 244).

The conclusion of the Cambridge criminologists West and Walker appears to be that Eysenck's theory presents a challenging subject for further research but that the evidence so far available shows that the theory remains unproved[7]. In defence of Eysenck's theory of crime, we have some spirited replies from Eysenck himself, the results of his own further researches together with his wife, and the results of other studies tending to support the theory. One new development is the introduction of a further dimension, the predisposition to a psychotic breakdown, which the Eysencks claim can be measured and is significantly related to crime. We shall now review these matters.

Eysenck's 1970 edition of his book on *Crime and Personality* attempts to provide an answer to some of the criticisms[8]. He summarises a dozen studies whose results he claims are favourable to his theory, and lend it mild support. He accepts that there are difficulties over the question of finding suitable control groups, which beset all crime studies. He considers the notion that an offender's personality may be profoundly affected by the trauma of trial and conviction to be improbable, at least so far as the degree of extraversion is concerned. He accepts that there are large numbers of inadequate offenders who are not extraverts, but says his theory is not concerned

5 p. 250.
6 p. 252.
7 West (1967) p. 146; Walker (1968) p. 79.
8 (1970) pp. 193 et seq. The 1977 edition does not include this discussion.

with these but rather with the actively antisocial psychopathic offenders, the 'tough-hostile' group identified by Pierson and Kelly in their 1963 study of American male offenders[9].

Psychoticism

We have referred to the introduction of a new dimension (the P factor = Psychoticism) in later versions of Eysenck's theory. He believes now that 'there appears to exist a continuum from normal to psychotic, along which predisposition to psychotic breakdown (psychoticism) can be measured'[10]. Prisoners appear to score high on the P factor, corresponding in this respect with psychotic males and females. Further work needs to be done on this dimension, he suggests, and we now have the results of further studies.

In 1970 Eysenck and his wife[11] published the results of their investigation of the application of the three dimensions, extraversion, neuroticism and psychoticism, to a population of English prisoners drawn from four different institutions, and compared with various control groups. They conclude that their results 'strongly support our prediction as far as P is concerned, moderately strongly support our prediction as far as N is concerned, and rather weakly, if at all, our prediction as far as E is concerned'[12]. Regarding the new concept of psychoticism, they claim that recent studies reinforce their view 'that psychoticism in general may share certain important features with criminality, without implying of course that all (or even a large proportion) of criminals are in fact psychotic'[13]. They conclude that one needs to pay more attention to the differences within the offender group in respect to the scores for P, E and N. It might be possible to construct a typology of crime and criminals on this basis which would be useful for diagnostic and treatment purposes.

Other researchers have attempted to verify Eysenck's theory, including Burgess, Crookes, the Smiths and Passingham. We shall now review these studies before reaching a general conclusion.

Burgess[14] found some evidence to support Eysenck's theory in three

9 G. R. Pierson and R. F. Kelly, 'Anxiety, Extraversion and Personality – Idiosyncrasy in Delinquency' J Psychol Vol. 56, p. 441 (1963).
10 (1970) p. 198.
11 S. B. G. Eysenck and H. J. Eysenck, 'Crime and Personality: An Empirical Study of the Three-Factor Theory' BJC Vol. 10, No. 3, p. 225 (July 1970).
12 pp. 235–236.
13 p. 230.
14 P. K. Burgess, 'Eysenck's theory of criminality: a new approach' BJC Vol. 12, p. 74 (1972).

studies designed to test it, the first being a small sample of Canadian prisoners, the second and third being prisoners from several English prisons. He suggests a different way of going about testing the hypothesis about extraversion and neuroticism, and using this method his results confirmed Eysenck's theory, though he does say that in the more extreme form he does not believe it can be sustained. He proposes that a new way of looking at the relationship between neuroticism and extraversion would be to devise a new variable ('h' = for hedonism) by calculating the product of the E and N scores. He predicted that among individuals scoring high on 'h' there would be an over representation of criminals, and this was confirmed by his data. The Eysencks' 1974 study tried out this measure and found that it made little difference compared with the score for E alone, but in combination with P it did appear to discriminate between recidivists and non-recidivists[15].

Crookes[16] applied the 'h' score to a population of patients in a psychiatric hospital and concluded that it did not provide a very useful index of criminality but that it might be used to provide an index of social adaptation. He suggested that instead of multiplying the scores for E and N one should add them. When one did this however, the scores for prisoners and psychiatric patients appeared very similar, though the contribution of E was greater for prisoners. He considers that many other factors are involved, and not surprisingly suggests that psychoticism is of considerable relevance for psychiatric patients. His conclusion that personality variables must still play an important part in producing maladaptive behaviour and that E and N are well-established dimensions of personality, shows him to be on the side of Eysenck but with some qualifications. A later study by Crookes[17] explores the sociability components such as impulsiveness which he considers to be of less importance specially when combined with high neuroticism.

The Smiths' study[18] was of a large sample of male probationers tested on the Eysenck scales at the commencement of their probation order. They found that when these scores were related to reconviction and certain other factors, psychoticism proved highly relevant to

15 Eysenck and Eysenck, loc. cit., note 3.
16 T. G. Crookes, 'Burgess "h" score in Psychiatric Patients' BJC Vol. 14, No. 3, p. 273 (July 1974).
17 T. G. Crookes, 'Sociability and Behaviour Disturbance' BJC Vol. 19, No. 1, p. 60 (January 1979).
18 D. E. Smith and D. D. Smith, 'Eysenck's Psychoticism Scale and Reconviction' BJC Vol. 17, No. 4, p. 387 (October 1977).

reconviction within a year, and to age and number of previous convictions. Offenders with high scores on psychoticism were also regarded by their probation officers as high risk cases, having serious criminal tendencies. They were also described as immature and of low intelligence, more likely to suffer from ill-health, drug and drink problems and to possess a variety of other negative factors.

Passingham[19] reviewed a large number of studies and found the evidence far from equivocal regarding the dimension of extraversion but he was prepared to believe that high impulsiveness and neuroticism had more relevance, since it was known that these factors were characteristic of slum sub-cultures. One might point out that Eysenck himself drew attention to the fact that the sociability component in extraversion had not 'on the whole, produced good differentiation between criminals and normals'[20]. It is on the impulsivity side of human personality that he prefers to concentrate: 'it is the impulsive side of extraversion rather than the sociability side which we may consider to be associated with criminal behaviour'.

Passingham criticises Eysenck for adopting an imprecise notion of criminal behaviour, not specifying what types of offence and offender are covered by his theory. Some attempt has been made by Eysenck to remedy this in his later work, but there is still a tendency to generalise the theory and apply it to criminality as a whole.

Another major review of those studies which have tested Eysenck's theory or have applied similar tests is that by Feldman[1]. The results of previous research, as summarised by Feldman[2], may be stated as follows:

1 In general, the prediction for E has not been supported, but prisoners tend to be high on impulsiveness and low on sociability. It is the combination of these two that goes to make E.

2 The prediction relating N to offending has been supported.

3 The prediction relating P to offending has also been found to be true.

4 The combination of scores on two or three of these factors (E, N and

19 R. E. Passingham, 'Crime and Personality: A Review of Eysenck's Theory' in *Biological Bases of Individual Behaviour* (1972), eds. V. D. Nebylitsyn and J. A. Gray.
20 Eysenck (1970) p. 143.
1 M. P. Feldman *Criminal Behaviour: A Psychological Analysis* (1977).
2 p. 149.

P) is more strongly associated with criminal behaviour than any one dimension taken alone.

He sets out the conclusions of research to date on three aspects of the matter:

1 the acquisition of criminal attitudes and criminal behaviour;

2 performance of criminal behaviour;

3 maintenance of criminal behaviour.

He suggests that personality measurements may be more use in relation to explaining the acquisition of criminal attitudes than to its performance and maintenance, and that this is more true of the extreme cases of high scores than in the case of median scores. But 'even in acquisition, by extreme scorers, personality will be only part of the story; situational variables will play a significant role'[3].

It is to a discussion of these situational or environmental factors that we turn in the next chapter. First we must consider another personality theory developed by Gordon Trasler[4]. This is drawing upon many of the same strands as Eysenck but is expressed rather differently. In some ways it is easier to comprehend and seems more acceptable, perhaps because it offers more hope for improving the methods of treatment of offenders.

Trasler's explanation of criminality

According to Trasler recent developments in psychology suggest the possible relevance to understanding criminal behaviour of the theories of those European psychologists like Wilhelm Wundt and O. H. Mowrer who built upon the foundations provided by the work of Pavlov. Trasler believes that social learning behaviour is powerfully influenced by what he terms 'passive avoidance conditioning' or 'passive avoidance training'. In other words individuals order their behaviour in such a way as to maximise pleasurable experiences and reduce to a minimum painful experiences. They learn to behave in a socially acceptable manner mainly during childhood and early up-bringing when experiences of pain and pleasure mould the personality. Some people learn (or condition) more readily than others. This is

3 p. 161.
4 G. Trasler, *The Explanation of Criminality* (1962).

because they are by nature introverts. The extraverts in contrast are slower to learn or more difficult to condition. They do not learn so readily from experience. They are less amenable to those stimuli which could attract an avoidance response. Anxiety is not so easily generated in such persons. This discovery by psychologists may have extremely important implications for social training including retraining those who become deviant and commit delinquent behaviour. Perhaps this is its most important feature.

Trasler, like Eysenck, attaches some importance to the twin studies and thinks that genetic factors play an important role in deciding a person's personality. He also appears to accept that part of Eysenck's theory which relates to extraversion[5]. He draws up a list of practical conclusions which flow from this explanation of criminality. Walker[6] describes this theory as one concerning ethical learning, which he distinguishes from prudential learning or intellectual or motor learning.

Notes. Personality theories

1 Once again, as with the psychoanalytical theories, one must point out that the part of the personality theories relating to crime represents only a small part of the total writing on the subject. There is a vast literature concerning psychological tests of the human personality, discussing the methods used and the results, their objectivity and validity. Eysenck's contribution in this field is considerable. The student who requires further reading in addition to the books mentioned in the text and footnotes, should consult the following: H. J. Eysenck and S. B. G. Eysenck, *Personality Structure and Measurement* (1969); *Handbook of Abnormal Psychology* (1973), ed. H. J. Eysenck.

2 Eysenck in 1952 in his book *The Scientific Study of Personality* gives an account of the various ways in which one goes about measuring different traits in the personality together with illustrations, and many tables and figures. The 1969 book by the Eysencks gives an account of the development of the Maudsley Personality Inventory (M.P.I.) and assesses its value compared with two other personality inventories, that of Cattell and Guilford. The M.P.I. is seen to be superior in that it is more objective and therefore more reliable. Extensive research findings using the latest statistical techniques support this conclusion. Eysenck comments that the age-old practice of creating traits by rather subjective observation may well be responsible for the low regard in which personality research is held by experimental psychologists. 'The

5 p. 63.
6 Walker (1968) pp. 76–77.

outstanding fact about such systems as those of Cattell and Guilford is not that they are objective, and based on correlation and factor analysis, but that they are subjective, and based on arbitrary and intuitive judgements. The building stones of a questionnaire are the items and objectivity demands that factor analysis should begin at this level, i.e. with the intercorrelation and factor analysis of items . . . only E and N escape from this criticism': (1969) pp. 326–327. He continues: 'There are now many studies in the literature based on intercorrelations between items which yield these two factors, and it can be documented that identical items go to make up each factor on different occasions. It is difficult to over-emphasize the importance of this point'.

Eysenck frequently admits that more work needs to be done on these factors. This is especially true of P (psychoticism).

3 There are doubts about what exactly each of the Eysenck factors actually measures. Hoghughi and Forrest (1970) say 'there is very little acceptable evidence that the scales . . . actually measure what they purport to measure'. This is in reference to the Junior Eysenck Personality Inventory (J.E.P.I.) and the Junior Maudsley Personality Inventory (J.M.P.I.) developed by Eysenck which were used by Hoghughi and Forrest to measure extraversion and neuroticism among approved school boys. On the subject of psychoticism, Crookes (1979) observes that 'the psychometric status of this scale is far from clear' and because 'it contains a number of items asking explicitly about anti-social behaviour, so it is not surprising that criminals score high on it, but it has not yet been related to any basic psychological or physiological mechanism which might increase the probability of such behaviour' (p. 60). On the subject of N (= neuroticism) scores it has been observed that the self-report studies of delinquency are ones where it is very likely that the subjects would score high on neuroticism.

4 A highly critical account of Eysenck's theory of crime appears in I. Taylor, P. Walton and J. Young, *The New Criminology* (1973) pp. 47 et seq. They concentrate their criticism on the deterministic implications of the theory: 'The degree to which a person has been conditioned to avoid "anti-social" behaviour is central to Eysenck's explanation of criminality'. This depends on the autonomic system which he has inherited and the quality of the conditioning he has received in his family environment. All this takes place in a society where there is a general consensus about values, which defines certain kinds of behaviour as deviant. For Eysenck such matters are taken for granted just as for the radical socialist-minded criminologist they represent the very point at which the inquiry takes off, the very stuff of the subject.

'We wish to argue that Eysenck's analysis is misguided not because of his omission of social factors but because he constructs a false notion of the interplay between biology and society. For Eysenck the interaction between society and the individual potential for deviance is *additive*. He has a *steady state* notion of biological potential – it is something which is fixed and measurable and follows a man throughout his life' (pp. 55–56).

5 The heavy reliance by Eysenck's theory and that of Trasler on one particular kind of learning, that which is associated with conditioning by pleasurable or painful experiences, leaves out of account the many other types of learning which occur in common experience. Nigel Walker regards the type of learning which is here involved as ethical learning which he distinguishes from prudential learning and intellectual learning. Much of the criticism by the radical criminologists of Eysenck's theory stems from its failure to allow for these other types of learning: 'reason is not merely a set of deterministic reflexes – rather it is a consciousness of the world, an ability of the individual to give meaning to his universe, both to interpret and to creatively change the existing moral order. Man's reason, rather than being a conditioned amorality is a conscious optimizing of choices' (Taylor, Walton and Young p. 51).

6 Perhaps one should be less concerned with the question whether offenders tend to be high on extraversion, neuroticism and psychoticism, and instead ponder the question what it is which one is measuring by these characteristics. If the answer is present traits of the subject being measured, then there is another question to be posed, how did he get like that? The answer which relies mainly or entirely on inherited or innate characteristics leaves out of account the sub-cultural and social factors or minimises their influence. Yet, as Eysenck sometimes appears to admit, the latter can be decisive, at least in regard to the actual way in which the crime is carried out, and whether the culprit is found and punished: (Eysenck (1970) pp. 74–75). The question which also needs to be asked is whether the offenders were always like this, or whether they acquired their traits as a result of their experiences in pursuing a criminal career, or through living in a particular environment and absorbing its culture. Hoghughi and Forrest accept that delinquents are drawn from the unstable 'choleric' section of the population and point out that 'we know that the socialisation experiences of delinquents are more disturbed and inconsistent than those of normal children': (1970) p. 250. In its extreme form, as applied to psychopaths, the same question has to be raised, whether they were always like that or whether they have become like that through successive experiences at the hands of society, i.e. having been in and out of institutions, and having been repeatedly punished, they develop a psychopathic response.

7 West and Farrington (1973) examined their sample repeatedly at different ages according to the Eysenck scales for measuring extraversion and neuroticism. The results did not provide much support for Eysenck's theory, they say, and only at the age of sixteen was extraversion significantly correlated with delinquency. 'The results were remarkably consistent, and did not favour Eysenck's theory' (p. 113). It is not without interest to note, however, that maternal neuroticism and parental instability did play an important role in the lives of this sample of young delinquents.

Psychopathy and crime

1 In the chapter on Mental factors and crime (Chapter 3) and in this chapter on Personality theories about crime (Chapter 5) reference has been made to the psychopathic personality. Eysenck's personality theories apply most particularly to this type of offender. The concept of psychopathy and crime requires some explanation.

2 The term 'psychopathic inferiorities' was introduced almost 100 years ago, by the German psychiatrist Kraepelin, in 1891, though it seems likely that philosophers and physicians had recognised something of the kind as early as the seventeenth century. In the early part of the nineteenth century the idea of moral insanity appears to have been used to describe those who were not suffering from intellectual defect or any known mental disorder but whose behaviour was so violent or persistently anti-social as to point to a mental explanation. Originally the psychopathic disorders embraced all mental disorders which were not 'psychoses' (major mental illnesses with a known or suspected physical or organic origin). A wide variety of conditions was included, and some scholars adopted the description sociopathy in recognition of the fact that this was a condition which expressed itself in extremely anti-social behaviour. See the Report of the (Butler) Committee on Mentally Abnormal Offenders, Cmnd. 6244, October 1975, Chapter 5, 'Psychopaths', in particular paras. 5.2–5.9, pp. 77–79.

3 In the United Kingdom Sir David Henderson's study of *Psychopathic States* (1939) provided a further impetus to the development of the notion of psychopathy. He adopted a three-fold classification of psychopaths into aggressive, inadequate and creative psychopaths: see para 5.10 of the Butler Report, p. 80.

4 The Royal Commission on Capital Punishment 1949–1953 in its Report, Cmd. 8932 (September 1953) received evidence concerning the relevance of psychopathy to crime, and discussed the question of its definition. They noted that there was 'no generally accepted definition of this term, and no consensus of opinion about the scope or nature of the mental condition which it is intended to describe' (para. 393, pp. 135–136). They heard evidence from Sir David Henderson concerning his classification and description of the different types of psychopath (para. 396, pp. 136–137). They also heard evidence from Dr. D. Stafford Clark and Dr. F. H. Taylor about the results of EEG examinations of cases of apparently motiveless murder. The Commission concluded that 'the available evidence justifies the conclusion that in many cases the responsibility of psychopaths can properly be regarded as diminished . . . ' (para. 401, p. 139).

5 The Percy Commission in 1957 were sufficiently impressed to include the category of 'psychopathic disorder' in their recommendations for the definition of mental disorders for the purposes of the law. The result was that

section 4 of the Mental Health Act 1959 recognises this type of disorder, which is defined in section 4(4) as being 'a persistent disorder or disability of mind (whether or not including subnormality of intelligence) which results in abnormally aggressive or seriously irresponsible conduct on the part of the patient, and requires or is susceptible to medical treatment'.

6 Strong arguments have been raised against the recognition of psychopathy, particularly in connection with criminal responsibility. These arguments are reviewed in the Butler Report: para. 5.20. Briefly they are as follows:

1 There is no general agreement among psychiatrists as to the use of this term.

2 The concept involves circular reasoning by inferring mental disorder from anti-social behaviour and then using that diagnosis to explain or excuse the anti-social behaviour. Lady Wootton subjected the concept of psychopathy to a devastating analysis in her *Social Science and Social Pathology* (1959).

3 There is a danger in labelling a person in this way. A harmful consequence is the stigma which follows, and a harmful effect is that it serves only to confirm or reinforce the person's anti-social behaviour.

4 Both Scotland and Northern Ireland have managed very well without adopting this heading of mental disorder.

7 The Butler Committee agreed with these criticisms, especially with 3. They discuss the possibility that the term should be abandoned, as being no longer a useful or meaningful concept (para. 5.23). They consider that the alternative course might be preferable, that is to substitute 'personality disorder' in the definition in section 4(1) and to delete section 4(4). They examine the consequences this would entail for the making of a hospital order under section 60 of the Mental Health Act 1959, and consider that it might be necessary to import something like section 4(4) into section 60, together with the provision that sexual deviation alone or alcohol or drug addiction alone would not be sufficient to bring a person within the section. The present law contains a provision broadly to the same effect (section 4(5)) but the Committee would like to see it strengthened.

8 Efforts to agree on the international classification of disease have grappled with the problem of whether to include recognition of psychopathy. The 1968 Revision of the World Health Organisation's International Statistical Classification of Disease recognises three major groups of mental disorders:

1 The psychoses

2 Mental retardation,

3 The neuroses.

There are nine sub-categories of 3, the neuroses, of which 'personality disorders' is one. The terms 'psychopath' and 'psychopathic disorder' or 'psychopathic personality' are not used. (Butler Report, paras. 5.16 and 5.17, pp. 82–83).

9 Under the heading of 'personality disorders' the British Glossary prepared by a sub-committee of the Registrar-General's Advisory Committee on Medical Nomenclature and Statistics, acknowledged that 'psychopathic personality' is included in the category 'personality disorders', and provides a description of this type of personality disorder. The W.H.O. glossary published in 1974 for international usage also includes 'psychopathic personality' in the category of 'personality disorder'. (Butler Report, para. 5.17 and 5.18, p. 83).

10 The treatment of psychopathic offenders in the prison system and in the health service is not a subject which can be explored within the compass of this book. Suffice it to say that the category of 'psychopathic disorder' is frequently used, on its own or together with another category of mental disorder, for the purpose of diagnosis under the Mental Health Act 1959 and for the purpose of diagnosis of prisoners suffering from mental disorder, according to the statistics. Increasingly, however, it is becoming accepted that, standing alone, it is a shaky concept. In the practice of probation and parole it is still widely used as a form of 'shorthand' to describe the most intractable cases. Dr. Peter Scott argued that there was no difference between a psychopathic offender and an incorrigible recidivist: P. D. Scott, 'The Treatment of Psychopaths' BMJ (May 28 1960) Vol. 1, p. 1641. See also P. D. Scott, 'The Psychopathic Patient in General Practice' The Practitioner, Vol. 218, p. 801 (June 1977).

11 There is some evidence suggesting a link between certain physiological characteristics and psychopathy the precise meaning of which is not yet clear. Dinitz reviews the evidence, suggesting possible genetic or biological differences. The galvanic skin response (GSR) of psychopaths is abnormal which suggests that they are less sensitive to pain and anxiety than normal persons. Research in Broadmoor special hospital showed an abnormally low physiological response to stress so far as the accretion of adrenaline is concerned. A normal person subject to stress experiences an accretion of adrenaline, enabling him to more easily defend himself or take avoiding action (the 'fight or flight' syndrome). A psychopath may react differently. Also when a normal person becomes aggressive there is an increase in nor-adrenaline, but it seems that psychopaths experience an abnormal increase in nor-adrenaline. This is regarded by the researchers as being more than a difference in degree, being in fact a difference in kind, 'an alteration of the character of the response'. More work is needed on this subject. See S. Dinitz in J. C. Conrad and S. Dinitz, *In Fear of Each Other* (1977); D. D. Woodman, 'What Makes a psychopath?' New Society, 4 September 1980; Shah and Roth in *Handbook of Criminology* (1974), ed. D. Glaser pp. 101 et seq.

Chapter 6

Social and cultural factors

Having reviewed the evidence concerning physical and inherited factors in relation to crime, and psychological and psychoanalytical factors, we are now free to broach the subject from a sociological point of view. It is necessary to subdivide the sociological discussion of crime into various sub-headings, and we propose to adopt the following arrangement:

1 Family factors;

2 Area influences;

3 Gang studies;

4 Structural and cultural theories;

5 Symbolic-interactionist and labelling theories, and 'control' theory.

1 Family factors

It is natural that we should begin our search for the sociological explanation of crime with a study of family influences, for sociologists can agree with psychologists and psychoanalysts that nothing is more likely to influence human behaviour than the experiences of the child as it is growing up in the family[1]. No more potent factor exists than this, although the influence of other factors will also sometimes be considerable.

The family factors which require discussion can be grouped into five headings, as follows:

A. The broken home;

B. Family tension;

1 P. W. Tappan, *Juvenile Delinquency* (1949) pp. 133–134.

C. Home discipline and relationships;

D. Criminality in the family;

E. Neglect.

A. The broken home

Discussion of delinquency frequently centres on the influence of a broken home. It is often suggested that the broken home, broken by the death of one or both the parents, by divorce or separation of the spouses or desertion, is a major cause of crime. There is a good deal of evidence to support this belief, and yet from a scientific point of view the 'broken home' syndrome has proved unsatisfactory. It is possible that we have too readily jumped to a conclusion that here at last was a major criminogenic factor. We shall review the evidence of American and British studies before reaching a conclusion.

The American studies at first sight suggest that the broken home is an important factor. The Gluecks in their 1950 study found broken homes occurred nearly twice as frequently in the case of their sample of delinquents compared with their controls. (60.4 per cent: 34.2 per cent)[2]. It was also estimated that 40 per cent of delinquents in America came from broken homes, but this figure must be interpreted in the light of the evidence that in the United States, because of the prevalence of divorce, a very high proportion of all children come from broken homes, possibly as high a proportion as 25 per cent[3]. Shaw and McKay found[4], in their review for a U.S. National Commission in 1931, that with regard to boys, the ratio of broken homes comparing delinquents and controls was 1.18:1.0, which, as Sutherland says, 'indicates that the broken home is not closely linked with the delinquency of adolescent males'[5]. It was thought at one time that a higher ratio for girls indicated that the broken home was a more powerful factor in their case. A ratio of 1.49:1.0 was found by Margaret Hodgkiss[6], but that result was challenged by H. Ashley Weeks[7]. The

2 S. and E. Glueck, *Unraveling Juvenile Delinquency* (1950) p. 122.
3 Tappan, op. cit., p. 134.
4 C. R. Shaw and H. D. McKay, 'Social Factors in Juvenile Delinquency' in Report on the Causes of Crime, National Commission on Law Observance and Enforcement (1931) Vol. II, No. 13, pp. 261–284.
5 E. H. Sutherland and D. R. Cressey, *Principles of Criminology* (6th edn., 1960) p. 176.
6 M. Hodgkiss, 'The Influence of Broken Homes and Working Mothers' Smith College Studies in Social Work, Vol. 3, p. 259 (March 1933).
7 H. Ashley Weeks, 'Male and Female Broken Home Rates by Types of Delinquency' 5 Am Soc Rev 601 (August 1940).

modest finding of Shaw and McKay has been criticised as being unreliable on various grounds and tending to understate the incidence of broken homes among delinquents[8]. Apart from that of the Gluecks, these studies relate to the period between the two World Wars.

The Gluecks in 1962 published a special study entitled *Family Environment and Delinquency*, in which they examined the influence of a host of family factors related to the personality of the individual and his traits. Although the broken home is among the factors mentioned the study gives more attention to the psychological quality of the overall family experience and attaches more significance to the differential effects of childhood experience on children possessing different personality and constitutional traits. As such it must be regarded as a development of the Gluecks' previous work on the physical types in relation to psychological traits, which throws little light on the subject of the broken home. The most that can be said, it seems, is that a broken home contributes to the development of certain traits such as an uninhibited motor response to stimuli, and that in children who are emotionally labile and possess a feeling of inadequacy, the broken home adds to their delinquency potential[9].

F. Ivan Nye's studies of family relationships have contributed a great deal to our understanding of family pathology[10]. In 1958 he published a study which compared delinquents who, because of their delinquency, had been committed to state training schools, with a population of high school delinquents who had not been so committed, and a population of non-delinquent school children. He found that broken homes were far more common among the committed delinquents than the most seriously delinquent of the non-committed group, which he thought was due to the selection factor – differential treatment of the children of broken homes. He found a small but significant difference in delinquent behaviour between youths from broken and unbroken homes, which he attributed to the loss of control over the children in single parent families and confusion where a step-parent was introduced into the home. One striking discovery was that there was less delinquency in broken homes than in the unhappy unbroken homes – which led him to suggest that the 'happiness factor' was far more closely related to delinquency than the formal family status[11].

8 D. R. Taft, *Criminology* (3rd edn., 1956) p. 192.
9 S. and E. Glueck, *Family Environment and Delinquency* (1962) pp. 123–124.
10 F. I. Nye and F. M. Berardo, *The Family: Its Structure and Interaction* (1973); F. I. Nye, *Role Structure and Analysis of the Family* (1976).
11 F. I. Nye, *Family Relationships and Delinquent Behaviour* (1958) p. 51.

Nye also has some data concerning the age at which the breach in the home occurs, suggesting that it is immaterial at what age this happens. This appears to be contradicted by the British evidence which points to the vulnerability of children approaching adolescence when the break occurs[12]. In the pre-pubertal period there are strong loyalties and attachment to parents which may be strained by the breach. The child becomes emotionally involved far more deeply than is often realised. By the time one reaches adult status, the effect of a breach is no longer significant, according to Tappan[13].

The British evidence concerning the influence of broken homes on delinquency is just as equivocal as the American. Sir Cyril Burt found that about twice as many broken homes occurred in his delinquent sample compared with his controls[14], a finding echoed by Carr-Saunders, Mannheim and Rhodes in 1942[15]. Yet Ferguson in Glasgow[16] and Hughes in Coventry[17] obtained results which appeared to challenge this conclusion. Mannheim's Cambridge study appeared to confirm the fact that a high proportion of delinquents come from broken homes[18]. He has suggested that to treat the concept of the broken home as a unitary concept cannot be satisfactory: it should be regarded as something to be investigated deeper and broken down into its sociological and psychological components[19].

This approach to the concept of the broken home commends itself to many scholars. Even John Bowlby supports it. In his 1952 Report Bowlby wrote that 'the concept of the broken home is scientifically unsatisfactory and should be abandoned. It includes too many heterogeneous conditions having very different psychological effects'[20]. Howard Jones writes that 'in the study of the actual process of causation, and also in the working out of measures of prevention and treatment . . . the broken home is a blind alley'[1].

A strongly critical attack on British criminologists for subscribing to the view that the broken home causes crime came from the pen of Lady Wootton, who subjected the broken home concept to devastating

12 T. Ferguson, *The Young Delinquent in his Social Setting* (1952).
13 Tappan (1960) p. 196.
14 C. Burt, *The Young Delinquent* (1945) p. 95 and Table IV, p. 64.
15 A. M. Carr-Saunders, H. Mannheim, E. C. Rhodes, *Young Offenders* (1942) p. 62.
16 T. Ferguson, *The Young Delinquent in his Social Setting* (1952).
17 E.W. Hughes, 'An Analysis of the Records of Some 750 Probationers' B J Educ Psychol Vol. 13, No. 3, p. 113 (1943).
18 H. Mannheim, *Juvenile Delinquency in an English Middletown* (1948) pp. 20–21.
19 H. Mannheim, *Group Problems in Crime and Punishment* (1955) p. 135.
20 J. Bowlby, *Maternal Care and Mental Health* (1952) p. 12.
1 H. Jones, *Crime and the Penal System* (1962) p. 90.

analysis[2]. She asserts that the hypothesis about the etiological effect of the broken home in relation to crime is 'of all the hypotheses as to the origins of maladjustment or delinquency, perhaps the most generally accepted'. Our discussion has shown that this is by no means the case. She makes more cogent points when she complains about the absence of agreement among scholars about the precise definition of a broken home, and the absence of any information as to the frequency of broken homes among the population in general. She also acidly observed that every home is eventually broken in one way or another so that the important point is to observe when precisely the break occurs.

Trevor Gibbens' study of borstal youths[3] revealed that an exceptionally high proportion of borstal boys came from a very disturbed home background, but he observed this may be due to the way they are selected, as with approved school boys. He also makes the point that the unbroken home may on occasions be just as bad as any other (p. 69). In a third of the cases where both parents were living together their relationships were strained (55 per cent of the total cases). There was no evidence of more homes being broken by death of a parent than in some non-delinquent populations, and no reliable information about maternal separation could be obtained (p. 200).

The most recent British evidence on this matter comes from the Cambridge study of delinquency development. West discussed the broken home in the first volume of the series[4] and, like Lady Wootton, he observed that it is not easy to find a satisfactory definition of a broken home. Just over 10 per cent of their sample came from what they describe as anomalously constituted or incomplete families. Like so many other studies the 1973 study found that twice as many delinquents as controls came from homes which were broken before the age of ten by separation or desertion[5]. They also investigated a number of other factors concerning parental pathology including parental attitudes, discipline, conflict, degree of supervision, and so on. The Table overleaf gives in summary form the relevant findings, comparing delinquents and controls.

The general conclusion seems to be that unsatisfactory parents increase the chances of a child becoming delinquent as much as twofold. Broken homes which were not broken by death of a parent were found to be significantly related to delinquency where the offenders

2 Barbara Wootton, *Social Science and Social Pathology* (1959) pp. 118 et seq.
3 T. C. N. Gibbens, *Psychiatric Studies of Borstal Lads* (1963).
4 D. J. West, *Present Conduct and Future Delinquency* (1969) pp. 60 et seq.
5 D. J. West and D. P. Farrington, *Who Becomes Delinquent?* (1973).

Factors identified as relevant to delinquency judged by significant differences in per centage delinquent between those having or not having the factor in question

Factor	Factor present	Factor not present
1 cruel, passive or neglecting mother	33.3%	17.4%
2 mother's discipline very strict or erratic	26.7%	15.8%
maternal discipline harsh in emotional quality	37.2%	17.4%
3 parental conflict	35.0%	16.2%
4 parental supervision poor	31.1%	16.5%
parent joining in child's leisure	35.5%	16.8%
5 broken homes by separation or desertion before age 10	38.7%	19.0%
separation	32.2%	17.1%
6 maternal neuroticism	24.8%	16.8%
7 maternal instability	44.9%	15.3%
paternal instability	34.0%	17.5%

Source: Compiled from D. J. West and D. P. Farrington, *Who Becomes Delinquent?* (1973).

were convicted both as juveniles and as adults (p. 143) and where the delinquency itself was of an anti-social nature (p. 155). West concedes that 'it may seem that a great deal of effort has been spent documenting the obvious, namely that socially deprived, unloving, erratic, inconsistent, and careless parents tend to produce badly behaved boys'[6]. But we needed to demonstrate this scientifically. In the process of doing so, it would appear that the relative importance of the broken home has declined and other family factors have assumed more significance, principally the quality of the family relationships and the degree of warmth and loving care experienced. Also mentioned is tension and stress or conflict in the home.

6 (1969) p. 97.

B. Family tension

As we have seen, and as Howard Jones[7] points out, 'all the main psychological theories . . . lean heavily upon the family'. The over-whelming importance of the family atmosphere and the degree of warmth or affection exhibited by either or both the parents towards the child must be recognised. The Gluecks in their most recent studies of juvenile delinquency[8] attached great significance to such matters. One conclusion of Shaw and McKay's report from the 1930s can surely be accepted: that it is not so much the formal break in family membership that operates as a causative factor in delinquency but the cumulative effect of internal tension and discord[9]. Paul Tappan puts it well when he observes:

'tension, discord, and conflict in the home are often found in the delinquent *Gestalt*; it is these, rather than a formal breaking of the home, that possess significance in the child's maladaptations. In fact, it is undoubtedly true that a child's adjustment has often been improved when the desertion, divorce, or death of a parent has put a decisive period to a family atmosphere made morbid by hostility'[10].

The distinguished American psychiatrist David Abrahamsen stresses the significance of tension in relation to delinquency[11]. The most significant finding of a four-year study carried out under his direction at Columbia University was

'that those families which produced criminals showed a greater prevalence of unhealthy emotional conditions among the family members—that is, family tension—than did the families of the non-delinquent group. This family tension, manifested through hostility, hatred, resentment, nagging, bickering or psychosomatic disorders, engendered and maintained emotional disturbances in both children and parents alike'[12].

More recently Rutter in his review of the research to date 'suggests that it may be the discord and disharmony preceding the break (rather

7 H. Jones (1962) p. 88.
8 S. and E. Glueck, *Unraveling Juvenile Delinquency* (1950).
9 C. Shaw and H. D. McKay, (1931) p. 285.
10 P. W. Tappan, (1949) pp. 135–136.
11 D. Abrahamsen, *The Psychology of Crime* (1960). See also his article 'Family Tension: Basic Cause of Criminal Behaviour' 40 J Crim L & Crim'ogy & Pol Sci p. 330 (September/October 1949).
12 p. 43.

than the break itself) which led to the children developing antisocial behaviour'[13].

C. Home discipline and relationships

Whether home discipline or the absence of it is a significant etiological factor is a question which has been explored by many criminologists. Sir Cyril Burt placed defective discipline at the top of his list of significant factors, having found that 60.9 per cent of his delinquents came from homes with defective discipline, compared with 11.5 per cent of his controls[14]. The Gluecks too regarded the absence of sound discipline as sufficiently important to include this factor in their social prediction table which was designed to forecast the probability of a child becoming delinquent[15]. They concentrate on the role of the father in this respect, but they also use the factor of supervision of the boy by the mother, which must be closely related. The earlier Glueck studies had also found 'unsound' discipline involving either extremely lax or extremely rigid control in about seven-tenths of criminal men and nearly two-thirds of delinquent women[16]. The Gluecks' volume on *Family Environment* also explores the relationship between discipline in the home and the development of the child's personality traits[17]. Healy and Bronner found that 40 per cent of their 4,000 cases came from families with lack of discipline[18]. Carr-Saunders, Mannheim and Rhodes also found less striking but highly significant differences with regard to the factor of discipline[19].

The McCord study[20] which retrospectively analysed material from a pre-war survey in America known as the Cambridge-Somerville Youth study, attached more importance to consistency of parental discipline than to whether it was rigid or firm, or relaxed and weak. As Mannheim puts it, 'there was, surprisingly perhaps, no evidence that

13 M. Rutter, *Maternal Deprivation Reassessed* (1981) p. 110.
14 C. Burt, *The Young Delinquent* (1945) p. 606 and p. 53.
15 S. and E. Glueck, *Unraveling Juvenile Delinquency* (1950) pp. 130–133 and p. 261.
16 D. R. Taft, *Criminology* (1956) p. 201.
17 S. and E. Glueck, *Family Environment and Delinquency* (1962) summarised by H. Mannheim, *Comparative Criminology* (1965) Vol. 2, p. 614.
18 Taft (1956) p. 201, citing W. Healy and A. F. Bronner, *Delinquents and Criminals, Their Making and Unmaking* (1926) p. 125.
19 A. M. Carr-Saunders, H. Mannheim and E. C. Rhodes, *Young Offenders* (1942) as reported by H. Mannheim (1965) p. 614.
20 W. McCord and J. McCord, *Origins of Crime* (1959).

consistently punitive discipline was a criminogenic factor; on the contrary. Consistency was more important than the choice between punitive and love-oriented methods'[1]. The Gluecks too attach significance to what they term 'erratic' disciplinary methods 'swinging from overstrictness to laxity, without any consistency'[2]. It is frequently the case that one parent treats a child firmly and the other is indulgent, and the contradictory signals the child receives may well cause confusion. There may also be discrimination in the way different children are treated in the same family, to which Mannheim draws attention[3]. Questions of birth order, and the effect of being an only child, have also been considered by criminologists, as well as the effect of being one of a large family, or an unwanted child[4].

There seems to be an unusual degree of unanimity among criminologists about the significance of home discipline in the explanation of delinquency. This is coupled with emphasis on the importance of the emotional climate of the home, and the degree of warmth or affection which exists between the family members – or what Nye called 'the happiness factor'. The Gluecks come up with the two factors 'degree of affection of father for boy' and 'degree of affection of mother for boy' as important in their social prediction table[5].

One final word about home discipline and the quality of family relationships. Paul Tappan has observed the difficulties of appraising or comparing the standards which prevail in these matters in different social classes, groups or cultures. 'It seems probable', he says, 'that disciplinary practices are "defective" by the standards of good mental hygiene in a great proportion of the homes of all social classes, although the techniques of family control vary a great deal. It is not sound to impute poor discipline only to lower socio-economic groups'[6]. Moreover one might add that standards change from one generation to another.

---

1 Mannheim (1965) p. 615.
2 S. and E. Glueck, (1950) p. 132. The Cambridge Study of Delinquency Development tested factors such as inconsistency in parental handling and strict or erratic discipline by either parent, and found the more delinquency-prone boys had had such experience more often than the rest: D. J. West (1969) p. 96; West and Farrington (1973) pp. 51–52.
3 H. Mannheim (1965) p. 616.
4 Some of these questions are dealt with in B. Wootton, *Social Science and Social Pathology* (1959) and in H. Mannheim (1965) pp. 610–617. See also G. Rahav, 'Birth Order and Delinquency' BJC Vol. 20, No. 4, p. 385 (October 1980).
5 S. and E. Gluecks (1950) p. 261.
6 Tappan (1949) p. 137, note 4.

D. Criminality in the family

The influence of other members of the family who are already delinquent, including not only siblings, but other relations, has been examined by criminologists interested in exploring family pathology in relation to crime. Burt found that vice and crime were present already in the homes of his delinquents five times as frequently as in the homes of his controls[7]. The Gluecks in their earlier studies had observed that a high proportion (over 80 per cent) of offenders had been reared in homes where there were other criminal members[8]. In their 1950 study of juvenile delinquency they found over 90 per cent of the delinquent boys came from homes where drunkenness, crime or immorality occurred, compared with only 54 per cent in the case of the controls[9]. From this evidence Sutherland and Cressey concluded that 'the homes in which delinquents are reared are in an extraordinary degree situations in which patterns of delinquency are present'[10].

West and Farrington[11] provide the most recent discussion of this matter. They point out that the fact that crime tends to be concentrated in certain families and that criminal parents tend to have criminal children has been known for years. Lady Wootton[12] discussed this in 1959, and Ferguson's Glasgow study[13] had shown that boys with criminal fathers were twice as likely to be delinquent as other boys, and that boys with delinquent older brothers were three times as likely. West and Farrington regard these propositions as still remaining valid. What is not clear is the precise mechanism whereby criminality comes to be transmitted. They carried out a special investigation of this matter. They conclude that 'the self-perpetuating characteristics of family criminality cannot be denied'. Striking results were obtained when the criminality of the youths in this study was compared with that of their parents. Forty five such families out of nearly 400 accounted for nearly half the individuals convicted, and an even more striking concentration occurred when they found that eighteen families accounted for nearly half of all the convictions[14]. They say that the reason for this is not clear, and various possible

---

7 C. Burt, *The Young Delinquent* (1945).
8 See the studies cited by E. H. Sutherland, *Principles of Criminology* (1960) p. 174.
9 S. and E. Glueck, *Unraveling Juvenile Delinquency* (1950) pp. 110-111.
10 Sutherland (1960) p. 175.
11 D. J. West and D. P. Farrington, *The Delinquent Way of Life* (1977) pp. 109 et seq.
12 B. Wootton (1959) pp. 87 et seq.
13 T. Ferguson (1952).
14 p. 111.

explanations were explored without success. The explanation does not appear to lie in instruction of sons by their fathers in criminal techniques, or the communication of hostile attitudes towards society, or any factor connected with child-rearing. Nor is it necessarily the result of increased vulnerability to police attention or any factor connected with police prosecution policy. They suggest that other adverse social factors, such as residence in a delinquency area and attendance at a school with a high delinquency rate, could be responsible[15].

The effect of having a criminal brother was found to be almost as great as that of having a criminal father[16]. The general conclusion is that the self-perpetuating characteristics of family criminality cannot be denied, but the explanation for this remains elusive[17]. West and Farrington do appear to suggest however that where the child has a criminal father it is likely to be less well supervised[18].

E. Neglect

A few criminologists have studied the effect of child neglect on the pattern of behaviour of the child as it grows up, and in particular delinquent behaviour. This has been linked with interest in what is described as 'the problem family' and more recently with growing awareness of the extent of 'baby-battering' and, indeed, the battered wife syndrome. Of course such behaviour as cruelty and wilful neglect constitutes criminal offences on the part of the perpetrator. What we are here concerned with is the effect on the child. Harriet Wilson's study of 52 problem families in Cardiff[19] shows they had a delinquency rate eight times as high as the general rate for that city and well over twice the rate for non-problem families living in the close vicinity. Moreover the problem families living in the low-delinquency areas showed a delinquency rate similar to those residing in the high-delinquency areas, which tends to suggest that the area has little to do with it[20]. Wilson explored various factors which might explain the

15 p. 121.
16 p. 123.
17 p. 124.
18 D. J. West and D. P. Farrington, *Who Becomes Delinquent?* (1973) p. 42, quoted in West and Farrington (1977) at p. 117; see also p. 121.
19 H. Wilson, *Delinquency and Child Neglect* (1962).
20 p. 122, and see H. Mannheim (1965) p. 624.

high level of delinquency found among her sample and concluded that 'the mere fact of child neglect was the primary causative factor'[1].

Notes. Family factors

1 Discussion of the part played by criminality already present in the family reminds one of the studies of so-called criminal families carried out in the early period of criminological research, such as Richard Dugdale's study of *The Jukes* (1877), A. H. Estabrook's follow-up in 1916, Estabrook and Davenport's study of *The Nam Family* (1912) and H. H. Goddard's study of *The Kalikaks* (1912). These studies all used family trees to prove that crime was inherited, by tracing the very high incidence of criminal members of the same family. Deviant behaviour of other kinds such as prostitution was noted, as well as venereal disease, feeble mindedness and pauperism. The reliability of these early studies is questionable, the families selected being unrepresentative, the data being incomplete and not tested in accordance with modern scientific methods, according to Mannheim (1965) p. 229. Mannheim's conclusion was that 'family histories of this type are not convincing evidence'. See also E. H. Sutherland (1960) pp. 98 et seq.; P. W. Tappan (1960) pp. 104–105; H. Jones (1962) pp. 34–35; S. Hurwitz, *Criminology* (1952) pp. 58 et seq. H. Mannheim (1965) and S. Hurwitz (1952) cite a number of European studies of criminal families.

One might add the reflection that we are quite familiar with families where the attainment of success and high office in the law runs in the family, and the same might be said of banking, commerce and other professions. Yet no one seriously regards this as entirely due to inheritance.

2 The tendency to point to the broken home as a cause of crime is very widespread. Thus two probation officers writing a book of practical guidance for social workers, while recognising that a constellation of factors centred on the relationships in the home and environment are relevant to understanding delinquency, remark at one point that 'few practising social workers will agree with the conclusions drawn' from the statistics, and deplore the tendency in recent years for the effects of the 'broken home' on children to be discounted: H. L. Herbert and F. V. Jarvis, *Dealing with Delinquents* (1961) p. 68. The psychiatrist Dr. Eustace Chesser regards broken homes as a major tragedy of modern life: E. Chesser, *The Sexual, Marital and Family Relationships of the English Woman* (1956). There is a sense in which practitioners use the 'broken home' syndrome as a kind of convenient shorthand to indicate a disturbed family pathology. But in scientific terms the concept must be viewed with extreme caution, as we have shown.

1 p. 145.

3 As in the case of low intelligence, so in the case of the broken home, some modern criminologists are beginning to challenge conventional scientific wisdom. Thus Karen Wilkinson has re-examined the status of the broken home as an aetiological factor in crime: see Karen Wilkinson, 'The Broken Home and Delinquent Behaviour' in *Understanding Crime: Current Theory and Research* (1980), eds. T. Hirschi and M. Goffredson, p. 21.

2 Area studies of crime

The American area studies

One of the earliest sociological approaches to the study of crime was that which originated in Chicago in the 1930s, principally associated with the names of Clifford Shaw and Henry D. McKay. Already in Chicago the sociologists Park and Burgess had developed what can be described as an ecological approach to the study of urban areas. They used the biological concept of ecology[2] and adapted it to the study of human beings, in their book *The City* published in 1925. Soon their students and colleagues applied the same method of the study of crime. Frederic Thrasher in 1927 published his classic study of *The Gang*, in which he included a map plotting the distribution of juvenile gangs operating in Chicago. In 1929 Clifford Shaw's book *Delinquency Areas* was entirely devoted to the ecological approach to the study of crime. He later collaborated with Henry D. McKay in the preparation of two volumes on juvenile delinquency, one published in 1931, and a later revised edition in 1942: *Juvenile Delinquency and Urban Areas*, a book which became a classic in this field.

There had been in America some earlier writing in this field, for example, by the social workers Abbott and Breckinridge in 1912[3]. In Britain in the eighteenth and nineteenth centuries social observers like Fielding, Mayhew, Charles Dickens and Charles Booth had chronicled the existence of areas of high crime, sanctuaries or refuges for thieves known sometimes as rookeries[4], and in Europe Guerry in France and Quetelet in Belgium had pioneered the study of social data relating to criminal behaviour, an approach which was echoed in

2 The biological concept of ecology refers to studies of the way plants and animals are influenced by or are the product of their environment, in terms of soil, climate, habitat, etc. It also refers to the way they adapt to their surroundings.
3 E. Abbott and S. P. Breckinridge, *The Delinquent Child and the Home* (1912).
4 J. J. Tobias, *Nineteenth-century Crime: Prevention and Punishment* (1972).

Zone maps for three juvenile court series.

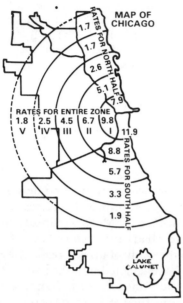

A. Zone rates of male juvenile
delinquents, 1927-33 series

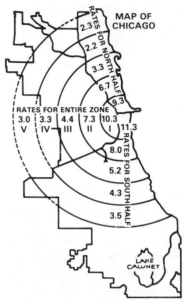

B. Zone rates of male juvenile
delinquents, 1917-23 series

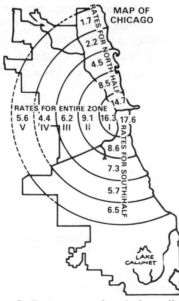

C. Zone rates of male juvenile
delinquents, 1900-1906 series

Source: Shaw C. and McKay H.D.
Juvenile Delinquency and Urban Areas
(1942).

Rates of male juvenile delinquents, Chicago 1927-33.

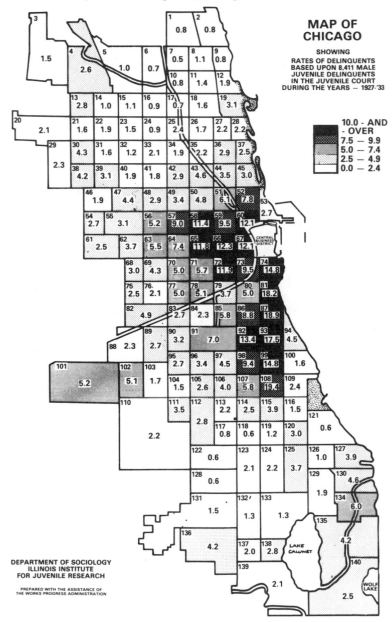

Source: Shaw C. and McKay H.D. Juvenile Delinquency and Urban Areas
(1942).

Britain by Rawson and Fletcher[5]. It was natural to see a connection between certain poor areas of the city and high rates of crime. As Lady Wootton remarked rather acidly in 1959 'even the most unprejudiced sociological eyebrows will hardly be raised at the discovery that delinquency tends to be concentrated in particular areas, and that in general those are the slummy ones'[6].

The distinctive contribution of Shaw and McKay, however, was to place these observations on a better scientific footing. They had available, as T. P. Morris has pointed out, more accurate social data and more refined statistical techniques[7]. Using these they were able to show by a variety of methods such as spot maps of the city of Chicago, radial maps, and by plotting the rates of crime in mile square areas of the city, the pattern of distribution of crime (see maps ante, pp. 102–103). This they demonstrated was higher in the centre of the city and tended to diminish as one approached the outer suburbs. 'Delinquency areas' could be discerned. These were what Burgess had called 'areas of social disorganisation' or what Thrasher described as 'interstitial areas'. They tended to be zones where industry and commerce had forced out all but the poorest and least eligible members of community and in these slums there tended to reside the poorest citizens including large numbers of immigrants and coloured people. Crime was much higher in these areas, and tended to remain high over several generations. Here we may see the seeds of the notion of a delinquent sub-culture which has developed and is passed on to children and adolescents growing up in such areas.

Sutherland[8] summarised the conclusions reached by Shaw and McKay in the form of five propositions, as follows:

1 the rates of delinquency vary in different neighbourhoods. The neighbourhoods with the highest rates may be designated 'delinquency areas';

2 the rates of delinquency are generally highest in the low-rent areas near the centre of the city and decrease with the distance from the centre of the city;

3 the areas with high rates of delinquency also have high rates of truancy from school, and the areas with a high rate of delinquency for boys also have a high rate for girls;

5 T. P. Morris, *The Criminal Area: A Study in Social Ecology* (1957).
6 B. Wootton, *Social Science and Social Pathology* (1959) p. 65.
7 Morris (1957) p. 71.
8 Sutherland (1960) p. 158.

4 the areas which had a high rate of delinquency in 1930 also had a high rate of delinquency in 1900;

5 the delinquency rate of a particular national group shows the same general tendency as the delinquency rate for the entire population.

The original Shaw and McKay study was severely criticised on a number of grounds, as we shall see, but the method of ecological study of crime was applied to many other American cities, so that by 1942 no less than eighteen cities were included in Shaw and McKay's revised edition. The 1942 edition introduced refinements and embodied reformulations designed to accommodate some of the criticisms and make the work more acceptable. It is perhaps right to point out at this juncture that linked with the ecological analysis Shaw and McKay proposed a social programme of community based activities which was put into effect in the well-known Chicago Area Project, with the help of voluntary contributions from business and commerce. The messianic character of Shaw is well described in Snodgrass's recent rather critical biographical account[9].

Criticisms and extensions of area studies

One of the fiercest critics of Shaw and McKay's thesis was Sophia M. Robison. In her book *Can Delinquency Be Measured?* (1936) she made a fundamental attack on their conclusions, which she said were wrong in three respects:

1 they were based on court records of appearances which did not allow for the differential rate of reporting offenders or bringing proceedings against them;

2 they were based on legal definitions of delinquency which sociologists regard as an inadequate test of deviant behaviour;

3 they were based on calculating rates of delinquency for mile square areas which bore no necessary relationship to natural neighbourhoods.

Moreover she pointed out that the concentric idea of the organisation and growth of a city was inapplicable to New York City so far as Manhattan is concerned. She 'felt that the gradient of delinquency rates from the city centre outwards was merely coincidental with a

9 J. Snodgrass, 'Clifford R. Shaw and H. D. McKay: Chicago Criminologists' BJC Vol. 16, No. 1, p. 1 (January 1976).

particular type of urban development'[10]. While there is much substance in her criticism in respect of the artificial character of the mile-square areas, there must be doubt whether one can do better than rely on court figures as an index of levels of criminal behaviour, and the legal definition of delinquency seems a firmer base than any other. Morris points out that the notion of the radial development of a city is not central to the Shaw and McKay position but of secondary importance[11]. What is crucial is the significance of the various stages of a city's growth, and the invasion of residential zones by industry and commerce, and their decline as desirable areas to live which is correlated with high rates of delinquency, as successive waves of settlers, often immigrants and blacks, take the place of those who have moved on. He considers that the most important criticism made by Robison is 'that Shaw did not consider adequately the differences between groups of approximately the *same* socio-economic status, living in *similar* areas'[11].

Another American scholar who found that the zonal hypothesis did not work too well when applied to his chosen area was Bernard Lander, whose study of Baltimore tested various of Shaw's hypotheses[12]. Lander found no evidence to support the zonal hypothesis in Baltimore, and was unable to confirm the view that high rates of delinquency were found in areas populated by large concentrations of immigrants[13]. Moreover, he found that delinquency was not correlated with poverty, bad housing, and other socio-economic conditions of an area. He thought that stable communities had low delinquency rates despite having some of these characteristics, and that social instability and normlessness—what Durkheim called *anomie*—characterised high delinquency areas[14].

Further highly critical analysis of the ecological approach was provided by Alihan in 1938[15]. She felt extremely unhappy about the application of the ecological analogy, i.e. applying to man the lessons of plant and animal life, remarking that 'generally the analogy is labored and, if anything, distorts rather than describes or explains reality'[16].

Despite these criticisms, with the help of increasingly sophisticated methods of statistical correlation, other American scholars such as

10 Morris (1957) p. 85.
11 p. 88.
12 B. Lander, *Towards an Understanding of Juvenile Delinquency* (1954).
13 pp. 81 and 83.
14 pp. 88 and 89.
15 M. A. Alihan, *Social Ecology: A Critical Analysis* (1938)
16 p. 249.

Shevky and Bell[17] and Schmid[18] took the ecological approach still further. Using multivariate analysis they came up with little that was new or enlightening, and have themselves been criticised for shortcomings over both concepts and methods[19]. The better view appears to be that merely to develop these analyses without a theory to test will not advance our knowledge of the subject, for the facts will not simply 'speak for themselves'.

One feature of the area hypothesis which has attracted attention is the possibility of selective migration, i.e. that 'birds of a feather flock together' in the sense that people with bad character congregate, and at the same time 'bad money drives out the good' in the sense that other persons resident in a district will choose to leave rather than remain in those areas which are 'going down' or getting a bad reputation or are in other ways undesirable. There is constantly taking place a process of social selection and migration, as Donald Taft showed as long ago as 1933[20] and although Sutherland found this argument unconvincing[1], it derives some support from the field of mental health where studies of suicide and mental disorder have been made along ecological lines. Spencer asserted that 'the "attraction" hypothesis is supported by evidence in the field of mental disorder', and thought there was undoubtedly a certain amount of social selection and segregation going on[2]. This may be linked up with a comment made by Lady Wootton to the effect that the value of ecological studies lies not so much in what they have discovered about the static position in the community, but more in the light they throw upon the mechanisms whereby an antisocial culture can be absorbed and communicated – the process of social dynamics[3]. As we shall see, the British area studies tend to confirm the significance of social selection and migration. We shall also see that often there is precious little choice involved. Factors such as

---

17 E. Shevky and W. Bell, *Social Area Analysis: Theory, Illustrative Application and Computational Procedures* (1955). Also E. Shevky and M. Williams, *The Social Area of Los Angeles: Analysis and Typology* (1949).

18 C. F. Schmid, 'Urban Crime Areas' 25 Am Soc Rev 527 et seq and 655 et seq (1960).

19 See John Baldwin's pungent criticism in his essay 'Ecological and Areal Studies in Great Britain and the United States' in *Crime and Justice: An Annual Review of Research* (1979), eds. N. Morris and M. Tonry, p. 29 at pp. 40 et seq. Also B. T. Robson *Urban Analysis* (1971) pp. 48 et seq.

20 D. R. Taft, 'Testing the Selective Influence of Areas of Delinquency' 38 Am Jo Soc 699 (March 1933).

1 Sutherland (1960) p. 161.

2 J. Spencer, 'Delinquency Areas' BJD Vol. VII, No. 2, p. 146 (October 1956).

3 B. Wootton (1959) p. 73.

public housing policy, social attitudes and other constraints may be more important than any ecological factors. To see the problems solely in terms of spatial analysis is now regarded as somewhat naive. It is to the British area studies that we must now turn.

The British area studies

The British studies of delinquency which parallel the American area studies have proceeded upon slightly different lines and have produced different results. Some of these have tended to concentrate attention on particular areas of the city rather than attempt a city-wide analysis, and have as a result of this microscopic approach achieved a remarkable picture of the differences occurring between different streets or sectors of the same community or area. There has also been a realisation of the necessity of distinguishing between areas of crime commission and areas where the delinquents reside. This was stressed by T. P. Morris in his Croydon study of 1957, and he points out that it is a distinction ignored by Shaw who made a fundamental error in this respect[4]. The importance of this distinction had been realised by other scholars such as Lind[5] in his study of Honolulu in 1930, and Hasan El Saaty[6] in his study of Cairo, Egypt, in 1946.

Morris studied crime patterns in Croydon, a town some twenty miles south east of London which is not only a commuter base but has an identity of its own (and now a splended new town centre). At the time of the study it had attracted some notoriety due to the attentions of the press engendered by the Craig and Bentley case. Morris collected data of the number of offences known to the police, the types of offences, and the ward distribution of crime. This information was related to such factors as population density, overcrowding, and the proportion of middle-class households. He found that 25 per cent of the crime in Croydon was committed within a quarter of a mile of the centre of the town. It was here that the shops, unguarded warehouses and offices existed which provided the best opportunities for property crime. When the distribution of the offenders' places of residence was plotted on a ward basis, it was found that the four wards with the

4 T. P. Morris, *The Criminal Area* (1957) pp. 20–21 and p. 73.
5 A. W. Lind, 'Some Ecological Patterns of Community Disorganisation in Honolulu' 36 Am Jo Soc 206 (1930).
6 H. El Saaty, *Juvenile Delinquency in Egypt*; unpublished doctoral dissertation, University of London, 1946.

highest delinquency rates were the ones where property was in decline, due to the effects of bombing and re-development plans, and where the worst housing conditions existed. Also the rate of delinquency was high on the two large housing estates built between the wars. A positive correlation was found between delinquency and population density and overcrowding, and a negative correlation with the proportion of middle-class households.

Two earlier studies had emphasised the significance of a delinquent culture prevailing in a particular area of the city or town. John Mays[7] had described graphically the attitudes and behaviour of boys growing up in certain areas of Liverpool. Jephcott and Carter[8] had shown how two neighbouring streets in the same Derbyshire mining town could be contrasted with regard to their cultural attitudes and their social behaviour, including criminal behaviour. Dyke Street will forever be remembered by British criminologists in contrast with Gladstone Road. Howard Jones[9] examined delinquent behaviour in housing estates in Leicester, and John Spencer and Roger Wilson[10] surveyed the pattern of crime and social behaviour in a Bristol housing estate, as part of the Bristol Social Project. The Bristol study showed that part of a new housing estate had developed quite a different character from the rest of the estate in terms of the incidence of social problem families and high rates of delinquency, partly due to the influence of social selection and migration, partly due to deliberate housing management policy. Jones found something similar in Leicester in the contrasts between two newly built housing estates, one of which had a much better record than the other in these respects. Delinquency also persisted in the older more stable slum areas near the city centre. One conclusion deriving from this study which also receives some support from Ferguson's study of Glasgow[11] is that simply to rehouse people gives no guarantee that their behaviour will improve.

Two further British studies must be mentioned to complete the picture. In 1967 Wallis and Maliphant[12] published their study of

7 J. B. Mays, *Growing up in the City* (1954).
8 M. P. Carter and P. Jephcott, *The Social Background of Delinquency* (unpublished manuscript (1954)), referred to in T. P. Morris (1957) at pp. 104 et seq. See also W. J. H. Sprott, 'Delinquency Areas' BJD Vol. VII, No. 2, pp. 137–138 (October 1956).
9 H. Jones, 'Approaches to an Ecological Study' BJD Vol. VIII, p. 277 (1958).
10 J. Spencer, 'Delinquency Areas' BJD Vol. VII, No. 2, p. 146. R. Wilson, *Difficult Housing Estates* (1963). J. C. Spencer, *Stress and Release in an Urban Estate* (1964).
11 T. Ferguson, *The Young Delinquent in his Social Setting* (1952).
12 C. P. Wallis and R. Maliphant, 'Delinquency Areas in the County of London' BJC Vol. 7, p. 250 (July 1967).

delinquent areas in London which was based on a study of 350 boys who were sent to either prison, borstal or detention centre, and whose home addresses lay in the old London County Council (LCC) area. The 29 metropolitan boroughs were grouped into 46 areas and the boys were allocated to each. The delinquency rate was calculated for each area per 1,000 of the male population aged 17–20. The conclusions which emerged were as follows:

1 The areas of high delinquency were similar to those found by Sir Cyril Burt in 1922–1923. Only slight shifts of emphasis had taken place.

2 As in other studies, a high correlation was observed with areas of poverty and over-crowding, and areas with many children in care matched the high delinquency areas closely.

3 Low correlations were found with areas of high divorce rates, illegitimacy and suicide rates. The authors observe that this has not been found in other cities such as Liverpool, but London seems to be different from other cities. Sainsbury's study of suicide[13] showed that unlike Chicago, the areas of poverty and social disorganisation are not identical, and the authors suggest that here economic rather than social disorganisation factors are of relatively greater importance in determining juvenile delinquency. They also suggest that the concept of social disorganisation is not a unitary one, and the distribution of its parts are not the same in all communities. Thus in London we find areas of high delinquency rates with many children in care on the one hand, and on the other hand quite different areas, with high rates of suicide, divorce and mental illness.

The Sheffield study by Baldwin and Bottoms[14] provides further evidence to support previous findings. Here areas of crime commission are distinguished from areas of residence of delinquents by calculating the distance travelled to commit the offence. The role of council housing estates, areas of rented accommodation, and areas with a predominance of owner-occupation is examined. Working on the basis of official crime reports to the police and census data on wards and enumeration districts, they show how Sheffield is a unique city in that it has been relatively crime free for many years. The characteristics of juvenile and adolescent and adult crime in Sheffield seem to be

13 P. Sainsbury, *Suicide in London* (1955); T. P. Morris (1957) p. 178.
14 J. Baldwin and A. E. Bottoms, *The Urban Criminal* (1976).

different, Generally offenders were concentrated in the so-called 'twilight areas' where there were relatively high proportions of immigrants, and on certain council housing estates, and areas close to the main areas of heavy industry. The juveniles committed their offences predominantly in their local area, whereas the age group sixteen and over travelled some distance to commit their crimes. There is a great deal of information given about such variables as social class, housing type, and type of offence, which it is difficult to summarise. The book ends with a detailed examination of the problem of 'difficult' housing estates. The theory based on social disorganisation did not fit and the researchers were left with certain ideas and hypotheses concerning housing policy and social space and social networks. Further research is being carried out in a second stage to test some of these questions.

John Mays[15] has regretted the tendency among criminologists today to react against the idea of the criminal area and to belittle the contribution of the Chicago School. He believes the central tenets remain valid, and are not vitiated by the fact that some people residing in a delinquency area do not commit delinquency. There can be no doubt that some areas are 'delinquency-producing': any chief constable could verify this. One needs to evaluate the significance of police discrimination or selection, of the under-reporting of crime in middle-class areas, and the greater opportunities for crime in areas with many warehouses, offices, etc. Mays believes there is more to it, and that some areas have a 'crime-tolerant social atmosphere' or ethos which makes them delinquency areas. He discounts various criticisms of the area approach, and observes that 'delinquency areas or delinquent communities . . . are comparatively small in British cities and towns, and for this reason the concept of the large criminal zone as originally described by the Chicago School is not viable in this country'[16].

The contribution of human geography and urban sociology

We cannot form a rounded view of the situation concerning area studies today without taking cognizance of the contribution which human geography and urban sociology has made to the further elucidation of these matters.

The human geographers have repeated and extended the study of

---

15 J. B. Mays, 'Delinquency Areas–A Re-assessment' BJC Vol. 3, No. 3, p. 216 (January 1963).
16 pp. 222–223.

the city and urban areas, as has been already mentioned, by the application of various kinds of statistical analysis to census data and other social data. By now a vast number of cities have been studied in a wide variety of different countries. Excellent summaries of the work which has been done are provided by Robson[17] and Herbert[18]. It is a comfort to find several of the conclusions agree with those reached by criminologists. There is recognition that the purely ecological approach leaves out of account significant human factors such as community attitudes, values desires and needs. Thus Robson asserts that 'geographers, no less than ecologists, are not interested in spatial patterns per se but rather in the dynamics and the factors which are responsible for the existence of spatial associations or spatial patterns'[19]. There is some emphasis on the process of adaptation to the environment and the importance of avoiding 'the danger of assigning to the environmental factors a determinative influence which they do not exert'[20] The cultural anthropologists too have stressed the importance of recognising the powerful influence of man over his environment and the significance of adaptation[1]. There seems to be general agreement concerning the importance of culture in relation to area. Thus Robson found in Sunderland that the milieu had an important influence upon urban social structure. 'Within the term "milieu" is included not only the physical environment of housing conditions, but also the less tangible factors of room density and area density, of the whole complex of such psychological factors as attitudes and of spatial location relative to the facilities within the town and other people or types of people within a given local area'[2].

Herbert's account of the research studies also recognises the importance of cultural attitudes and values. He points out that one of the great difficulties has been that of establishing causality through correlational analysis, and many past studies have inferred causality where it has been spurious[3]. 'The basic question concerns the relevance of neighbourhood and geographical location in the understanding of life styles'[4]. Here Herbert believes that the social geographical referent must always be of some significance, though

17 B. T. Robson, *Urban Analysis: A Study of City Structure with Special Reference to Sunderland* (1971).
18 D. Herbert, *Urban Geography: A Social Perspective* (1972).
19 Robson (1971) p. 33.
20 A view expressed by H. H. Barrows as long ago as 1923. Ann Ass Am Geogr XIII, p. 1 (1923) quoted by Robson (1971) at p. 29.
1 Y. A. Cohen, *Man in Adaptation: The Bio Social Background* (1968).
2 Robson (1971) p. 244.
3 Herbert (1972) p. 212.
4 p. 225.

other factors, social, psychological or economic, will often be of equal or greater relevance.

The urban sociologists have approached the subject more from the point of view of the constraints of social class and the effect of the environment on social networks and also the influence of what is described as social space. Timms[5] sees the city as a mosaic of social worlds. The modern city is highly differentiated between neighbourhoods, as a result of social rank, family status, ethnicity and urban mobility. At the individual level there is an element of choice about residential location but various constraints powerfully influence the result. There is still room in this discussion for testing out the zonal hypothesis, for looking at areas of social disorganisation and areas of transition. 'The zones in transition around the central business district and on the rural–urban periphery provide a haven for despised minorities and an attractive location for all those who welcome the anonymity and freedom from traditional social controls characteristic of the urban way of life'[6].

Pahl[7] places more emphasis on the constraints than upon the element of freedom of choice. By reason of social class, economic status, housing arrangements, people are locked in to a way of life in a particular environment with its own attendant values and attitudes. This is a much more deterministic (and hence pessimistic) interpretation which invites compassion or a political solution to mitigate or resolve. The contrast with the views of the human geographers is noted by Herbert[8] but perhaps it is more a matter of emphasis than of substance.

To return to the views of criminologists, for the present we can do no better than quote the opinion of John Baldwin[9] co-author of the Sheffield study, that social area analysis and the use of multi-variate statistical methods are unlikely to add significantly to our knowledge. According to the other co-author of the Sheffield study, A. E. Bottoms[10], it seems likely that the promising directions for theory and research lie in the exploration of ideas of social space, social networks

5 D. Timms, *The Urban Mosaic: Towards a Theory of Residential Differentiation* (1971).

6 p. 252.

7 R. E. Pahl, *Patterns of Urban Life* 1970; *Readings in Urban Sociology* (1968), ed. R. E. Pahl.

8 D. Herbert (1972) p. 224.

9 J. Baldwin, 'Ecological and Areal Studies in Great Britain and the United States' in N. Morris and M. Tonry, *Crime and Justice* (1979) Vol. I, pp. 29 et seq. at pp. 53–54.

10 J. Baldwin and A. E. Bottoms, *The Urban Criminal* (1976), Introductory Essay by A. E. Bottoms, p. 1, at pp. 18 et seq.

and housing policy. These are the directions in which to look for the future exploration of the subject.

Notes. Area influences

1 In their book *Delinquency Research: An Appraisal of Analytic Methods* (1967), T. Hirschi and H. C. Selvin take as an example of the dangers of multivariate statistical analysis Bernard Lander's study of juvenile delinquency in Baltimore: *Towards An Understanding of Juvenile Delinquency* (1954) which they think contained 'some serious methodological errors' (p. 146). Typical of many area studies of crime is to infer causality from the discovery of a correlation without observing that further testing is required before assuming such a relationship. There is what is described as a failure 'to consider the problem of causal order' (p. 149). As the geographer D. Herbert puts it in *Urban Geography* (1972) p. 212: 'Hirschi and Selvin have carefully spelt out the dangers in correlational analysis and have shown that in many past studies, causality has been inferred where it has been spurious and that the necessity for careful testing before assuming a relationship has been ignored'.

2 John Baldwin in his review of 'Ecological and Areal Studies in Great Britain and the United States', in *Crime and Justice* (1979), eds. N. Morris and M. Tonry, argues that there is a great difference between the ecological studies of the city carried out by Burgess and his followers and the 'areal' studies of Shaw and McKay. This is also a point stressed by A. E. Bottoms in J. Baldwin and A. E. Bottoms, *The Urban Criminal* (1976): 'Shaw and McKay . . . did not . . . rely much on Park's biotic model' (p. 15). Alihan had pointed this out in 1938: M. A. Alihan, *Social Ecology: A Critical Analysis*. Instead their theory of delinquency was a social and cultural one. They still used some of the ideas contained in Burgess's work concerning the zones of transition and migration but they were mainly interested in social disorganisation and socialisation into a delinquent culture: J. Baldwin and A. E. Bottoms (1976) p. 16. It is as such that it has to be evaluated.

3 'The ecological fallacy', effectively exposed by Alihan in 1938 was further demonstrated in 1950 by W. S. Robinson, 'Ecological Correlations and the Behaviour of Individuals' 15 Am Soc Rev 351 (1950). To quote J. Baldwin (1979) again, 'Robinson argued that it is a mistake to assume that there is a simple correspondence between properties of areas and the properties of the individuals who live in the areas. This means that, at the very least, the greatest care is needed in interpreting areal data' (p. 35). Baldwin echoes Hirschi and Selvin in emphasising the dangers of social area analysis and factor analysis.

4 The effect on different ethnic groups of migration into and out of delinquency areas has been the subject of some research. The Chinese and

Japanese communities seem to have such a strong culture of their own that they remain impervious to the criminogenic influences of a delinquency area. Sutherland (1960) cites the study by Hayner of the Japanese in Seattle (p. 162) and Pauline Young's study of the Moloccans in Los Angeles. The former group had a very low rate of delinquency although they settled in a high delinquency area, in contrast to the Moloccans whose rate of delinquency increased dramatically after they settled in a high delinquency area: see N. S. Hayner, 'Delinquency Areas in the Puget Sound Area' 39 Am Jo Soc 314 (November 1933); Pauline V. Young, 'Urbanization as a Factor in Juvenile Delinquency', Publications of the American Sociological Society Vol. 24, p. 162 (1930).

5 Another dimension of the area studies approach to crime is to consider the relation between urban and rural crime. This has been the subject of extensive studies by Marshall B. Clinard: see his *Sociology of Deviant Behaviour* (1957) Chap. 3, and his essay on 'The Relation of Urbanization and Urbanism to Criminal Behaviour' in E. W. Burgess and D. J. Bogue, *Contributions to Urban Sociology* (1965) pp. 541 et seq. Attempts to replicate Clinard's American research have been made in Sweden. In the summary and conclusions of Clinard's 1965 essay he asserts that 'an adequate theory of criminal behaviour must take into account the wider societal influences (in addition to individualistic explanations based on constitutional or psychological factors). One well-documented fact is the nearly world-wide variation in crime between rural and urban areas and by city size in the amount and type of crime' (p. 558). One difference observed between rural and urban offenders was the absence in the former of the criminal career type of offender identified in the latter.

3 Gang studies

Closely linked to the discussion of area influences on crime is the subject of the gang. This subject has been extensively studied in the United States, where the main pre-occupation has been with the study of juvenile and adolescent gangs. The study of adult gang behaviour has been less energetically pursued, perhaps because it is more difficult and dangerous. The subject of organised crime is linked with adult gang activities, and it is in that connection that adult gang behaviour is best studied. Organised crime is such a special subject that it deserves to be reserved for separate consideration. It is not proposed to discuss this here, but to concentrate on juvenile and adolescent gangs, about which most of the writing has taken place. As we shall see, there have been some attempts to study youth gangs in Europe, particularly in the United Kingdom, and in other parts of the world, but first we must review the American literature.

The American literature on youth gangs

The classic study by Frederic Thrasher in 1927 in Chicago must be the starting point of this review. Thrasher analysed over 1,300 gangs in Chicago, mapping them according to area and describing their characteristics. According to Thrasher a proper gang possessed certain characteristics: it was a structured group consisting of leaders and followers, it had a definite meeting place, and territory, an initiation procedure and secret signs, a tradition handed down to newcomers, and it developed as a response to the environmental conditions. Most gangs had an ethnic base, a fact reflected in the musical 'West Side Story' many years later. In 1943 another sociologist William F. Whyte published his study *Street Corner Society* in which he described the different aspirations and values of the 'college boys' as contrasted with the 'corner boys' in a vivid example of successful research by means of the technique known as participant observation. Both these studies were updated in post-war editions[11]. It was not until 1955, however, that the next major development occurred, with the publication of Albert K. Cohen's, *Delinquent Boys: The Culture of the Gang*[12]. This work proved a seminal influence in that several other studies followed tending to disprove, expand or vary the thesis proposed by Cohen.

Cohen's thesis was that certain characteristics of the behaviour of adolescent youths in gangs portrayed a delinquent subculture whose characteristics were the institutionalisation of violence, destructiveness and pointless delinquent behaviour as a kind of defiant reaction towards the respectable middle-class values which prevailed in society at large. These youths found themselves growing up in a society which offered them little opportunity for success in terms of the conventional goals of position and wealth, and sought a solution in the delinquent subculture of violence which at that time seemed endemic in most

11 An edited abridged edition of Frederic Thrasher, *The Gang*, (ed. James F. Short Jr.) was published in 1964. A second edition of William F. Whyte's, *Street Corner Society* appeared in 1955.

12 Albert K. Cohen's, *Delinquent Boys: The Culture of the Gang* was published in the United States in 1955 and in the United Kingdom in 1956.

American cities. The characteristics of this subculture were that it was non-utilitarian in that no economic reward flowed from the behaviour, and it was malicious and negativistic.

The delinquent youths took their norms from the larger middle-class culture and turned them upside down, so that what was good in middle-class eyes was bad for them: they inverted the values and behaved in a way which demonstrated their contempt and rejection of those values. In this way they gained status and respect within their group which was denied to them or not available otherwise. Whereas in the past the corner boy had reacted passively and with indifference, the delinquent reaction today was a positive and active one. He refused to temporise and engaged in violent and destructive behaviour.

There can be little doubt that at this period the behaviour of youths in violent gangs was a source of grave concern in America. The media had highlighted the situation, and various popular accounts appeared describing the activities of the gangs[13]. A tremendous amount of research attention and resources were focussed on the situation. Cohen's theory was disputed, tested and extended.

There was from the beginning doubt whether the behaviour of American youth gangs really corresponded with Cohen's model. Dietrick and Kitsuse[14] argued that the theory did not fit the behaviour of contemporary gangs, much of whose activities displayed extremely utilitarian motives. The way Cohen had located the problem essentially as being situated in youths of the lower socio-economic groups did not account for the phenomenon appearing in many middle-class communities among the children of the relatively affluent and favoured.

The theory might explain how the delinquent subculture emerged but failed to explain its persistence over time and how it was maintained. Walter Miller[15] attacked the theory on the grounds that what was described in terms of the stress on violence and aggression was simply characteristic of the working-class cultural tradition generally. The 'focal concerns' of people in the lower socio-economic group had always centred around such matters. These youths came from female-dominated families and their aggressiveness was an

13 For example, Harrison Salisbury, *The Shook-Up Generation* (1959) and in the United Kingdom T. R. Fyvel, *The Insecure Offender* (1961).

14 J. I. Kitsuse and D. C. Dietrick, 'Delinquent Boys: A Critique' 24 Am Soc Rev 208 (April 1959).

15 W. B. Miller, 'Lower Class Culture as a Generating Milieu of Gang Delinquency' Jo Soc Issues Vol. 14, p. 5 (1958) reprinted in M. E. Wolfgang, L. Savitz and N. Johnston, *The Sociology of Crime and Delinquency* (1962) pp. 267 et seq.

assertion of their masculinity. Being tough and smart conferred status within the peer group and thus provided satisfaction and reassurance.

Another angle was provided by the social pyschologists like the Sherifs[16], as well as by the sociologists Bloch and Niederhoffer[17], who regarded the gang as an important reference group for the adolescent at a period of uncertainty when he faced the necessity of making significant adjustments in his concept of himself and others as he approached adulthood. The absence in the West of any ceremonial *rites de passage* (save in the Jewish community with the bar mitzvah) means there is a vacuum which is likely to be filled if only temporarily by peer group values and attitudes. The group or gang shares 'certain ways of looking at the world' to use James Short's happy phrase[18], and this is its value and importance.

Attempts to validate Cohen's theory in respect of the rejection of middle-class values have failed to reveal any large-scale rejection of those middle-class values, and Matza[19] has given at least a partial explanation why this should be so, as we shall see. As James Patrick[20] puts it:

'the wealth of empirical research, stimulated by the publication of Cohen's book, has not been supportive of his original ideas and a mass of evidence has been collected . . . which seriously questions the hypothesis that gang members reject middle-class values'.

With these doubts about Cohen's theory in our minds it is time to move on to discuss the remarkable contribution made by Richard Cloward and Lloyd Ohlin in 1960 in their book *Delinquency and Opportunity*. These authors managed to draw together some of the threads from various theories and researches in order to provide a fresh and apparently convincing explanation for the emergence of the delinquent subculture of the violent type (here called the 'conflict' subculture). In stable slum communities, they argued, it had been possible to locate and join in the criminal subculture which was characterised by theft and other utilitarian crimes. As these slum areas broke up under the influence of rehousing policies and other social

16 M. Sherif and C. W. Sherif, *Problems of Youth: Transition to Adulthood in a Changing World* (1965) pp. 6 et seq.
17 H. A. Bloch and A. Niederhoffer, *The Gang: A Study in Adolescent Behavior* (1958).
18 James F. Short Jr. in the Introduction to *Gang Delinquency and Delinquent Subcultures*, which he edited in 1968: p. 14.
19 D. Matza, *Delinquency and Drift* (1964).
20 J. Patrick, *A Glasgow gang observed* (1973) p. 172.

pressures, the disorganised slum community was unable to provide the avenue or opportunity for recruitment into the criminal subculture which had previously existed. Instead the young adolescents turned towards a conflict subculture which emphasised the use of violence and aggression in order to gain status. This accounted for the violent subculture identified by Cohen.

There was an alternative subculture, described by Cloward and Ohlin as the retreatist subculture, which was adopted as a solution by those who failed to locate and be recruited to the criminal subculture and rejected or were rejected by the conflict subculture. Such persons indulged in the abuse of drugs and alcohol as a means of escape or resolution of their problems.

Cloward and Ohlin were able through this analysis to account for both the emergence and the maintenance of these subcultures. They drew on the cultural transmission theories favoured by the Chicago school of criminologists such as Shaw and McKay as well as the 'anomic' theories which had been advanced by Merton based on Durkheim, and used by Cohen. By 'anomie' is meant the state of normlessness which comes into existence when values and attitudes accepted by society at large cease to prevail in a particular area or sub-group[1]. The key to Cloward and Ohlin's explanation lies in their recognition not only of different attitudes and values, but of different opportunities presenting themselves to persons growing up in particular areas. Hence the different responses adopted in different situations.

This was a highly conceptual approach which had immediately an immense appeal, though like Cohen's theory, it was not based on much solid empirical data. Attempts to verify it by field studies proved disappointing, both in America and in the UK, as James Patrick has pointed out[2]. He remarks on the inability of theory in this field to stand up to research[3].

One researcher who claimed to get near to the activities of adolescent gangs of the conflict type was Lewis Yablonsky in New York[4]. On the basis of extensive research and participant observation, he reported that the descriptions given by Thrasher of gangs proper, and those more recently advanced by modern sociologists, did not adequately portray the true situation. He preferred to describe the groups of

---

1 For a discussion of anomic theories, in particular Merton, see post p. 136.
2 Op. cit., p. 173.
3 Ibid., p. 176.
4 L. Yablonsky, *The Violent Gang* (1962).

youths he observed as 'near groups' standing midway between the group and the mob. The structure of a 'near group' contained three elements:

1 the leaders, who were the most psychologically disturbed members of the group, who needed the group membership most of all. These could be termed the core members;

2 those who casually participated in the group's activities but claimed membership;

3 those who would join the activity of the group on occasions but would deny membership; these might be described as peripheral members.

Yablonsky was unable to confirm the existence of retreatist gangs since the retreatist subculture of the addict is not a gang activity of any sort, most drug addicts being social isolates. It is true that there is a certain amount of sharing of values and attitudes with other addicts, on whom one depends for supply and support. Nor was there evidence of criminal gangs as distinct from social gangs of teenagers who combined together for leisure purposes. When a member of such a group committed delinquency it was 'on his own in a bizarre way'[5]. The violent gang was to a large extent an invention of the press and other observers who misinterpreted and misreported what they observed. That there were occasions when group activity erupted in violence cannot be denied, but this behaviour was sporadic and more time was spent talking about violence or behaving in threatening ways than actually fighting. As we shall see, research in England and Scotland tends to confirm these findings.

Another researcher who threw light on the behaviour of young persons in group situations was Howard W. Polsky. His study of a closed community of delinquents in a public institution, *Cottage Six*, in 1962, makes the point that so far the theories concerning delinquent subcultures had been constructed from fragmentary data, and few researchers had been able to get close enough to the scene to assess the subculture's content and functioning in its milieu. This is what Polsky was able to do, albeit in an institutional setting. He found that the peer social system was a critical factor in the persistence of the deviant ideology. Polsky gives a convincing picture of the way in which the boys in Cottage Six relate to one another and how they derive their

5 p. 151.

values and attitudes from the group and what he calls 'the peer social structure'. It is this which 'provides the stability for deviant patterns of aggression, manipulation and exploitation and an appropriate negative value system'[6].

Further research by many American scholars has tested the theories concerning the various types of delinquent subculture and gang behaviour. Short and Strodtbeck[7] found little evidence in Chicago of the criminally oriented or retreatist gang, but several negro 'conflict' gangs were located. Gangs of middle-class youths were rare. The research went beyond testing the conventional theories and tried to establish more about attitudes and value systems, and to discover whence the boys derived their image of themselves (self-concept). They recognise the difference between the gang activities chronicled by Thrasher and others in the 1930s and the gang of today, but believe that much still depends on the neighbourhood and the criminogenic or anti-social influences to which the youths are exposed. This is exemplified by a negro gang situated in an area noted as a centre of the drug traffic. They found little evidence of a rejection of middle-class values, and noted that for most offenders delinquency was essentially a part-time activity. They discuss the relevance of the notion of short-run hedonism and this is reinterpreted in the context of the known fact that much lower-class life is lived in these terms, of crisis-solving and living from day to day, rather than long-term planning and aspirations.

Klein[8] edited a valuable collection of papers in 1967, the product of a conference held in California, and in 1971 reported on his own research with a 'conflict' type gang. He remarked that the changes since Thrasher's day were more a matter of emphasis than of structural change, and that observers and research workers have tended to bring with them their preconceived ideas and impose them on the data. Though Short and Strodtbeck argued that what is new is that gang delinquency had become a major problem since World War II[9], it now seemed that there was evidence that gang activity may be declining. Like Short and Strodtbeck, Klein stresses the significance of neighbourhood variables. He also points out that non-gang delinquency has to be accounted for, as well as gang delinquency. The best approach

---

6 H. W. Polsky, *Cottage Six – The Social System of Delinquent Boys in Residential Treatment* (1962) p. 173.
7 J. F. Short Jr. and F. L. Strodtbeck, *Group Process and Gang Delinquency* (1965).
8 *Juvenile Gangs in Context: Theory, Research, and Action* (1967), ed. M. W. Klein; M. W. Klein, *Street Gangs and Street Workers* (1971).
9 Op. cit., note 7, p. 1.

seems to be to view the problem in terms of adolescent stress and go along with those theorists like the Sherifs who see the group or gang as providing a means whereby the tensions and anxieties of adolescence may be acted out or resolved.

The British studies of gangs

As with area studies, so with gang studies, Britain has contributed to the general pool of knowledge in a somewhat distinctive way. Elsewhere in Europe and other parts of the world, great interest has been shown in studying gangs, particularly adolescent gangs, as the problem seems world-wide in urban societies[10].

The early British studies like that of John Mays[11] in Liverpool were related more to the prevalence in certain areas of a delinquent subculture. The psychiatrist Peter Scott[12] in 1956 tried to establish the extent of gang activity of the Thrasher-type among young people referred by the courts to a remand facility. Although this study may properly be regarded as one concerned with pre-adolescent youths[13] it provides a useful starting point for discussing the subject in British terms. Scott divided gangs into three types as a result of his observations extending over ten years while working as a psychiatrist in the remand situation. These were as follows:

1 adolescent street groups;

2 structured groups (gangs proper);

3 loosely structured or diffuse groups.

We shall summarise his findings as to each type.

10 C. Debuyst, *Criminels et valeurs vécues* (1960); P. Parrot and M. Gueneau, *Les Gangs d'adolescents* (1959); P. Robert and P. Lascoumes, *Les Bandes D'Adolescents: Une Theorie de La Ségrégation* (1975); W. Middendorff, *New Forms of Juvenile Delinquency: Their Origin, Prevention and Treatment* (1960); T. C. N. Gibbens, *Trends in Juvenile Delinquency*, W.H.O. (1961); E. W. Vaz, 'Juvenile Gang Delinquency in Paris' Social Problems Vol. 10, No. 1., p. 23 (Summer 1962); J. Monod, 'Juvenile Gangs in Paris: Toward a Structural Analysis' Jo Res Crime & Delinq Vol. 4, No. 1, p. 142 (January 1967); D. P. Ausubel, 'Psychological Acculturation in Modern Maori Youth' in *Problems of Youth* (1965), eds. M. Sherif and C. W. Sherif, pp. 110 et seq.; L. B. Defleur 'Delinquent Gangs in Cross-Cultural Perspective: the case of Cordoba' Jo Res Crime & Delinq Vol. 4, No. 1, p. 132 (1967).
11 J. B. Mays, *Growing Up in the City* (1954); *On the Threshold of Delinquency* (1959); *Crime and Social Structure* (1963).
12 P. D. Scott, 'Gangs and delinquent groups in London' BJD Vol. 7, p. 4 (1956).
13 J. Patrick, *A Glasgow gang observed* (1973) pp. 158–159.

(i) *Adolescent street groups*

This group consisted typically of youths between the ages of fourteen and eighteen, who gathered together in the evenings or at weekends in loosely structured street groups comprising about five to 30 members, sometimes mixed in sex, but more often with girls occasionally tolerated. They occupied themselves by strolling along well-lit thoroughfares, gossiping at streetcorners and coffee-stalls, or frequenting cheap cafes and dance halls. Foremost among the purposes of such groups were self-display and mutual support in the difficult process of extricating themselves from an uncomfortably close emotional dependence on the home, and developing a self-determined existence. The majority of such street groups were quite innocuous. Occasionally some of the members got into trouble with the law, but when they did it was usually as individuals not as members of the group. Consequently they do not figure in the statistical analysis of types of association given below.

(ii) *Structured groups (gangs proper)*

According to Thrasher there were certain characteristics possessed by a gang proper, in that it was a structured group (with leaders and followers), it had a definite meeting place and territory, an initiation procedure, secret signs, and a long tradition handed down to new members. Scott's observations led him to conclude that in London such gangs were exceedingly rare. Indeed he found it difficult to discover one which fitted all the criteria. His impression was that such gangs may exist among ten-year-old boys but not among the older youths. They were usually pretty disturbed youths, having 'a gross anti-social character defect and come from homes in which the emotional atmosphere has been obviously disturbed and detrimental'. Out of 151 consecutive groups noted for the purpose of this study, only seventeen appeared to be of this character. The police and probation officers were not unduly worried about such groups.

(iii) *Loosely-structured or diffuse groups*

These may consist of three sub-types:

1 fleeting casual delinquent associations;

2 groups of usual companions (siblings or friends);

3 loose anti-social groups.

The age ranges for 2 and 3 are wider than for 1 where the delinquents are usually between ten and thirteen years of age. The most serious · threat comes from 3, which consist of very anti-socially inclined youths who combine promiscuously in loosely-structured, unorganised, fluid groups. They are so unhappy and disturbed in their home life and in regard to society at large as to be careless of the consequences of their actions, indeed often hoping the result will be their removal from home. They are regularly looking for delinquent opportunities in an indiscriminate and unplanned manner.

To summarise, we may present Scott's findings concerning the distribution of the groups he studies as follows:

Types of Association

Structured groups (gang proper)	17
Unstructured groups (86%)	
1 fleeting associations	18
2 usual companions	69
3 loose anti-social groups	43
Uncertain	4
Total	151

It would appear that gangs and loose anti-social groups do the most damage, while solitary offenders and those acting in fleeting association the least.

There is some echo in Scott's findings of the notions of Cloward and Ohlin concerning the conflict gang, and Yablonsky's violent gang. Mannheim commented that it may be doubted whether gangs proper were not greatly under-represented in Scott's findings[14]. The evidence of other researches does seem to confirm however that proper gangs hardly exist in the United Kingdom. Moreover even the conflict gangs proved hard to locate at least in the East End of London[15], though the situation appears to be different in Scotland, where Glasgow's reputation as a violent city is confirmed in this respect by James Patrick and others[16]. David Downes remarks that the available evidence indicates that delinquent group structure in England is different in kind from that of American metropolitan centres, insofar as the latter rests on the notion of the gang proper. 'In England, delinquent group structure is more fluid and less tangible than in the

---

14 H. Mannheim, *Comparative Criminology* (1965) Vol. II, p. 68.
15 D. Downes, *The Delinquent Solution* (1966).
16 Op. cit., note 13.

States' and 'a kind of delinquent freemasonry operates' for a certain section of the male adolescent urban working class[17].

Downes carried out his study in the East End of London, where he found no evidence to support Cloward and Ohlin's view about the three types of delinquent subculture.

'The English evidence lends no support for the existence of delinquent subcultures on the Cloward-Ohlin basis. . . . Gangs of the distinctive "criminal"/"conflict"/"retreatist" subcultural varieties clearly do not exist and there is faint support for the clear-cut demarcation of delinquent activities which the Cloward-Ohlin typology delineates'[18].

Such groups as existed were also dissimilar to those described by Yablonsky in New York though there was some approximation to the 'near-group' in the way youths combined together in their leisure pursuits. Downes believed however that the London groups differed from the American counterparts:

'Delinquent groups in the East End lacked both the structured cohesion of the New York gangs described by Cloward and Ohlin, and the fissile impermanence of Yablonsky's "near-group"'[19].

He remarks that the delinquent gang so far as the East End of London is concerned is 'a thoroughly atypical collectivity'. The possible exceptions heard of were by repute conflict-oriented and 'near-group' in structure. The bulk of delinquency however resulted from the activities of small cliques whose members committed illegal acts, sometimes collectively, sometimes in pairs, sometimes individually, in some cases regularly, in others only rarely. Average group size was four or five, with a few individuals on the periphery. These street corner groups persisted over time and usually possessed a dominant personality as leader but portrayed none of the other characteristics of a proper gang: 'The norm . . . is the fluid, street-corner clique, averse to any form of structure and organisation, but with persistence over time'[20].

Interest in England and Wales shifted to the discussion of other phenomena such as the violence between groups of 'mods' and 'rockers', and football hooliganism. Stan Cohen[1] showed that the

17 Op. cit., p. 122.
18 p. 134.
19 p. 198.
20 p. 199.
1 S. Cohen, *Folk Devils and Moral Panics: The Creation of the Mods and Rockers* (1972).

behaviour of 'mods' and 'rockers' had been exaggerated if not induced by the manner in which the media reported incidents. The picture of riots and gang warfare depicted by the media was not borne out by patient sociological investigation. The amount of serious violence or property damage on these occasions was small. One cannot deny that these events occur from time to time, and it has been suggested that the greater mobility of modern youth afforded by the motor bike has transported these confrontations far from home, to seaside towns at bank holiday weekends. There is almost a ritual quality to it, which the police frustrate by their preventive measures and active intervention. Much the same conclusions have been reached by those who study football hooliganism. Psychologists like Peter Marsh[2] and sociologists like Eugene Trivizas[3] agree substantially about these matters. The degree to which the public are endangered or damage occurs to property has been exaggerated. Yet there are interesting parallels between the behaviour of groups in football crowds and group behaviour of the more obviously delinquent kind. There is an age structure, much role playing occurs, and the leaders are often rather disturbed individuals. Such characteristics have also been observed in the Glasgow gang studied by James Patrick[4].

More than any other study, Patrick's study draws together the different threads in the American and British research studies concerning adolescent gangs. He also contributes fresh information about the situation in Glasgow, which appears to be rather different from that observed by Downes in the East End of London. Here in Glasgow we find a subculture of violence which contrasts with that prevailing south of the border, but has many parallels with the American research on violent gangs. All the familiar arguments are explored to describe and explain this phenomenon. The relevance of short-run hedonism, of adolescent anxieties, the role of core members of the group, the fact that the leadership is vested in the most disturbed and violent boys – these points are reinterpreted in relation to the data obtained and the observations made in Glasgow. What appears to be clear is that the influence of group norms is extremely tenuous if non-existent. The short-run hedonism is not seen as more than a recognition of the hopelessness of the situation which the boys faced growing up in this lower working-class environment, a hopelessness

2 P. Marsh, *The rules of disorder* (1978); *Aggro: the illusion of violence* (1978).
3 E. Trivizas, 'Offences and Offenders in Football Crowd Disorders' BJC Vol. 20, No. 3, p. 276 (July 1980); 'Sentencing the "Football Hooligan"' BJC Vol. 21, No. 4, p. 342 (October 1981).
4 J. Patrick, op. cit.

shared with the adults who live there. The subculture of violence is persistent and survives rehousing, as the Easterhouse example shows. If it is true that gang activity is waning elsewhere, it may endure in these situations while the conditions last. Some kinds of intervention such as the well-publicised attentions of the singer Frankie Vaughan in 1968, are likely to be self-defeating since they have a re-inforcing effect on the solidarity of the gang.

In Liverpool Howard Parker[5] found evidence to support many of the conclusions of other gang studies. He documents the emergence of a group, which he studied for some three years, in a district of Liverpool, which centred itself in a relatively isolated set of buildings. The group formed its own values and definitions. There was a cohesive core of members at the centre and a loose aggregate of associate members. Over time there was some continuity, but the contribution of each generation was different. So far as delinquency was concerned, it was sporadic and the stake of the gang members in crime was rarely complete. Delinquency in general was regarded as an opportune and rational solution to particular problems rather than providing the foundations for a conscious career of crime. When it led to an arrest, delinquent behaviour could provide a watershed or turning point and lead to a halt being called to the behaviour. Sometimes this crisis would simply confirm a person's commitment to and involvement with crime.

Conclusion

We are now in a position to reach some conclusions, however tentative, concerning the phenomena of adolescent gang crime:

1 The researches have often been coupled with the development of theories concerning adolescent gang behaviour of a highly conceptual kind.

2 These concepts have not been verified by field observation and indeed research studies have frequently thrown doubt on their assumptions.

3 In particular there is doubt concerning the following matters:
   (a) the degree of social organisation or disorganisation which exists

5 H. Parker, *A View from the Boys* (1974).

in so-called delinquency areas, and which is thought to spawn gang delinquency;

(b) the degree of solidarity or acceptance of group norms among gang members;

(c) the amount of criminality which directly stems from gang activities;

(d) the degree of alienation of gang members from middle-class values;

(e) the qualities of the leadership;

(f) whether one can discern any cultural homogeneity between American gangs in, say, New York and Chicago, or British gangs in, say, East London and Glasgow;

(g) the degree of commitment to the gang;

(h) the extent to which short-run hedonism is characteristic;

(i) the question whether the gang provides a reference group during adolescence at a time of stress and anxiety;

(j) the sources of information about gangs, specially the police and the media;

(k) whether adolescent gang behaviour is declining;

(l) differences in gang activities even within the same neighbourhood, e.g. the negro gangs observed in some US studies.

With so many doubts, what can be said except that more research is needed to clarify these matters. This point was emphasised by James Short Jr. in his review of the evidence. What seems to be clear is that researchers have too often, to use James Patrick's felicitous expression, carried with them 'the stamp of the outsider'[6]. It has not been easy for researchers to get close enough to the gangs to make valid and reliable observations. New techniques and methods need to be devised. One feature mentioned by very few writers in this field is the tremendous influence of pop culture and membership of so-called beat groups which has overtaken the subject in the last twenty years. A study of pop culture might be quite revealing particularly insofar as it made the differentiation between 'punk' and 'rock' explicit, as well as exploring 'soul' music. Clearly the criminologist must give way here to the wider interests of the urban sociologist and the cultural anthropologist. We might help them however to ask the right questions.

6 Op. cit., p. 197.

Notes. Gang studies

1 Police figures for arrests of persons under 21 are available for the Metropolitan Police area. They have consistently shown that while the majority of youths are arrested when operating in the company of other persons, the number in the group is rarely more than four persons, and most often two or three persons only. Some are arrested while acting in association with adults. The following figures for the Metropolitan Police area are derived from the Report of the Commissioner of the Metropolitan Police for the year 1963, Cmnd. 2048 (1964):

Of the 20,000 persons under 21 arrested in 1963 for indictable offences, 60 per cent were operating with other persons. Twelve per cent were associating with adults in committing these crimes. The position regarding the remainder is shown below.

Arrest of groups whose members were all under 21 years of age

No. in group	Number of groups
2	2854 ⎫ 89%
3	922 ⎭
4	296
5	93
6	26
7	11
8	1
9	2
10	1
11	1
	4207

2 Malcom W. Klein has observed how in Los Angeles for the purpose of police records of gang activities, the definition of a gang is anything from a group consisting or three or more members, 'a gang incident', to any group of eight or more. Criminologists have not been too precise about the notion of a gang either. Most juvenile delinquency is group delinquency, but it does not necessarily mean that a gang is involved. Klein argues for a precise definition of a gang, and provides one as follows:

'For our purposes, we shall use the term *gang* to refer to any denotable adolescent group of youngesters who (a) are generally perceived as a distinct aggregation by others in their neighbourhood, (b) recognize themselves as a denotable group (almost invariably with a group name) and (c) have been involved in a sufficient number of delinquent incidents to call forth a consistent negative response from neighbourhood residents and/or enforcement agencies'. M. W. Klein, *Street Gangs and Street Workers* (1971).

On this basis, youth gangs are very rare even in American cities. It is not clear whether such gangs are on the decline in the USA. Solid empirical data are still lacking.

Hood and Sparks point out that nearly all studies of convicted juvenile delinquents in the USA and in European countries 'have found the normal number of persons involved to be two or three' (p. 87). This is not of course conclusive evidence since the arresting officers may not be able to handle more, and the prosecution policy may influence the choice of subjects to proceed against.

3 David Downes regards the introduction of the opportunity structure theory by Cloward and Ohlin as for the first time integrating previous sociological theories into a coherent whole, while at the same time remaining flexible. While originally used to explain gang delinquency, it seems likely to be helpful in explaining other forms of delinquency. It combines the ecological theories of the twenties and thirties, the 'anomie' theory developed by Merton, and Cohen's two-pronged theory of status frustration and the delinquent sub-culture. Empirical research had shown that none of these theories was wholly satisfactory by itself. Opportunity theory combines all three, although it discards the status frustration component of Cohen's theory.(D. M. Downes, 'Social Theories' in *Frontiers of Criminology* (1967), eds. H. J. Klare and D. Haxby, pp. 41 et seq.)

Downes maintains that the theory of opportunity structure is useful, and has a factual basis. Many changes have occurred in the social system since working-class subcultural theories first appeared, which make such theories less relevant today. He also sees many differences between the American and the British situation. The English counterpart of the American gang de-linquent has a stable working-class tradition which enables him to transcend the humiliations of failure at school and lack of advancement at work. Only in one area, leisure pursuits, is there any real problem for him. This was written in 1966, before the recent sharp rise in unemployment. With an almost prophetic insight Downes saw however that changing patterns of employment must be reckoned with: 'the streets of our urban slums are slowly filling with young men who have no prospect of finding manhood through work: who are coming of age in a society which neither wants them nor needs them' (D. M. Downes, *The Delinquent Solution* (1966) p. 264).

4 Taylor, Walton and Young in *The New Criminology* (1973) appear to agree with Walter Miller's point about there being a close correspondence between the delinquent subculture and adult working-class culture generally, but they criticise Cohen for failing to draw the distinction which they think is essential between instrumental and expressive behaviour, which may go a long way in their view towards explaining the non-utilitarian features of adolescent deviant behaviour (p. 136).

These authors provide a useful discussion of Cloward and Ohlin's theory, under the heading of 'Differential Organisation' (p. 130). They see Cloward and Ohlin as extremely significant. There is one criticism however and that is concerning the failure of Cloward and Ohlin to recognise and explain the groups which actively reject what they regard as bourgeois values and ideals and are to be found located in bohemian subcultures of the drug-culture type.

Crowd criminology

1 Interest has shifted among criminologists from the investigation of small groups and gangs to the larger more amorphous groupings which can be described as crowds or mobs. Here the degree of organisation involved is only rudimentary and short-lived, according to Mannheim, and there is rarely any continuity: H. Mannheim, *Comparative Criminology* (1965) Vol. II, pp. 643 et seq. What constitutes a crowd is a matter for discussion, mere numbers not being sufficient without 'an environmental and a mental "something" which transforms the purely factual agglomeration into a crowd in the psychological sense': ibid., p. 644.

2 It is possible to exaggerate the dangers of the crowd and its anti-social tendencies. Mannheim believes that this occurred in the earlier writings on the subject in the late nineteenth century (p. 645). The French scholar Le Bon had identified several changes which occur through joining or being in a crowd: G. Le Bon, *Psychologie des foules* (1895). A loss of inhibitions occurs and profound psychological and moral changes (p. 645). The anonymity of the situation contributes to this effect. That the resulting behaviour is not always anti-social but may possess heroic and valuable qualities should be recognised. In recent times the behaviour of trade unionists in Poland in the Movement *Solidarity* provides an instance.

3 There may be a parallel here with the argument sometimes advanced about road traffice offences, viz. that when a person sits behind the wheel of a motor vehicle he is somehow transformed. The better view, supported by modern research, is that this is not the case, and that 'people drive as they live': see T. C. Willett, *The Criminal on the Road* (1964). This view has the support, so far as crowds are concerned, of the distinguished psychologist F. H. Allport, *Social Psychology* (1924), quoted by Mannheim pp. 647-648.

4 Modern scholars have focussed on such crowd behaviour as football hooliganism, the sporadic trouble between 'mods' and 'rockers' at bank holiday weekends at various seaside holiday resorts, and political crowds: see the studies by P. Marsh, E. Trivizas and S. Cohen. The ritual quality of much crowd behaviour may be compared with the interpretations by some sociologists of gang behaviour in terms of its ritualistic character: see *Resistance through Rituals: Youth Subcultures in post-war Britain* (1976), eds. S. Hall and T. Jefferson.

5 The role of the leader in a crowd may be compared with the role of the leader in a gang. It is clear that this is central to the activity: Mannheim pp. 648 et seq., and Nathan L. Gerrard, 'The Core Member of the Gang' BJC Vol. 4, No. 4, p. 361 (April 1964). Sometimes modern gangs appear to coalesce without an obvious or nominated leader: see the two articles by P. Marsh and Anne Campbell, *New Society* 12 and 19 October 1978, on the youth gangs of New York and Chicago, and G. Kaiser, *Randalierende Jugend* (1959) (Mannheim pp. 650–651).

6 Studies of riots are a separate variety of crowd studies. Here one can list the different types of riot, e.g. prison riots, race riots, inner-city riots, and study the factors associated with each. See, for example, the studies carried out by the Prison Department psychologists into the factors associated with prison disturbances.

4 Structural and cultural theories

Sociologists have developed various theories designed to explain criminal behaviour. These theories are expressed in terms either of crime being a natural response to the situation in which the offender finds himself (structural theories) or in terms of explaining crime by reference to cultural or subcultural differences (cultural deviance theories). Sociologists have also borrowed from social psychology to develop symbolic-interactionist and labelling theories, and much of the modern writing on the sociology of deviance derives support from these latter sources. Another way of approaching the explanation of crime from a sociological or socio-psychological angle has come to be known as 'control' theory, which is based on regarding the loosening of the moral bind of the law as in some way enabling offenders to commit their crimes. We thus have the following four types of sociological theory about crime[7].

A. Structural theories.

B. Cultural theories, or theories of the subcultural nature of deviance

7 There is no agreement among sociologists concerning these classifications, but Hirschi follows Ruth Kornhauser, while Lamar Empey and Gwynn Nettler provide certain extensions and variations. See: T. Hirschi, *Causes of Delinquency* (1969); Ruth R. Kornhauser, *Social Sources of Delinquency: An Appraisal of Analytic Models* (1978); Lamar T. Empey, *American Delinquency: Its Meaning and Construction* (1978); Gwynn Nettler, *Explaining Crime* (1974). Downes has followed Hirschi, 'Interpreting Delinquency' in Laurie Taylor, Allison Morris David Downes, *Signs of Trouble: Aspects of Delinquency*, (1976) (BBC).

C. Symbolic-interactionist and labelling theories.

D. 'Control' theory.

We shall first consider A. & B., leaving C. and D. to be dealt with later.

A. Structural theories

These have their basis in the way society is structured into social classes, and the way some people are disadvantaged compared with others. When they perceive their poor status it is argued that a situation of strain develops, and delinquency may be the result. These theories are hence described by some writers (Kornhauser, Hirschi) as 'strain' theories. Two authors may be regarded as having developed 'strain' theories, Thorsten Sellin and Robert K. Merton. Both published their theories in 1938.

(i) T. Sellin's culture conflict theory

Sellin's book was entitled *Culture Conflict and Crime*[8]. Here he propounded the thesis that a major cause of crime lay in the conflicting cultures offered to the American immigrant child growing up in a metropolitan environment. On the one hand, the child's parents offered him the values and aspirations of their own culture which they brought with them as immigrants and were anxious to preserve and pass on. On the other hand, the child was exposed at school and in the street to the rather different values and aspirations of the host society. Tensions built up in such situations, and it was not surprising that sometimes these were resolved by resort to crime.

Sellin found support for this theory in the writings of E. H. Sutherland whose *Principles of Criminology* had already been published in 1934. He also derived support from the work of Clifford Shaw on delinquency areas. Sutherland and Sellin had been commissioned to make a survey of existing knowledge in criminology, and in writing the report Sellin drew on a wide range of anthropological and historical evidence to provide illustrations. It was not his intention to limit the 'culture-conflict' notion to immigrants, or to suggest that immigrants were largely responsible for the high crime rate. The suggestion is made however that the second generation immigrant faces more severe problems of adjustment or that more serious conflict

8 Thorsten Sellin, *Culture Conflict and Crime* (1938).

of culture occurs in the second generation immigrant growing up in an American city. It should be remembered that Sellin was writing after several decades of high rates of immigration into the United States.

That this theory deserves to be better known and more widely researched is certainly true. Events in Britain several generations later make one wish that the theory had received more attention. Sellin's contribution to the sociological theory of crime has been re-assessed by Donald R. Cressey[9], who regrets that, perhaps because of some ambiguities in the basic concepts used, the theory had less impact on criminological studies than it deserved. Cressey believes that the distinction which Sellin made between conflict of cultural norms as a result of transfer from one culture to another and conflict of norms which develops as a result of increasing societal complexity has been overlooked. Sellin pointed out that 'as a modern industrial and mercantile society has arisen, the process of social differentiation has, by itself, produced a conflict of conduct norms'[10]. Cressey prefers to use the phrase 'normative conflict' to 'culture conflict' in order to avoid any danger of limiting the discussion to the different culture of immigrant groups. He also points out how close Sutherland got to expressing his theory of differential association (see post) when he discussed 'culture conflict' in the third edition of his *Principles of Criminology* in 1939. Sutherland later admitted that he rather inadvertently stated the fundamentals of that theory before he realised he had a theory[11].

Some use has been made of culture conflict by modern criminologists. For example, Shoham has used it to explain certain aspects of crime in Israel[12]. It is possible that we have not yet fully exploited the potential of this theory in criminological explanation. On the other hand, it falls short in failing to tell us why, for example, an immigrant child should fail to adjust satisfactorily to the norms of the host society, when it is quite clear to anyone who has the slightest acquaintance with North American cities, not to mention Europe or other parts of the world, that countless families of immigrants have been satisfactorily absorbed. On special days each year they celebrate their cultural

9 Donald R. Cressey, 'Culture Conflict, Differential Association, and Normative Conflict' in *Crime and Culture: Essays in Honor of Thorsten Sellin*, (1968), ed. M. E. Wolfgang, pp. 43 et seq.
10 Cressey pp. 46–47.
11 Cressey p. 47.
12 S. Shoham, 'Culture Conflict as a Frame of Reference for Research in Criminology and Social Deviation' in *Crime and Culture: Essays in Honor of Thorsten Sellin* (1968) pp. 55 et seq.

differences with gusto, as anyone who has witnessed St. Patrick's Day in New York or Kosciusko day in a New England town will know. Even today Canadian cities such as Montreal are host to many different cultures bourne by immigrant families. No doubt strains and tensions arise but these do not necessarily result in deviancy or criminal behaviour. The same can be said of the immigration of coloured people, whether from Asia or the West Indies, into Britain. Indeed the evidence suggests overwhelmingly that crime occurs less frequently among the immigrant population.

Studies of immigration played a considerable role in American criminology in the 1930s. As Cressey points out, there was considerable emphasis on problems of immigration in the social science culture of that period[13]. There was also concern about the high negro crime rate, and Sutherland, among others, set about examining the factors which could be associated with this, such as the fact that the negro population of the northern American cities contained an undue proportion of the young-adult male age group, which generally speaking has a high crime rate, together with the likelihood that differential treatment occurred towards the negro population in respect of arrest and court disposal. Sutherland also found support here for his theory of differential association[14].

Modern criminology has taken less interest in problems of immigration and race. While an extensive literature has grown up on race in relation to problems of discrimination over housing, employment, and police attitudes, criminologists have largely neglected the subject, so that there is very little we can say, as criminologists, in answer to current concerns about racial riots and public disorder. Study of the problems of the inner-city has been left largely to others, including not only those concerned with race relations but also representative groups of immigrants themselves[15]. Surveys show that there is comparatively little crime among immigrant populations, who seem to strive to behave well and keep out of trouble, possibly because of some sensitivity about their position in the host society, possibly because of internal social controls exercised by families and by their own communities. If

13 Cressey p. 50.
14 See, on Race and Crime, the discussion in H. Mannheim, *Group Problems in Crime and Punishment* (1955) pp. 194 et seq.
15 J. R. Lambert, *Crime, Police and Race Relations* (1970); P. Mason, *Race and Society* (1970); K. Little, *Negroes in Britain* (1948); R. Glass, *Newcomers* (1960); Sheila Patterson, *Dark Strangers* (1963); J. B. Mays, *Crime and Social Structure* (1963) Chap. 10. But see P. Stevens and C. F. Willis, *Race, Crime and Arrests* (1979) Home Office Research Study No. 58, and M. Tuck and P. Southgate *Ethnic Minorities, Crime and Policing* (1981) Home Office Research Study No. 70.

these controls are now showing signs of weakening, in the presence of extremely high rates of unemployment, high rates of police activity and intervention, and political feelings of resentment, fear and hostility, it is likely that it is the second generation coming from an immigrant family, the youth born and brought up here, who responds and behaves in a deviant and anti-social way, either by rejecting the standards and values of the host society, or by claiming, often with more truth than we care to admit, that these standards and values are applied selectively and with discrimination. Sellin's message of 1938 is as relevant today as it ever was, and should be heeded. Yet what answer does it provide to a situation of diverse and diverging cultures, and the attitudes and values derived therefrom? Do we want cultural uniformity and is not variety itself something to be cherished and nurtured? In our approach to surviving rural customs and village cultures we are keen to seek their survival and preservation. Can any lower standard apply to ethnic differences?

(ii) *Robert K. Merton's anomic theory*

In 1938 Robert K. Merton, the Harvard sociologist, published an article[16] on 'Social Structure and Anomie' in which he outlined a theoretical model as an explanation of crime which derived from the writings of Durkheim about the state of 'anomie' or normlessness[17]. Merton postulated that, American Society being premised on the achievement of economic success, the social structure was such that success was denied to many by legitimate means. People responded in various ways to the situation in which they found themselves. Some accepted the situation, some rebelled, some retreated, some innovated so as to achieve the goal by different means. Hence the various response could be described in terms of the acceptance or rejection of the goals and legitimate means of achieving them. This Merton expressed as follows, giving plus signs as a symbol for acceptance and minus signs for rejection of goals and means, and characterising the response pattern accordingly. In one case (Adaptation V) there is rejection of both the goals and the means and substitution by the person of his own goals and means:

16 Robert K. Merton, 'Social Structure and Anomie' 3 Am Soc Rev 672 (1938). See also his *Social Theory and Social Structure* (1957) pp. 131 et seq. For a review of the theory, see 24 Am Soc Rev No. 2 (April 1959). The article of 1938 is reprinted in M. E. Wolfgang, L. Savitz and N. Johnston, *The Sociology of Crime and Delinquency* (1962) pp. 236 et seq.

17 For an explanation, see *A New Dictionary of Sociology* (1979), ed. G. Duncan Mitchell, sub tit. *Durkheim, Émile* pp. 58–59, and *Anomie* p. 7.

	Culture goals	Institutionalised means
I. Conformity	+	+
II. Innovation	+	−
III. Ritualism	−	+
IV. Retreatism	−	−
V. Rebellion	±	±

The view that delinquency is the result of the discrepancy between culturally prescribed goals and the socially structured avenues available for their realisation, giving rise to a state of *anomie* or normlessness, is superficially attractive with its egalitarian overtones, but hardly serves to explain those types of delinquency which are non-materialistic or non-utilitarian.

Merton's theory assumes that most people share the same values and goals but that the social order gives them very different opportunities to achieve their goals. The theory has been termed a 'strain' theory by sociologists like Kornhauser, Hirschi and Downes. This is because the notion of pressure is crucial, pressure to achieve or respond. As Nettler points out, this type of explanation of crime sees delinquency as adaptive and views crime as partly or mainly reactive[18].

The 'strain' theory has been severely criticised by Hirschi for a variety of reasons. It locates delinquency only in the lower classes. It requires us to assume economic motivation for delinquency. It is both inadequate and misleading:

'It suggests that delinquency is a relatively permanent attribute of the person and/or a regularly occurring event; it suggests that delinquency is largely restricted to a single social class; and it suggests that persons accepting legitimate goals are, as a result of this acceptance, more likely to commit delinquent acts'[19].

Merton's theory has not received much support from criminologists but it may have influenced the development of the cultural or sub-cultural theories of deviance such as those of Cohen and Cloward and Ohlin. These we can conveniently discuss under the same heading of structural theory.

18 G. Nettler, *Explaining Crime* (1974) pp. 154–158.
19 T. Hirschi, *Causes of Delinquency* (1969) p. 10.

(iii) *Albert K. Cohen's theory of the delinquent subculture*

This theory has already been discussed in the section on gang studies (p. 116, ante). We there noted its reliance on the notion of status and the view that the lower class boys who found themselves at the bottom of the pile in those terms and without much chance of acquiring economic status reacted through resort to delinquent behaviour of a non-economic kind, which conferred status within the group. We also noted the many criticisms of the theory. The theory was criticised on theoretical grounds and had not been borne out by empirical research. Nevertheless it proved to be a seminal work of great distinction. Nettler describes it as plausible but unproven[20].

(iv) *Cloward and Ohlin's opportunity structure theory*

The most prominent application of Merton's theory was by Cloward and Ohlin in their development of the work of Cohen in terms more of delinquent opportunity than of delinquent reaction. They located three distinct subcultures of delinquency, as we have seen, viz. the criminal, the conflict and the retreatist subcultures. Whether the response was in the direction of one or the other depended on the chance factor of the local situation and the opportunities available to join in such a subculture. There seemed to be a ring of truth about this analysis, which conveniently explained 'conflict' crime and 'retreatist' crime, and combined some elements of earlier subcultural theories such as those of Shaw and McKay and the Chicago School with Merton's structural theory based on *anomie*. Nettler says this type of explanation, because it located crime in poor social and economic conditions, was the social worker's favourite[1]. But upon analysis the theory fails to satisfy for a number of reasons. Nettler claims that the key concepts are not clear, the opportunity-structure thesis does not accurately describe gang delinquency, nor does it explain how the subcultures are produced in the first place, and the recommendations which flow from the theory are neither feasible nor effective[2].

This may seen a harsh judgment on the theory, but it must be admitted that, despite its intellectual neatness, there has been little empirical support in the United States or Britain for the Cloward/Ohlin thesis. Its attempt to draw on the Shaw and McKay

20 p. 172.
 1 p. 158.
 2 pp. 159–167.

material to explain the origin of a delinquent subculture and Sutherland and Merton to explain its nature was attractive but unconvincing.
There remained too many unexplained features in the analysis.

B. Cultural theories or theories of the subcultural nature of deviance

Sociological theories tending to explain crime in terms of cultural or
subcultural differences, which may be termed cultural deviance
theories, have their origin in the work of the Chicago School of
sociologists and criminologists, who, as we have seen in section 2
(p. 101, ante), perceived the different areas of the city where crime
was concentrated as areas of social disorganisation, where a different
set of values or subculture prevailed which powerfully influenced
behaviour in the direction of deviant behaviour, so that the area
became a high crime area or a delinquent area. Shaw and McKay and
Thrasher were followed by Bernard Lander and others in the field of
area studies. Many of the theories on gang delinquency also derive
support from this approach. Thus Travis Hirschi asserts that Cohen's
Delinquent Boys and Cloward and Ohlin's *Delinquency and Opportunity* 'are heavily influenced by the cultural deviance perspective'[3].
Walter Miller's work on lower-class culture described in section 2,
p. 117, ante, also belongs here.

Drawing on the tradition deriving from the Chicago School, and
providing a separate theory of cultural deviance based on the deviant
values and attitudes acquired in such delinquency areas, came
Sutherland's theory of differential association, which can be appropriately termed a theory of cultural deviance, according to Ruth
Kornhauser and Travis Hirschi[4].

E. H. Sutherland's theory of differential association

In 1939 Professor Sutherland announced his theory of differential
association. This relied heavily on the notion that crime was essentially
learned behaviour. Sutherland argued that people become criminal
due to an excess of contacts with criminal patterns of behaviour and
isolation from non-criminal patterns, or, to put it his way, from an

3 p. 13, note 36.
4 Though Professor Hirschi may be having second thoughts about this, tending
towards regarding Sutherland's theory as a symbolic-interactionist theory
(personal communication).

excess of definitions favourable to law violation over definitions unfavourable to violation of the law[5]. This theory admits that such associations may vary in frequency, duration, priority and intensity. On this view criminal behaviour is essentially something which is learned not inherited. It is therefore a wholly environmental theory. It places heavy reliance on human relationships and what sociologists call 'interaction processes', and assigns a secondary and insignificant role to such impersonal agencies of communication as the media.

Sutherland was never wholly satisfied with his theory, and 'at the time of his death, he was actively engaged in (its) revision'[6]. The formal statements of the theory in the text 'were not conceived as final statements but rather as tentative formulations to guide and stimulate theoretically oriented research'[7].

This approach to the explanation of crime has much to commend it, according to Paul Tappan, but its major weakness is its failure to take into account psychological and physiological considerations[8]. Others have been more critical, arguing that it attempts to explain the widely different types of criminal behaviour by a single over-simplified theory. Nettler regards the theory as so general and so loosely phrased as to be impossible to falsify or disprove[9], echoing the judgment of Sheldon Glueck that this was a superficial and superfluous generalisation[10].

The main difficulty appears to be that Sutherland fails to explain why a person experiences different definitions in the way he does, whence they arise and what weight attaches to them. Clearly individuals differ in their response to such stimuli, and this flows not only from their circumstances but derives from their personality. Notwithstanding these criticisms and shortcomings, the theory had a very good reception among sociologists. Taft regarded it as 'one of the most nearly accepted generalisations purporting to explain all crime'[11]. It was used by Sutherland in his discussion of 'white-collar crime', where it seemed to fit quite well. Nevertheless the theory has been overtaken by more recent sociological theories deriving more from social psychology. These are the symbolic-interactionist and

5 E. H. Sutherland, *Principles of Criminology* (6th edn., 1960).
6 *The Sutherland Papers* (1956), eds. A. Cohen, A. Lindesmith and K. Schuessler, Introduction, p. 2.
7 p. 3 and pp. 5–6.
8 P. W. Tappan, *Juvenile Deliquency* (1949) p. 82.
9 G. Nettler, *Explaining Crime* (1974) p. 197.
10 S. Glueck, 'Theory and Fact in Criminology' BJD Vol. VIII, p. 92 (1956–7).
11 D. R. Taft, *Criminology* (1956) p. 223.

labelling theories. Already Vold in 1958 was writing about the theory of differential association in the past tense:

'The differential association theory has provided an exciting episode in criminological thinking. Through a fortunate combination of words and illustrations in its first formulation, it seemed to offer much more than it has been able to deliver'[12].

Relation to other theories. It appears to be open to argument whether to regard Sutherland's theory of differential association as belonging to the group of cultural deviance theories or whether it is really a theory relating to symbolic interaction. The latter view is shared by Hirschi and Empey. Since however Sutherland derives so much support from Shaw and McKay and the work of the Chicago School of criminology, and his work was done in that period, it seems preferable to regard him as representing one version of the cultural deviance theories. One should also consider whether Cohen and Cloward and Ohlin are properly regarded as examples of structural theory or whether they belong in the group of cultural deviance theories. There is less room for doubt about Walter Miller, when he writes about the 'focal concerns' of the working class, or other criminologists who see crime as a function of social class. They see the factor of social class as influencing criminal behaviour more directly than Merton and Cohen, not as producing a definite reaction so much as producing behaviour normal for the group, at least so far as some kinds of behaviour is concerned, e.g. violence. For the present these matters must be left to speculation and reflection.

5 The Symbolic-interactionist and labelling theories, and 'control' theory

The preceding discussion will have prepared the way for an examination of two varieties of sociological theory relating to crime, whose influence has been very considerable in recent years. These are the symbolic-interactionist theory and the labelling theory of crime. The literature on these theories overlaps so that it is barely possible to separate the sources and there is some congruence of ideas. We shall

12 G. B. Vold, *Theoretical Criminology* (1958) p. 198.

provide an outline of each together with some assessment of their significance. There is also a development of sociological theories of deviance described by some sociologists as 'control' theory.

The symbolic-interactionist theory

This theory stems from work done by sociologists on closed institutions such as mental hospitals and prisons, and work done on cultures such as the drug culture or subculture. Erving Goffman showed in his book on *Asylums* (1961) and his later work on *Stigma* (1963) how persons become labelled and stigmatised by mental illness and criminality. Howard S. Becker in his book *Outsiders* (1963) described the processes by which a person breaking society's rules becomes an outsider and perceives himself as different, in other words, how the process of alienation occurs. These two scholars provided the basis on which labelling theory rests. They also may be regarded as having contributed to the symbolic-interactionist view of deviant behaviour.

The central point about symbolic-interactionist theory is that behaviour should be regarded not so much in terms of what it means to others and society in general but what it means to you, the actor. Also the way other people react or respond to your behaviour powerfully influences your own response and reaction. We all live in a world made up of our own perceptions of reality, which may or may not correspond with the truth, and we act and interact in accordance with our reading of the situation, which includes of course our perception of the way other people are reading it. Studies of the self are very much in vogue in social psychology today. Sociologists have been quick to benefit from these new ways of looking at behaviour, and what the language used symbolises for the actor, as well as how other people's behaviour is described and interpreted. Hence symbolic-interaction.

This approach, dependent as it is very heavily on looking for 'explanations of social behaviour in learned dispositions identified through their expression in symbols', as Nettler puts it[13], is not very far removed from Sutherland's 'definitions' as the basis for differential association theory. The difference lies in its complete reliance on interaction as the source of meaning and interpretation. Nettler believes that both Sutherland's differential association theory and

13 Nettler, *Explaining Crime* (1974) pp. 192-193.

symbolic interactionism are types of explanation which are more American than European or Asian[14].

Jock Young has described in his account of the drug culture some of the steps by which a drug user becomes a member of that culture or subculture by a process of alienation and incorporation, involving the use of a special language or *argot*, and symbolic interaction[15]. The same is true of offenders, especially those in institutions, or well adjusted to a life of crime.

The mention of deviancy amplification in the title of Jock Young's essay prompts a reference here to this aspect of modern deviancy theory. It is now recognised that the mere fact of having become known to the police in connection with crime, whether by way of arrest, summons, or caution, or simply having been the subject of attention, increases the chances of a person once again coming to notice in connection with crime. This is known as 'deviancy amplification' and is linked with the notion of 'secondary deviance' which may be ascribed to the essay by Lemert in 1967[16]. Secondary deviance is conceived as a means of adaptation, whether by attack or defence or otherwise, to the overt and covert problems created by society's reaction to primary deviation, when the original causes of that deviation recede giving way to 'the central importance of the disapproving, degradational and labelling reactions of society'[17].

Another feature of modern theory concerning deviance is to concentrate on the actual process of becoming deviant, as distinct from the consequences in terms of official action. Deviancy on this view is a process rather than a static condition. The processual nature of delinquency is stressed rather than the static aspects, the dynamic business of getting labelled or coming to be regarded as deviant. So many factors contribute to this process, some relating to the individual himself, others relating to the environment, to other persons who experience individual's behaviour and their perception of him and of the behaviour and what is required in the nature of a response.

So we can identify four strands in this development as follows:

1 symbolic interaction;

2 the labelling perspective;

14 At p. 193.
15 J. Young, 'The Role of the Police as Amplifiers of Deviancy, Negotiators of Reality and Translators of Fantasy' in *Images of Deviance* (1971), ed. S. Cohen, p. 27.
16 E. M. Lemert, *Human Deviance, Social Problems and Social Control* (1967); see also I. Taylor, P. Walton and J. Young, *The New Criminology* (1973) pp. 150 et seq.
17 E. M. Lemert p. 17.

3 deviancy amplification;

4 the processual nature of deviancy.

The labelling perspective

The labelling theory of crime has been attributed to the writings of Howard S. Becker, Lemert, Goffman and others. Influential as it has been, the theory has not been without its critics, and recently some reassessment has taken place[18]. Howard Becker has pointed out that it was never intended to put forward labelling as a theory but more as a perspective or a particular way of looking at a general area of human activity[19].

'The original proponents of the position . . . did not propose solutions to the aetiological question. They had more modest aims. They wanted to enlarge the area taken into consideration in the study of deviant phenomena by including in it activities of others than the allegedly deviant actor'[20].

Enlarging the area of debate was certainly the result of this *genre* of sociological writing. The result has been healthy even though misunderstandings have occurred so that one has sometimes lost sight of the fact, which Becker stresses, that the act of labelling 'cannot possibly be conceived as the sole explanation of what alleged deviants actually do'[20]. The important consequence of this approach has been that we can no longer be content with a study of isolated acts of deviance:

'By viewing deviance as a form of collective activity, to be investigated in all its facets like any other form of collective activity, we see that the object of our study is not an isolated act whose origin we are to discover. Rather, the act alleged to occur, when it has occurred, takes place in a complex network of acts involving others, and takes on some of that complexity because of the way various people and groups define it'[1].

18 *The Labelling of Deviance: Evaluating a Perspective* (1975), ed. Walter R. Gove.
19 Howard S. Becker, 'Labelling Theory Reconsidered' in *Deviance and Social Control* (1974), eds. P. Rock and M. McIntosh, p. 41, at p. 44. See also Ken Plummer, 'Misunderstanding Labelling Perspectives' in *Deviant Interpretations* (1979), eds. D. Downes and P. Rock pp. 85 et seq.
20 p. 42.
1 p. 49.

Becker argues that it has been beneficial to the study of deviance to look at it in this more rounded way. He is not troubled that this approach has been regarded as radical by some critics, or not radical enough and too establishment-minded. He points out the ethical and moral implications of studying deviance in this way, rejecting the view that one can have a value-free sociology, but limiting the role of value judgment rather rigorously within a scientific framework.

Whatever may be the correct view of the significance of labelling theory, it cannot be denied that this perspective, by standing the question on its head, as it were, concerning the origins and explanation of deviant and delinquent behaviour, has proved to be a fertile source of new ideas and, by approaching crime from an entirely different angle, has greatly enriched our appreciation of delinquent behaviour.

The 'Control' theory

Hirschi and others have described certain modern sociological thinking about crime as possessing the character of a theory of social control, or, for short, 'control' theory. The writings of Matza and F. Ivan Nye, Walter Reckless and Albert J. Reiss Jr. are placed in this category[2]. According to these writers, men are naturally inclined towards deviant behaviour, but yield to such temptations only because of a weakening of the moral authority which tends to counteract it, or failure to form moral bonds in the first place, through childhood influences, experiencing appropriate models of behaviour in the home and in the street, and so forth. For the majority of delinquents such bonds are not totally absent. The moral authority of the law and society is acknowledged but is somehow undermined or replaced by an alternative version, a re-definition of affairs and relationships, which makes the deviant behaviour acceptable or legitimizes it. Some sociologists even include the psychological theories of Eysenck and Trasler in their account of 'control' theory[3]. We shall not run over that ground again, but content ourselves here with a discussion of the best-known exponent of 'control' theory, David Matza.

2 D. Matza, *Delinquency and Drift* (1964); F. Ivan Nye, *Family Relationships and Delinquent Behaviour* (1958); Walter C. Reckless, *The Crime Problem* (1967); Albert J. Reiss Jr. 'Delinquency as the Failure of Personal and Social Controls' Am Soc Rev 196 (1951).
3 G. Nettler, *Explaining Crime* (1974) Chap. 9. For Eysenck and Trasler, see ante, Chap 5.

David Matza's theory of drift

Bursting upon the confused scene among modern deviancy theories in 1964, David Matza in his book *Delinquency and Drift* provided yet another dimension to the sociological debate. He fiercely opposed the deterministic implications of much of traditional criminology, and argued that much delinquent behaviour involved choice by the actor between competing courses of action, and a kind of soft determinism applied to influence his choice. Many delinquents were not firmly committed to a criminal way of life. At first they drifted between adherence to conventional norms and subscribing to criminal norms. They tended to drift into delinquency, but this drift might be accelerated or deflected by numerous events. There was no hard commitment to delinquency.

Matza has much to say about the subculture of delinquency and its relationship to the wider culture of society, a relationship which he described as 'subtle, complex, and sometimes devious'. He noted the importance of that subterranean tradition found in many localised deviant traditions. Delinquency, he claimed, involved at first merely flirting with this, but the result was to loosen the moral bind of the law, and feelings of guilt were neutralised by a variety of means – techniques of neutralisation involving such things as extending the range of legitimate defences beyond those recognised by the law, and other techniques of rationalisation. In so behaving the delinquent acknowledged the existence of the law and recognised its validity. This last part of the argument reflects the earlier contribution made by Sykes and Matza on 'Techniques of Neutralization'[4], about the way many lower-class delinquents acknowledge the middle-class norms and values embodied in the law and offset their guilty feelings about committing crime by different kinds of rationalisation.

Matza's later book *Becoming Deviant* (1969) developed the thesis further. He described the process whereby society creates delinquents by its labelling them, and the way the delinquents themselves become alienated from conventional norms. On this analysis there are three distinct stages of becoming a delinquent: 1) the *alienation* of the delinquent from conventional norms; 2) his *affiliation* with a subculture of delinquency; 3) his *signification* or definition as such by the law and the judicial process. There is a great deal of discussion about the

---

4 Gresham M. Sykes and David Matza, 'Techniques of Neutralization: A Theory of Delinquency' 22 Am Soc Rev 664 (December 1957), reprinted in M. E. Wolfgang L. Savitz and N. Johnston, *The Sociology of Crime and Delinquency* (1962) p. 249.

need to view delinquents not merely as objects but as subjects, acting and self-reflecting rather than merely reacting to the constraints of external stimuli. There is also an appeal for a return to a naturalistic view of man and his deviant behaviour[5].

Radical theories about crime

For some criminologists it was a short step from the expression of the symbolic-interactionist approach to deviance, and labelling theory, to the development of a radical theory about crime. In the United States this had its apostles in Alvin Gouldner, W. H. Chambliss, A. V. Cicourel, Richard Quinney and others[6], in Britain in the work of Taylor, Walton and Young[7], and others and the work of the National Deviancy Conferences held at York. Elsewhere in Europe, e.g. in Scandinavia, Holland and Western Germany there were parallel developments in the 1970s[8]. The radical seed had been sown, and was able to thrive, usually dependent on a fiercely socialist root derived from Marx and Engels, to provide a fundamental critique of the criminal justice system, and through this, of society itself, which was seen as an expression of power by an élite and repression of the working classes, involving much bias and discrimination in respect of law enforcement and the administration of justice.

Taylor, Walton and Young extended their criticism to condemn the whole tradition of empirical criminology, which was chastised for its belief in the quantitative method and scientific neutrality, and for adopting a deterministic view of criminal behaviour. Matza had already criticised some of these characteristics of 'positive' criminology, but now the criticism was elevated to the level of a major belief. Classical criminology stood condemned. In its place one could

5 D. Beyleveld and P. Wiles in their article 'Man and Method in David Matza's "Becoming Deviant" ' criticise Matza's view of man as subject not object and his resort to 'naturalism' to justify this approach on philosophical grounds: BJC Vol. 15, p. 111 (April 1975).
6 Alvin Gouldner, *The Coming Crisis of Western Sociology* (1971); W. H. Chambliss, *Crime and the Legal Process* (1969); *Law Order and Power* (1971); Richard R. Quinney, *The Social Reality of Crime* (1970); A. V. Cicourel, *The Social Organisation of Juvenile Justice* (1968).
7 I. Taylor, P. Walton and J. Young, *The New Criminology* (1973); *Critical Criminology* (1975); *Radical Issues in Criminology* (1980), eds. P. Carlen and M. Collison.
8 See Paul C. Friday 'Some Problems and Implications of Politicalization in Contemporary Criminological Thinking'; Denis Szabo, 'Some Thoughts on The New Criminology' (review article) 65 Jo Crim L & Crim'ogy & Pol Sci, No. 4 p. 554 (1975).

hope to provide a new criminology based on commitment and identification with the lot of the oppressed and the deprived, among whom crime had been located by traditional criminology. The way in which the criminal justice system had been used in the period of the industrial revolution to meet the needs of the rising bourgeoisie for protection would be exposed, as would the role it played at the present day as an instrument of social control and repression.

This radical approach to criminology gave expression to the feelings of many professional criminologists, feelings of disenchantment and disappointment over the poor results achieved by so much effort in the way of research and analysis by traditional criminologists, and the new criminology seemed to offer a way out. There was much that was exciting and valuable in the radical approach, and it is not surprising that it had a wide appeal, especially to the young student. It coincided with the corresponding developments in the political arena, nationally and internationally. There were several stands in the argument with which even 'non-believers' might feel inclined to agree. On a broad front it looked for a time as though the new criminology would indeed succeed in replacing the old, and that a new dawn had arrived in the history of criminology.

But there were too many diverse strands in the new criminology to make a coherent theoretical development. There were the naturalists whose beliefs were enshrined in the description 'ethnomethodology.' There were the extreme leftists who saw no alternative to a radical reconstruction of society in revolutionary terms. There were some who still clung stubbornly to the scientific methodology, and remained chary of commitment. Internal disputes and ideological differences led to the original promise of the deviance perspective becoming distorted and confused.[9] The weaknesses of the radical theory have been exposed by David Downes[9].

That there have been great benefits from this period of radical criminology cannot be denied. It is henceforth unthinkable to look at crime in such narrow terms as in the past, concentrating only on the offender and his offence. Our sensitivity to the part played by the whole system of criminal justice in identifying and processing the offender as such has been aroused, so that we strive for a more complete account of the events and relationships in a way which traditional criminology failed to do. These are very considerable gains. Moreover there are some types of offence and offender for which this

9 David Downes, 'Praxis Makes Perfect: A Critique of Critical Criminology' in *Deviant Interpretations* (1979), eds. D. Downes and P. Rock, p. 1.

approach is particularly valuable, e.g. drug offences, public order offences, vandalism and hooliganism. How far the deviance perspective can help over the more serious crimes against the person, like homicide, rape, incest, may be questioned, but undoubtedly society's attitude, values and expectations powerfully influence what is done even in those situations. The approach has been applied to the study of such property crimes as shoplifting, receiving, blackmail and organised crime. Some would argue that all crimes must be viewed in this light while others would see less room for the deviance perspective in emotional crimes and crimes stemming from abnormal or pathological conditions. There are signs of a continuing adherence to the scientific method even among radical criminologists. As for the more extreme forms of the radical thesis, it is necessary to point out that the analysis seems to embrace elements of that very positivism and determinism which is criticised when it is discerned at the root of traditional criminology. In the end the debate becomes a question of political belief or value system. Traditional values have not yet been entirely superseded and the political system, supported and protected as it is from drastic change by the institutions of parliamentary democracy and the forces of law and order, remains so far relatively unchanged, though its survival has often been assured only by means of skilful adaptations, which some would regard as the secret of its success.

Notes. Sociological theories about crime

1 Sections 4 and 5 dealing with sociological theories about crime do no more than provide an outline or brief sketch. The literature on this subject is extensive and, for the non-sociologist, rather difficult to comprehend. The matter is best approached through reading as many of the original monographs as possible. Useful summaries are provided by Laurie Taylor, *Deviance and Society* (1971), Travis Hirschi and Gwynn Nettler in the books cited in the text. Also see Lamar T. Empey, *American Delinquency: Its Meaning and Construction* (1978).

2 On labelling theory, discussed in section 5, see in addition to the sources cited, E. M. Schur, *Labeling Deviant Behaviour: Its Sociological Implications* (1971); Ruth-Ellen Grimes and Austin T. Turk, 'Labeling in Context: Conflict, Power and Self-Definition' in *Crime, Law and Sanctions: Theoretical Perspectives* (1978), eds. M. D. Krohn and R. L. Akers p. 39; S. G. Shoham, 'Labeling and Beyond: Social Stigma Revisited, in *New Paths in Criminology: Interdisciplinary and Intercultural Explorations* (1979), eds. S. A. Mednick and S. G. Shoham, p. 135; Ken Plummer, 'Misunderstanding Labelling

Perspectives' in *Deviant Interpretations* (1979), eds. D. Downes and P. Rock p. 85. For a development of Schur's position, see E. M. Schur, *The Politics of Deviance: Stigma Contests and the Uses of Power* (1980).

3 On the development of the radical theory, see the following books which have appeared in Britain, apart from Taylor, Walton and Young: M. Phillipson, *Sociological Aspects of Crime and Delinquency* (1971); P. Carlen and M. Collison, *Radical Issues in Criminology* (1980); *Permissiveness and Control: the fate of the sixties legislation*, National Deviancy Conference (1980) (Critical Criminology series); Jason Ditton, *Controlology: Beyond the New Criminology* (1979). For a critical assessment of the contribution of radical criminology, see Geoff Mungham, 'The Career of A Confusion: Radical Criminology in Britain' in J. A. Inciardi, *Radical Criminology: The Coming Crises* (1980).

4 A critique of criminology of the traditional kind written from a different angle is Terence Morris's *Deviance and Control: The Secular Heresy* (1976). For a different approach, by one of the outstanding young sociologists in Britain, see P. Rock, *Deviant Behaviour* (1973). Thoughtful reflections of a more balanced kind than most radical criminologists utter on the current situation in criminological theory come from Stan Cohen, *Crime and Punishment: Some Thoughts on Theories and Policies* (1979). See also his article in *The Listener*, 8 November 1973, 'The Failures of Criminology' p. 622, and his essay 'Guilt, justice and tolerance: some old concepts for a new criminology' in *Deviance and Social Control* (1979), eds. D. Downes and P. Rock, p. 17.

Chapter 7

The identification and measurement of crime

We now proceed to the vexed subject of criminal statistics, how they are compiled, and how they should be interpreted. The discussion falls into four parts:

1 How crimes are perceived and recorded.

2 Official records of crime: the criminal statistics in the United States and the United Kingdom.

3 Unofficial measurement of crime, such as is provided:
   A. by the self-report studies;
   B. by victim studies.
   Here we shall note the growth of the study of victimology.

4 The possibility of a crime index.

1 How crimes are perceived and recorded

The starting point in the discussion of criminal statistics is to consider how and where they originate. As we shall see in section 2, p. 157, post, in England and Wales official statistics are provided of the activity of the police and the courts and the penal system in relation to crimes committed and offenders processed in the criminal justice system. Criminologists usually begin their search for a measure of crime by looking at the figures provided for crimes known to the police. In England and Wales such figures are provided only in respect of serious offences[1] known to the police, but they are perhaps a fair guide. Figures for offences known to the police are considered to be a better guide than those relating to persons dealt with by the courts, since many crimes remain unsolved, and even when the offender is known it

1 Until 1978 these were known as 'indictable offences' for the purposes of the official criminal statistics.

may not be possible or desirable to institute criminal proceedings. As Thorsten Sellin put it in a graphic phrase 'the value of criminal statistics decreases as the procedure takes us further away from the offence itself'[2]. The nearest we can get to the criminal happening or event is the record kept by the police of crimes reported to them.

Yet this is by no means a perfect record. The police themselves may be instrumental in discovering the commission of an offence. This is more likely in the case of some property crimes like office-and shop-breaking and burglary of unoccupied dwelling houses. It is also true of what may be termed loosely 'street crimes' or offences against public order. But the majority of crimes become known to the police through reports emanating from members of the public, and the police role is largely a reactive one, to respond to calls for assistance. It has been estimated that 70 per cent of all recorded crime is reported to the police by the victim or some other person, leaving only 30 per cent as recorded by the police from their own observation and intervention[3]. It is not safe to rely on police records of crime for many reasons, most of which lie outside their control. Thus:

1 The victim may not be aware that an offence has been committed.
This frequently happens when employees are dishonest over deliveries of goods, receiving money and thefts by employees within the store or business. Such losses are often 'written off,' during stocktaking as shortages or breakages. There is an enormous amount of internal dishonesty which is never discovered or which is condoned[4].

2 The 'victim' may have been a willing partner to the crime and so it is unlikely to be discovered unless a third party reports it. This is the case for many sexual offences against children, and criminal abortion, and homosexual offences.

3 Even where the victim knows an offence has been committed and has not consented to it or partaken in it, he or she may decide not to report the offence to the police for a variety of reasons. It may be regarded as too trivial to warrant such a report, the victim may not wish to become involved in the consequences which may flow from the report, such as interrogation by the police or being called as a witness. He may not wish to see proceedings brought against the offender

2 T. Sellin, 'The Significance of Records of Crime' 67 LQR p. 489 at p. 498 (October 1957).
3 A. J. Reiss, *The Police and the Public* (1971).
4 J. P. Martin, *Offenders as Employees* (1962); J. Ditton, *Part-time Crime: an Ethnography of fiddling and pilferage* (1977).

because he is a child, relative, friend, or employee or employer. He may regard the sanctions of the law an inappropriate for the conduct in question. He may wish to avoid publicity. He may be too frightened to come forward. He may prefer to administer a more homely or less drastic remedy (a beating or the sack). The offender may simply be asked to pay for the goods or make restitution and be given a stern warning: this frequently happens in cases of shoplifting[5].

4 There may be no victim, since in some crimes such as those connected with drugs, alcohol and obscene publications, society condemns behaviour which involves no victim, unless the offender himself is so regarded.

Non-reporting of crime to the police is very extensive. The degree to which the occurrence of a crime is likely to be reported (its 'reportability') varies according to the nature of the offence. Some crimes like robbery and homicide have a very high degree of reportability. This is also true of burglary and car theft, since the insurance companies insist that the matter be reported to the police if it is the subject of a claim. Since personal theft, i.e. theft of a purse or wallet containing money, is less likely to be covered by insurance it is less likely to be reported to the police. Some crimes have a very low degree of reportability, for example, shoplifting, business fraud, certain sexual offences, and blackmail and handling (what used to be called receiving in English law now has a wider definition as 'handling'). The blackmailer's victim rarely reports the behaviour to the police. 'Handlers' or fences provide a service to the criminal who is unlikely to complain unless cheated. Business fraud or economic crime is so easy to hide and so difficult to detect that even when large sums of money are involved rarely do the victims seem inclined to report the events to the police, and only elaborate investigations lasting many years can determine what offences if any have been committed. Then there is the question of violence, and whether such behaviour has increased in frequency simply because there are more reported cases of violence is a debateable question, the answer to which depends in part on the period over which the comparison is being made. If one is comparing behaviour over several centuries, then there can be little doubt that our society has become less violent. There was a time when no gentleman would dare to walk down the Strand in London without

---

5 The various shoplifting studies include T. C. N. Gibbens and J. Prince, *Shoplifting* (1962).

an armed escort, and street violence was extremely common[6]. If, however, one is comparing behaviour over several decades, then there seems to have been an increase in violence, judged by the available statistics. But even here, caution is needed in interpreting the figures, since most violence is of a domestic nature, and it may well be that what we see is evidence of society's increasing disapproval of violence whether in the home or in the street. Standards and expectations have changed dramatically[7]. At the same time it is fair to observe that there appears to be an increasing tendency towards an explosive emotional response to situations of stress and tension which is hard to explain yet seems to exist not only in the domestic scene, as witnessed by the battered baby syndrome and the battered wives movement, but which also erupts in the street, between motorists and between pedestrians, more frequently than in the past. This observation is made independently from the quite separate question of crowd behaviour in relation to the police, such as occurred recently in our inner city areas. The latter needs to be studied separately in connection with the subject of race and crime, which is extremely complicated and involved[8].

We have arrived at the point in our discussion where we can agree with Wilkins that crime should be defined, for the purpose of statistics if not generally, as something that members of the public think the police ought to do something about[9]. This is not a sufficient definition, however, since it omits to include that the public expects the police to deal with it by recording and acting on the report as a crime report. It also omits to include behaviour which the police themselves define as such that it requires to be dealt with as crime. This draws attention to the vital role of the police in defining crime.

The police role in defining crime

There are several reasons why the police may decide that a matter reported to them as a crime should not be dealt with as such:

6 See various accounts by J. J. Tobias, *Crime and Industrial Society in the Nineteenth Century* (1967); *Nineteenth-Century Crime, Prevention and Punishment* (1972).

7 See A. K. Bottomley, *Decisions in the Penal Process* (1973) p. 11.

8 A study of criminology of crowds has been made by E. Trivizas, 'Offences and offenders in Football Crowd Disorders' BJC Vol. 20, No. 3, p. 276 (July 1980). The subject of race and crime has been studied by American criminologists, mainly in connection with the black population of the cities of the north eastern seaboard and Chicago. There have not been any definitive British studies.

9 L. T. Wilkins, *Social Deviance: Social Policy, Action and Research* (1964).

1 They may decide that it is not a crime, but should be regarded in some other way and dealt with accordingly. Thus a reported theft may be treated as lost property if the circumstances suggest that theft is unlikely. An event such as a motor vehicle collision may be regarded as an accident. Wayward behaviour may be treated as evidence of a mental or social problem. There are many ways in which the police may divert cases away from the criminal process.

2 They may decide it is not a serious offence, and, as has been mentioned above, the only record kept of offences known to the police is of serious offences. Offences regarded as summary offences will of course be investigated, and if the case goes to court, then there will be a record of it among the persons dealt with or proceeded against.

3 It may well be that although a serious offence has been committed it will be regarded as too stale to require investigation, or too trivial, so that it can be disregarded.

Procedural rules

Another matter which affects police recording of crime is the procedural rules. These derive in part from internal regulations and in part from Home Office directives concerning the way in which the criminal statistics are recorded. Changes may occur in either which can profoundly affect the crime figures. Several examples can be given:

1 The best-known example is the change which occurred in 1932 when the Commissioner of Police of the Metropolis decided to suppress the 'Suspected Stolen Book' and henceforth provide that only a 'Lost Property Book' should be kept in each police station, as well as a Crime Book. The result was that property reported as lost in circumstances suggesting theft now had to be included in the Crime Book. The effect on the statistics of recorded theft was dramatic. A rise in thefts in London was recorded from 26,000 known offences in 1931 to 83,000 in 1932[10].

2 Changes may be decreed by the Home Office in the way the figures are kept. This has happened in recent years with regard to minor thefts (under £5 in value) and criminal damage. Thefts under £5 in value were excluded in 1972 and 1973 but restored in 1975. Offences of

10 See H. Mannheim, *Social Aspects of Crime in England Between the Wars* (1940) pp. 72 et seq.

criminal damage of value between £20 and £100 were also excluded but are now restored in the statistics. Criminal damage of under £20 value is not included however.

3 There are elaborate 'counting rules' governing different situations[11]. For example, where a number of different offences are committed at the same time, the rule is different in respect of offences of sex and violence from the case of property crimes. In general in the former class of cases one offence is recorded in respect of each victim, in the latter, one offence in respect of each group of more or less homogeneous offences. Only the most serious offence is recorded out of a situation involving several distinct offences. No correction is made to any initial classification of an offence in the light of subsequent events such as the trial of the offender and conviction, which may well be for what lawyers call a lesser included offence, and result from a plea of guilty to the lesser offence or the jury's verdict. There is one exception to the rule, murder cases, where the need to keep as accurate a record as possible of the nature of the homicide has led to a rule that in this single instance a later correction may be made to the category of offence originally recorded. Many offences originally recorded as murder turn out to be manslaughter, and it is highly desirable for the statistics to reflect the social reality of the situation.

The dark number

Criminologists have frequently drawn attention to the so-called 'dark number' of offences which do not appear in the crime figures but are hidden from view[12]. There is undoubtedly an 'ice-berg' type situation here in that a very large proportion of offences lies beneath the surface and is never revealed or recorded. What proportion the 'dark number' represents it is impossible to say. Estimates have been made of 85 per cent of all crimes and perhaps 90 per cent of sexual offences being hidden from view or unknown. There is little point in pursuing the speculation. One aspect only is worthy of reflection and that is the way in which this 'iceberg' situation affects the interpretation of annual percentage changes in the crime figures. Suppose for example

11 N. Walker, *Crimes, Courts and Figures* (1971) p. 24. Report of the Departmental Committee on Criminal Statistics Cmnd. 3448 (1967) Chap. 5, pp. 18 et seq.

12 F. H. McClintock, 'The Dark Figure' in *Collected Studies in Criminological Research* (1970) Vol. V, European Committee on Crime Problems, Council of Europe, Strasbourg, pp. 9 et seq.

that it is announced that the figures show a 10 per cent increase in violence, comparing this year with last year. Suppose that 85 per cent of violence is unknown and not recorded. Then the 10 per cent increase is to be applied only to the known figures, i.e. the 15 per cent. This may mean that no more than 1.5 per cent more violence has actually occurred. If this sounds like special pleading by a liberal criminologist, let it be said that while *any* percentage increase is to be deplored, the point to remember is that annual rates of increase are somewhat suspect. If the trend is maintained over several years or a decade, then there is more cause for concern, but in respect of violence, including sexual assault, let it be remembered that such offences constitute altogether no more than some 4 per cent of criminal offences known in England and Wales[13]. It cannot be too strongly emphasised that in our society it is dishonesty in its various forms rather than violence which constitutes the most pressing problem, being far more widespread in its incidence and corrupting in its influence. The emphasis may differ in other western countries or in other continents for it is clear by now that for whatever reasons crime has a very strong cultural component. The figure overleaf gives a picture of the situation in England and Wales in 1979 regarding serious offences known to police, from which it will be seen that some 83 per cent of crimes known involve dishonesty of some kind, whether it be simple theft or handling, or violent theft such as robbery, or fraud or forgery.

2 Official records of crime

We have already made reference to the statistics of serious offences known to the police in England and Wales[14]. These are published annually in the Home Office Criminal Statistics (England and Wales) in a volume which contains a plethora of statistical information about crime and the working of the criminal justice and penal systems. There are comparative tables giving information about trends over recent years, and annual tables showing the work of the crown courts, magistrates' courts, courts of appeal, and the exercise of the prerogative of mercy and the working of legal aid and the mental health law relating to offenders. Trends in the use of remands in custody and

13 S. Klein, 'Crimes of violence against the person in England and Wales' Social Trends No. 3 (1972) p. 53.
14 p. 151, ante.

Serious* offences recorded by the police by offence group.

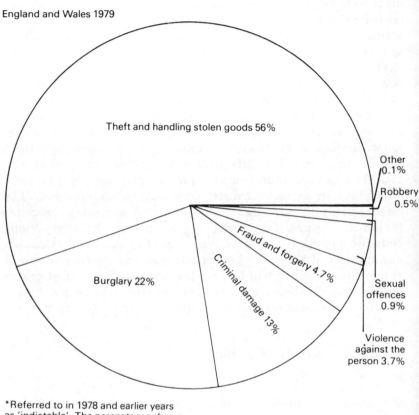

England and Wales 1979

Theft and handling stolen goods 56%

Other
0.1%

Robbery
0.5%

Fraud and forgery 4.7%

Criminal damage 13%

Burglary 22%

Sexual
offences
0.9%

Violence
against the
person 3.7%

*Referred to in 1978 and earlier years
as 'indictable'. The percentages shown
do not sum to 100 per cent because the
three largest figures are rounded to the
nearest unit.

Source: Home Office, Criminal Statistics (England and Wales)
1979 Cmnd. 8098, p.43.

trends) in sentencing can be studied from this source which is a
marvellous cornucopia of comprehensive, reliable and relevant
information. Not the least of the merits of this publication is that it is
reasonably up-to-date, in that last year's information is usually
available this year, which is quite an achievement, considering the
complexity and size of the operation.

Now it is true that, for many reasons, some of which have been outlined above in considering the way offences are identified and recorded, even the most experienced student of the criminal statistics finds difficulty in drawing a picture of the crime situation from a scrutiny of the criminal statistics. A former Head of the Home Office Research Unit, T. S. Lodge[15], put it graphically when he wrote that when the object is to draw conclusions about crime trends

'the criminal statistics do not contain such information; though they contain figures related to it. The interpretation of the statistics is not unlike attempting to draw a man's picture from his shadow on a wall – or, if non-indictable offences are in question, from his shadow on wire-netting'.

The amount of information which the statistics provide directly is strictly limited, says Lodge, but they do show the directions in which further inquiry should be made, and this is one of their essential functions.

The figures for serious offences known to the police may be studied further by relating them to the total population which might conceivably commit the offence, as is done in the graph on p. 160.

The figure for serious offences known may be used in a number of other ways. Thus the geographical distribution of certain offences may be demonstrated e.g. burglary and theft in dwelling houses may be shown, related to the proportion of dwellings in the area, as is shown in the map on p. 161.

Offences cleared up

One other use to which the figure for offences known is put relates to what is called the 'clear-up rate'. The Home Office has produced a definition of when an offence can be regarded by the police as 'cleared up' which is rather wider than simply having solved the crime. The definition is as follows:

'2.14 An offence recorded by the police is said to be cleared up if a person has been arrested, summoned or cautioned for the offence; if it is ascertained that the offence was committed by a child under the age of criminal responsibility; if the offence is taken into consideration by the court in sentencing an offender found guilty of another charge; or if, for various technical reasons, a person known or thought to be guilty

15 T. S. Lodge, 'Criminal Statistics' Jo Roy Stat Soc CXVI A p. 283 at p. 290 (1953).

Serious* offences recorded by the police per 100,000 population

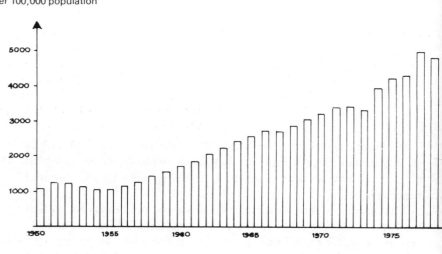

Number of offences +
per 100,000 population

*Referred to in 1978 and earlier
years as 'indictable'.

+ Excluding 'other criminal damage'
value £20 and under.

of the offence cannot be prosecuted or cautioned (e.g. if he is known to have died or if the proceedings cannot be pursued through death of the prosecutor or an essential witness). An offence is not regarded as cleared up if a warrant for the arrest of an offender remains unexecuted nor, except as described above, if there is insufficient evidence for proceedings to be taken against a known and available person who does not admit having committed the offence'[15a].

Each year the criminal statistics give the figures for offences cleared up and these are expressed as a proportion of the offences known, in relation to each serious offence, and in relation to the total volume of serious offences. These figures are regarded as some indication of police efficiency or effectiveness. The most frequently quoted figure is the overall proportion of offences cleared up, which has dropped to a mere 44 per cent in recent years. The figures for individual offences are perhaps more interesting in that one observes great differences

15a Home Office, Criminal Statistics (England and Wales) 1979, Cmnd. 8098, p. 57.

Offences of burglary, aggravated burglary and theft in a dwelling recorded by the police per 100,000 dwellings by police force area 1978.

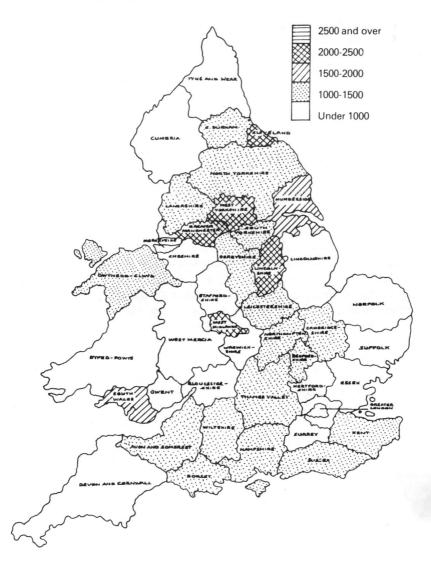

Source: Home Office Criminal Statistics (England and Wales) Cmnd. 7670.

between them in the clear-up rate. Violence against the person and sexual offences have a clear-up rate of some 80 per cent, which is understandable since they involve inter-personal confrontations. Robbery, burglary, criminal damage and theft have clear-up rates nearer to 40 per cent, sometimes falling nearer to or below 30 per cent. Little wonder that the robber is not deterred because he has such a good chance of escaping arrest or detection. This is why successive Lord Chancellors and Lords Chief Justice have urged that one must do everything in one's power to increase the certainty of detection[16].

Several important and interesting studies of crime in England and Wales have been carried out based on the official criminal statistics. McClintock and Avison[17] conducted a comprehensive survey of crime patterns in the different police areas of England and Wales, which showed marked divergences in the relative frequency of violence and sexual offences and breaking offences in different regions, as well as a pattern of some consistency over time. As Avison remarks, 'no satisfactory explanation for findings such as these has been forthcoming, although the part played by differences in police recording practices has to to be considered'[18]. McClintock has also studied sexual crime, violence and robbery, the latter limited to London, in separate volumes[19]. Another study, this time of a more international comparative nature, by Lynn McDonald, views the crime situation in England and Wales largely through the official criminal statistics[20]. It will be seen from these studies how criminologists use the official statistics of crime.

Yet it is possible to draw many false conclusions from the official statistics, and many myths about the crime situation and crime trends derive therefrom. This is something long recognised by criminologists[1]. There are so many pitfalls in their interpretation,

16 This is also a point frequently emphasised by chiefs of police. Increasing the probability of detection is more important than increasing the severity of punishment.
17 F. H. McClintock and N. Avison, *Crime in England and Wales* (1968).
18 N. H. Avison, 'Criminal statistics as social indicators' in *Social Indicators and Social Policy* (1972), eds. A. Shonfield and S. Shaw, p. 33, at p. 40.
19 F. H. McClintock and E. Gibson, *Robbery in London* (1961); F. H. McClintock, *Crimes of Violence* (1963). Report of the Cambridge Department of Criminal Science, *Sexual Offences* (1957).
20 Lynn McDonald, *The Sociology of Law and Order* (1976).
  1 F. H. McClintock, 'Facts and Myths about the State of Crime' in *Crime, Criminology and Public Policy* (1974), ed. R. Hood, p. 33; J. E. Hall Williams, 'Criminological myths and realities' International Annals of Criminology, Vol. 15, No. 1. (1976) p. 13; J. E. Hall Williams, 'Myths of criminal justice' in *Crime—Myths and Reality* I.S.T.D. Pamphlet (March 1969).

particularly when attempts are made to look at trends by comparing one year with another, that there seems now to be a growing preference for adopting other means for measuring crime, which we shall shortly describe.

First we must look at the American criminal statistics to see how far the situation resembles that in Britain. There the statistics are compiled by the FBI (Federal Bureau of Investigation) from figures supplied by local, county and state enforcement agencies throughout the United States. These statistics have been published annually since 1930 as the Uniform Crime Reports. Crimes known to the police are listed along with crimes cleared by arrest. The crimes are grouped into categories for the purpose of analysis, but there is much dissatisfaction with the grouping adopted and the reliability of the information is extremely suspect. While strenuous efforts have been made over the years to improve standards of reporting and recording crime, there is every reason to believe that one is left with a very imperfect picture of the actual incidence of crime in America. The President's Crime Commission reported in 1967 that there were many grounds for suspicion and there was much room for improvement[2].

What seems clear from the American literature is that there is a great deal of unreported crime, the reasons for not reporting being similar to those already described; that there has been a marked rise in crime in recent decades, such as we have witnessed here; that it is not clear how much of the increase in crime derives from increased reporting or improved efficiency; and that we need to look elsewhere than the official statistics for some sound guidance on crime trends and patterns. This is not to deny that crime has increased in terms of the volume of business experienced by the criminal justice system, including the police, the courts and the penal institutions.

The President's Crime Commission of 1967 found it very difficult to make an accurate measurement of crime trends by relying solely on official figures since, as Haskell and Yablonsky put it, 'it is likely that each year police agencies are to some degree dipping deeper into the vast reservoir of unreported crime. People are probably reporting more to the police as a reflection of higher expectations and greater confidence, and the police in turn are reflecting this in their statistics. In this sense, more efficient policing may be leading to higher rates of reported crime'[3]. The Commission made various recommendations

---

2 See the discussion in American criminology texts such as W. C. Reckless, *The Crime Problem* (1967) pp. 78 et seq.; M. R. Haskell and L. Yablonsky *Crime and Delinquency* (1971) pp. 32 et seq.
3 Haskell and Yablonsky (1971) p. 46.

for the improvement of the crime statistics but many of the problems remain and seem inherent in the system whereby the figures are compiled.

The federal criminal statistics include analysis of the age, sex and race of persons arrested for crime. Until an offender has been arrested or discovered we have no idea of his age, sex or any other characteristics such as previous convictions. Like the British statistics, detailed analysis is made of the characteristics of this population of known offenders. In England and Wales the figures are for persons dealt with by arrest or summons, and persons tried in the criminal courts. Everyone agrees that these persons may be unrepresentative of offenders as a whole. As Haskell and Yablonsky remark 'we know little or nothing about people who successfully commit crimes and are not apprehended'[4] who may be the majority, in the case of many offences.

Doubts about the representativeness of those offenders actually discovered, caught and dealt with, have been reduced to some degree by the evidence of certain scholars suggesting that we know more than we may think we know about the qualities and characteristics of those who dedicate themselves more or less consistently to a criminal career. Walker's study of 'the penal involvement rate'[5] and West and Farrington's study of juvenile delinquents in London[6] both suggest that sooner or later the persistent offender is picked up by the criminal justice system, and becomes 'visible'. Perhaps what we still require more information about is the casual offender or the one-off offender, and the way the system reacts to the different types of offender as they are filtered through its very early stages.

3 Unofficial measurement of crime

The doubts concerning the reliability of the official statistics of crime have led criminologists to consider using other means for measuring

---

4 Ibid, p. 53.
5 N. D. Walker, 'Caution: Some Thoughts on the Penal Involvement Rate' in *Progress in Penal Reform*, (1974), ed. L. Blom-Cooper, p. 221.
6 D. J. West and D. P. Farrington, *Who Becomes Delinquent?* (1973) p. 21: 'Whatever prosecution standards are in vogue, the individuals selected for official action are probably by and large, more seriously or more frequently delinquent in behaviour than the average citizen. . . . It may be justifiable to use official statistics to discover whether or not crime is increasing, but it seems reasonable to use them, as we have done, to isolate a relatively delinquent group'.

crime. Two such means have been employed so far: A. self-report studies, and B. victim studies.

A. Self-report studies

These have been carried out mostly by employing samples of students or school children or entrants to military service. The technique involves asking the subjects to record whether they have ever committed any of a given list of crimes or types of delinquent behaviour. The earliest self-report study was that carried out by Wallerstein and Wyle[6a] in New York State by sending out a mailed questionnaire to 1,800 men and women asking them to tick any of 49 offences against the penal law which they had committed. Two-thirds of the men admitted to having committed a felony, and a large number admitted multiple crimes. The women too reported high rates of criminal behaviour in a variety of situations[7].

Other studies include that of Empey and Erickson in 1966 in Utah, U.S.A.[8] of boys aged between fifteen and seventeen, and Elmhorn's study of schoolboys in Stockholm[9]. Common to both these studies was the extremely high proportion of offences which escaped detection, or were not cleared up. Other American studies such as that by Dentler and Monroe[10] and the Scandinavian studies[11] appear to confirm these findings. Some careful research carried out in London by W. A. Belson[12] on the incidence of theft among boys yielded similar findings.

Before one can accept the validity of these self-report studies certain methodological problems must be considered. One is the question

6a J. S. Wallerstein and C. L. Wyle, 'Our lawabiding lawbreakers' National Probation p. 107 (March–April 1947).

7 R. Hood and R. Sparks, *Key Issues in Criminology* (1970) gives a summary of the findings and reproduces them in a Table (Table 2:1, p. 48). They also summarise the other self-report studies at pp. 19 et seq.

8 L. T. Empey and M. L. Erickson, 'Hidden delinquency and social status' Social Forces Vol. 44, p. 546 (1966). See Hood and Sparks p. 24 (Table 1:3).

9 K. Elmhorn, 'Study in self-reported delinquency among schoolchildren in Stockholm' in *Scandinavian Studies in Criminology* (1965), ed. K. O. Christiansen, Vol. 1, p. 117. See Hood and Sparks p. 22 (Table 1:2).

10 R. A. Dentler and L. J. Monroe, 'Social correlates of early adolescent theft' 26 Am Soc Rev 733 (1961).

11 I. Antilla and R. Jaakola, *Unrecorded Criminality in Finland* (1966); N. Christie, J. Andenaes and S. Skinbekk, 'A study of self-reported crime' in *Scandinavian Studies in Criminology* (1965) ed. K. O. Christiansen, Vol. 1, p. 85.

12 W. A. Belson, *The extent of stealing by London boys and some of its origins* (1969). See also W. A. Belson, *Juvenile Theft: The Causal Factors* (1975). See Hood and Sparks, Table 2:3 at p. 50.

whether the conduct reported truly was criminal. Such are the vagaries of definition of theft or assault that it is possible that people may think they have committed such offences in circumstances where it is extremely unlikely that it would be treated as a crime if the matter became known to the police. There is a built-in danger of over-reporting which even the most stringent safeguards and precautions can hardly avoid. Nevertheless the studies do show the occurrence of acts of what may be loosely called anti-social behaviour in all social classes at some time or other. The second problem concerns the reliability of memory and the accuracy of recall. Various devices have been adopted to protect the studies from this danger of being based on incorrect recollection. Interviews with the subjects, repeating the tests after an interval, and built-in checks, even the use of a lie-detector, have been introduced. Hood and Sparks[13], after discussing these matters, are less pessimistic than some scholars about the potential of self-report studies, but it seems that their interest lies more in the general light thrown on the dimensions of the so-called 'dark figure' of hidden crime than in any increased accuracy they offer in regard to criminal statistics.

B. Victim studies

Although there were some criminologists many years ago who had proposed the study of victims as an important focus for criminology, it is only in the last few decades that the subject of victim studies—or victimology, as some have termed it—has really developed and caught hold. Now there is an upsurge of interest, a spate of international conferences has been devoted to the subject, there is a journal and even an institute concerned with victimology.

The early pioneers of victim studies were Mendelsohn[14] and Von Hentig[15], who in 1947 and 1948 drew attention to this neglected aspect of criminology. These were the 'seminal works that spurred research on the subject of the criminal–victim relationship', according to Drapkin and Viano[16]. Carson and Wiles believe that it was not until the Report of the President's Crime Commission in 1967 that victim studies first emerged as a viable approach[17]. Students of homicide

13 Hood and Sparks (1970) p. 70.
14 See S. Schafer, 'The beginnings of "Victimology"' in *Victimology* (1974), eds. I. Drapkin and E. Viano, p. 17.
15 H. Von Hentig, *The Criminal and His Victim* (1948).
16 I. Drapkin and E. Viano, *Victimology: A New Focus* (1973) p. ix.
17 W. G. Carson and P. Wiles, *Crime and Delinquency in Britain* (1971) p. 182.

however will recall that Wolfgang's *Patterns of Criminal Homicide* had drawn attention to the role of the victim in homicide, and coined the celebrated phrase 'victim-precipitated homicide'. The 1967 Crime Commission[18] did however bring the matter to the fore by commissioning several victim studies, using the survey method of social investigation. This involved sampling 10,000 households in the U.S.A. and also parts of the District of Columbia (Washington) and Boston and Chicago. The study of households revealed a far higher rate of involvement in crime as victim than had previously been supposed. In the year 1966 one in five households had been a victim of serious crime in one way or another, and about twice as many major crimes were committed as were known to the police. The smaller studies carried out in Washington, Boston and Chicago served to confirm this finding, and suggested even higher rates of victimisation prevailed in urban areas, particularly in big cities. Once again, as with self-report studies, there are a number of reservations to be made about these victim studies for methodological reasons[19]. Hood and Sparks after reviewing the limitations of these studies suggest that 'victimization studies shed a good deal of light on the reasons for not reporting crime and on the disparities between reported acts and those recorded by the police'[20].

The 1974 U.S. Commission known as the National Advisory Commission on Criminal Justice Standards and Goals reviews the history of victimisation studies[1], and revealed that a large-scale programme had been mounted to study burglary and stranger-to-stranger violence in several large cities of the U.S.A. In each of these cities a comprehensive victim survey was carried out. The preliminary findings revealed that criminal events such as assaults, robbery and burglary exceeded official estimates of these crimes as reported by the police by factors ranging from 1.5 to 5.0, depending on the type of crime. It also showed that only half the incidents of assault occured between strangers. The final report of this study covering thirteen cities has now been published, together with a series of comparisons of crime over time and space[2]. The Report of 1973 discusses the uses to

---

18 *The Challenge of Crime in a Free Society* (1967).
19 R. Hood and R. Sparks, (1970) pp. 25 et seq.
20 Ibid., p. 34.
1 National Advisory Commission on Criminal Justice Standards and Goals, *Criminal Justice System*, Appendix A: Victimization Surveying: Its History, Uses and Limitations (1973) p. 199 et seq.
2 Criminal Victimization Surveys in 13 American Cities (summary report) NCJ-18471.

which victim surveys may be put and their limitations. In some cases such as in connection with the study of shoplifting or consumer fraud they have been able to contribute little of value, since the truth has proved particularly elusive. Their value is greater in respect of inter-personal violence, particularly of the stranger-to-stranger variety, especially where robbery is involved. The conclusion is however that victim studies provide no panacea[3]. The U.S. Bureau of Census has now completed a representative survey involving 75,000 interviews of people drawn from different regions and social backgrounds which should provide some further information about public attitudes to crime based on their experience of it[4].

Victim studies have not been confined to the United States. There is a growing body of information deriving from studies carried out in many different jurisdictions. In Britain, the principal study has been that of Sparks, Genn and Dodd in 1978[5]. This was based on three areas of inner London, where a survey was carried out and the results regarding frequency of victimisation were compared with reports to the police in the same areas. It seems that a ratio of 11:1 existed of victim-perceived to police-recorded crime. Nearly half the population surveyed had experienced actual or attempted victimisation in the relevant twelve-month period. There were fewer differences in regard to such variables as sex, ethnic origin or social class than had been expected. There was also a surprising degree of consensus about the relative seriousness of offences in all social groups. Attitudes towards the police were mostly favourable. People who had been the victim of a crime did not panic but actually expressed less anxiety about safety on the streets than those who had not been victimised. There was impressive evidence to show how even quite minor changes in reporting and recording processes could generate the appearance of a crime wave. The authors contend that the measurement of crime by reference to what the victims perceived as crime should be regarded as an alternative way of measuring crime, additional to conventional means, but not necessarily superior. They do believe that valuable light can be thrown on certain key issues in criminology by this approach.

3 p. 201.
4 Edith E. Flynn, 'Issues and Priorities in International Cooperation in the Field of Criminology' International Annals of Criminology Vol. 16, No. 2 (1977) p. 19.
5 R. F. Sparks, H. G. Genn and D. J. Dodd, *Surveying Victims* (1978).

4 The possibility of developing a crime index

Several criminologists have suggested that, in view of the widely accepted unreliability of the official statistics of crime, what one should seek is the development of a crime index, rather similar to the Cost of Living Index and other economic indicators now widely used in public life.

Leslie Wilkins in 1963 proposed the construction of a crime index[6]. By means of correlation analysis of fifteen types of offence usually regarded as serious, he arrived at a short list of four groups of crimes, which might be used as the basis for constructing a crime index. These were:

1 Murder;

2 Attempted murder;

3 Serious crimes against the person;

4 Housebreaking, shopbreaking and robbery.

A subdivision of violence against the person would be needed in order to differentiate between fights and social disturbances on the one hand and the more serious personal attacks on the other hand. He discusses the ecological and statistical study of Seattle by Schmid in 1957 where the various crimes were differentiated by means of correlation analysis[7]. Schmid arrived at a group of six offences which were highly correlated with each other. These were:

1 Petty larceny;

2 Drunkenness and common drunkenness;

3 Disorderly conduct (fighting or other);

4 Vagrancy;

5 Lewdness (not indecent exposure);

6 Robbery (highway and car).

These provide an index of social disorganisation, distinct from the index of serious crimes such as murder and burglary, which is

6 L. T. Wilkins, 'The Measurement of Crime' BJC Vol. 3, No. 2, p. 321 (April 1963).
7 C. Schmid, 'Urban Crime Areas' 25 Am Soc Rev Nos. 4 and 5 (1960).

proposed. Wilkins suggests the transfer of robbery to the burglary group, to supply three separate indices, a crime index, a murder index, and an index of social disorganisation. His own proposals are that the following four categories of offence should be adopted to provide four separate indices:

1 Serious crimes against property, e.g. burglary, breaking and entering, robbery.

2 Social disorganisation, e.g. drunkenness, disorderly conduct and petty larceny.

3 Serious crimes against the person.

4 Homicide, divided into
   (a) murder, and
   (b) manslaughter.

It should be observed that no definition of category 3 is given, nor any examples, and that category 4 clearly overlaps Category 3[8].

In 1964 Sellin and Wolfgang[9] proposed a technique whereby crimes could be weighted according to seriousness by using the assessments made by several surveys of opinion carried out among university students, police officers, juvenile court staff and juvenile court judges. The students were taking an introductory course in sociology in two universities in Pennsylvania. The police officers were drawn from Philadelphia, and the juvenile court staff and judges were drawn from the state of Pennsylvania. They were asked to rate the seriousness of different offences on a scale. Tests revealed that there was a remarkable degree of agreement about the relative seriousness of the offences. From these surveys, scores were developed by which to rate the seriousness of different crimes, and the end product was to construct an index of crime which was not simply a collection of selected crime figures, but a collection of figures which were weighted according to their seriousness. The result would be 'an index that would, as accurately as possible, measure the real or actual incidence of delinquency during a given period or in a given area'. This is an immensely complicated study involving many advanced statistical techniques. According to Stanley Turner, in the introduction to the 1978 reprint edition, 'the Sellin-Wolfgang research has stood up over

8 Wilkins' ideas have been restated in his book *Social Deviance* (1964) pp. 166–177.
9 T. Sellin and M. E. Wolfgang, *The Measurement of Delinquency* (1964) reprinted 1978.

time'[10]. Despite strong criticism it has 'held up under repeated replications on diverse populations'[11].

Both in the United States and in Europe there have been criticisms and doubts expressed about the usefulness of the Sellin-Wolfgang method. Alfred Blumstein[12] concluded from a comparative study with the FBI's Uniform Crime Reports that the Sellin-Wolfgang scale contributed little additional information. Hindelang[13] too expressed serious reservations. In England and Wales Nigel Walker[14] delivered a blistering attack, and G. N. G. Rose[15] emphasised some statistical criticisms. The Council of Europe, through the European Committee on Crime Problems (ECCP) produced a collective study of the Sellin-Wolfgang method in 1970[16].

Walker's criticisms concern the wisdom of using first-year sociology students as one of the groups whose opinions were taken as the base for the rating of the relative seriousness of crimes. Also he regards the use of police officers and juvenile court judges as unwise. Furthermore, he doubts whether anything can be gained from a combination of weighted figures to produce a crime index. It is, he says, 'the most elaborate method so far devised for concealing differences in the patterns of crime'[17]. He makes much of the point that one should first make up one's mind for what purpose one wishes to have crime figures, for this will itself determine the figures one wishes to have. He believes that, if one must construct indices, the method devised by McClintock and Avison[18] of developing 'criminotypes' is less objectionable because it does at least distinguish between the different types of offence.

The Home Office appointed a Committee in 1963 to carry out a comprehensive review of the English criminal statistics. This Committee reported in 1967[19]. They restated the different purposes for which statistics are kept and used, and recommended far-reaching

10 Ibid., p. 300 (1978 edn.).
11 pp. xiii and xx.
12 Alfred Blumstein, 'Seriousness Weights in an Index of Crime' 39 Am Soc Rev 854 (December 1974).
13 M. Hindelang, 'The Uniform Crime Reports Revisited' JCJ Vol. 2, p. 1 (1974).
14 N. Walker, 'Psychophysics and the Recording Angel' BJC Vol. 11, No. 2, p. 191 (April 1971).
15 G. N. G. Rose, 'Concerning the Measurement of Delinquency' BJC Vol. 6, p. 414 (1966).
16 *The Index of Crime: Some Further Studies*, Council of Europe, Strasbourg (1970).
17 Loc cit., p. 193.
18 F. H. McClintock and N. H. Avison, *Crime in England and Wales* (1968).
19 Home Office, Report of the Departmental Committee on Criminal Statistics, Cmnd 3448, December 1967 (The Perks Committee).

changes, some but not all of which have been implemented. The Committee examined the case for developing an index of crime but concluded that no single figure could be constructed that would be a meaningful and generally acceptable index of crime as a whole. They did think that a small number of separate 'indicators' relating to different and relatively homogeneous groups of offences of high reportability might be provided[20]. They considered that the Sellin-Wolfgang method of weighting offences to indicate their seriousness was unacceptable 'because we feel that any weights that might be assigned would necessarily be controversial'. They conceded, however, that weighting within a class of offences would be less open to objection. Walker congratulated the Committee for 'keeping their heads' over this matter and for recognising the very limited scope for weighted indices[1].

The Committee did propose the adoption of a new system for classifying offences in the English criminal statistics, by using a standard list of offences which would include some of the more important non-indictable offences. They also proposed that a system of 'linkage' should be used, to link up information about offences deriving from different stages in the criminal process, so as to enable a continuous record to be traced from recorded offence to court and penal measure. For this purpose a new form of Standard Report would be introduced for use by the police. This had already been piloted successively in one county police force (Hertfordshire). Another recommendation was for the publication of more information about the victims and their relationship with the offender, the location of the crime, how it was reported and cleared up, if it was a property crime the type and value of the property, and if it was a violent crime the extent and nature of any injury received and the type of weapon used. It will be realised that such information could be of great value of criminologists. Another recommendation was for the publication of more regular digests of statistical information presented in a popular non-technical style for the information of the general public. The result of this has been the early presentation to Parliament of crime figures in general terms in advance of the publication of the detailed criminal statistics[2]. There has also been a great improvement in

---

20 See para. 128 and 129; pp. 37–38.
1 p. 194.
2 For comments on the Report see D. M. Downes, 'Perks v The Criminal Statistics' [1965] Crim L R 12; G. Millerson, 'Criminal Statistics and the Perks Committee' [1968] Crim L R 478.

communications emanating from the Home Office statisticians, and published in sources such as Social Trends[3], and other sources[4].

Notes. The perception and recording of crime

1 The police role in defining crime

Several studies have thrown light on the police role in defining crime. In the United States the best known studies are those carried out by Albert J. Reiss Jr., *The Police and The Public* (1971) and Jerome Skolnick, *Justice Without Trial* (1966). As Reiss points out the public generally regard the police role in detecting crime as proactive but research shows the opposite to be nearer the truth. The police were found to be mainly a reactive organisation, responding to calls for help and assistance from members of the public. Only in certain departments such as traffic, vice, narcotics and the like, could one characterise the police role as 'a proactive organisation' which 'seeks criminal violations on its own initiative': A. J. Reiss Jr. (1971) p. 88.

Moreover there are large areas of behaviour where the police are extremely reluctant to intervene. Domestic troubles and neighbour disputes constitute the principal examples but one could add to these certain cases of eccentric behaviour in public, and vagrancy, cases of shoplifting, depending on local police and store policies, and some reports of lost property. The list could no doubt be extended. Commercial fraud in many of its manifestations excites little attention unless there is a major scandal or much money and many victims are involved. The victims are left to their civil remedy.

One important British study by Sarah McCabe and Frank Sutcliffe *Defining Crime* (1978) throws considerable light on the situation in England and Wales. This is based on close observation of the work of the police at the police station in two different police areas – at the point where police and public interact. McCabe and Sutcliffe report that much of the behaviour mentioned in the previous paragraph is never recorded but the complainant is politely listened to, whether on the telephone or at the counter, and the matter is 'talked through'. This is described by the police as 'cuffing' (p. 29). The extent to which a police station serves as a refuge or inquiry centre is not generally realised (p. 23).

The official statistics of crimes known to the police depend entirely on a crime report which is filled in at the time. If there is no such record made, the incident has no place in the statistics of crime (p. 27). The discretion of the

3 C. M. Glennie, 'Crime in England and Wales' Social Trends No. 7, p. 32 (1976); D. Bruce, 'Crime in Scotland', ibid. 'Law Enforcement' Social Trends No. 10, p. 257 (1980).
4 For example the Home Office, *A Review of Criminal Justice Policy* (1977); *People in Prison* (1978). *Statistics of the Criminal Justice System* (*England and Wales*) (1969–79) (December 1980).

police at this point appears to be extensive and is more or less absolute and final.

One of the consequences of technological progress such as improving recording procedures by the use of tape-recording of telephone calls and computerised record-keeping may be to throw up more and more of this hidden activity and render it visible (pp. 28–29). Several important questions arise out of these developments. It seems at last that here, as with the preparation of probation reports and the making of sentencing decisions, we are beginning to recognise that an essentially human process is involved. This means that there is plenty of room for personal interpretation based on attitudes and values which may be deep-seated, as well as training experience and professional discipline.

McCabe and Sutcliffe report that in the process of interpreting the information received, the practice is diverse and sometimes quite idiosyncratic (p. 46). Reports of suspected theft may be classified as lost property, charges may be refused, or transferred to the 'domestic-no action' category. Where it is thought that the necessary element of criminal intent is lacking, or no useful purpose might be served by recording a crime since detection is out of the question, where the matter is not serious, and little harm would be done by avoiding making out a crime report, then the matter may not be recorded as a crime (p. 46). The same holds true of reports about vandalism and trouble-some behaviour by groups of young persons. As McCabe and Sutcliffe say, the police often exhibit 'antique virtue' in their dealings with members of the public, as well as 'swift pragmatism'.

2 Whether the result of police pragmatism is to deal fairly with all members of the community is a question which equally excites the attentions of sociologists and civil liberties groups. Lady Wootton in 1959 drew attention to the singular way in which the procedure deals with motoring offenders. They are not classed as criminals except for the few really serious traffic offences, and yet 'the typical criminal of today is certainly not the thief, nor the thug who hits an old lady on the head in order to possess himself of her handbag or to ransack her house: the typical criminal of today is the motorist': Barbara Wootton, *Social Science and Social Pathology* (1959) p. 25. It is surprising, she says, that research studies of crime habitually omit motoring crimes, and that police reports on previous convictions of offenders distinguish between 'crime' and 'traffic' offences. This failure to treat motoring offences as crime is seen by Lady Wootton as going a long way towards explaining the prevalence of crime in working-class areas and among members of the lower socio-economic group. Motoring offences are more prevalent among members of the middle and upper classes. 'The proposition that the residents in some areas, or the members of some social groups, are more disposed to criminality than are their differently placed neighbours ought therefore to be revised. The truth is that the anti-social behaviour of one social circle takes one form, while the members of other circles both behave and misbehave differently' (ibid., p. 70).

3 There can be little doubt about the preponderance of persons from the lower socio-economic groups (Social Classes IV and V according to the Registrar-General's classification) among those actually convicted of crime, and among those received into penal institutions. Lady Wootton cites the evidence of the borstal study by A. G. Rose, *Five Hundred Borstal Boys* (1954) and the Glasgow study of juveniles by T. Ferguson, *The Young Delinquent in his Social Setting* (1952) and says 'among persons committed to prison . . . there is undoubtedly a very heavy predominance of the lower ranks' (ibid., p. 48).

Self-report studies suggest, however, that crime is frequently committed by members of all socio-economic groups. As Travis Hirschi put it, 'social class differences with respect to self-reported delinquency are very small': T. Hirschi, *Causes of Delinquency* (1969) p. 81. What seems to be true is that more serious offences are admitted by middle and low status boys than by those of high status: R. Hood and R. Sparks, *Key Issues in Criminology* (1970) p. 58. In England and Wales criminologists have argued that the high representation of members of the lower socio-economic groups among offenders accurately represents the seriousness and persistence of their delinquency: N. Walker, 'The Penal Involvement Rate' in *Progress in Penal Reform* (1974), ed. L. Blom-Cooper, p. 221; D. J. West and D. P. Farrington, *Who Becomes Delinquent?* (1973) p. 188. West and Farrington believe that both self-report scores and official convictions constitute valid indices of delinquent behaviour. 'To a large extent, the two measures tend to pick out the same bad boys'. The social class factor in relation to crime has been specially studied by some criminologists: Lynn McDonald, *Social Class and Delinquency* (1969); J. Braithwaite, *Inequality, Crime and Public Policy* (1979); *Middle class juvenile delinquency* (1967) ed. E. W. Vaz; I. Nye, J. Short and V. J. Olson, 'Socio-economic status and delinquent behaviour' 63 Am Jo Soc 381 (1958); A. J. Reiss Jr. and A. L. Rhodes, 'Delinquency and Social Class Structure' 26 Am Soc Rev 720 (1961); W. R. Little and V. R. Ntsekhe, 'Social Class Background of Young Offenders from London' BJD Vol. 10, p. 130 (1959); J. W. B. Douglas et al., 'Delinquency and Social Class' BJC Vol. 6, p. 294 (1966). After reviewing all the available evidence Lynn McDonald concluded that 'the social-class factor will continue to be an important factor in influencing delinquency': Op. cit., p. 61.

4 The 'myth' of a crime wave

Frequently when the criminal statistics are published reference is made to the increase in crime, comparing one year with the previous year. The media tend to highlight this information and generate the idea of a crime wave. This is coupled with the tendency to focus on particular aspects of street behaviour from time to time, such as hooliganism, vandalism and 'mugging'. A few years ago in England and Wales there was a great scare about 'mugging', which led the Home Office to seek information from police authorities about the incidence of such behaviour. The difficulty encountered was that there was no legal category which was appropriate to describe this behaviour, so that a sociological description of 'mugging' had to be used. Even so, the evidence showed that apart from some metropolitan areas, the incidence of 'mugging' was not as great as the 'myth' had led one to believe. No one wishes to deny the seriousness of such behaviour when it does occur, or to condone it in any way. The point here being made is that one has to examine the evidence very carefully to discover what is going on, and not be rushed into panic measures or adopt the 'myths' as a form of truth simply because it is commonly accepted.

The present author spoke about the myths concerning crime waves as part of his discussion of criminological myths and realities in the ISTD pamphlet *Crime: Myths and Reality* (March 1969), and also in his lectures in Israel in 1962, reprinted in W. C. Reckless, *The Crime Problem* (4th edn. 1967) p. 94.

American scholars have addressed themselves to the same problem in relation to their own criminal statistics: see D. Bell *The End of Ideology* (1960) Chap. 8, pp. 137 et seq., 'The Myth of Crime Waves: The Actual Decline of Crime in the United States'; Albert J. Reiss Jr., 'Assessing the Current Crime Wave' in *Crime in Urban Society* (1970), ed. B. N. McLennan, p. 23.

Daniel Bell argues that there is probably less crime in America today than existed 100 or 50, or even 25 years ago, and that 'today the United States is a more lawful and safe country than popular opinion imagines' (p. 137). He draws attention to changes in police recording practices involving increased efficiency in Philadelphia and New York City, and to the artificial effect generated every ten years by the availability of the revised census figures and the effect on the calculation of rates of crime in the years between the censuses in artificially inflating the rate of crime in relation to the population at risk. He also recognises that changes have occurred in the attitudes of the black population of the United States towards law enforcement, and the effect this has had in inflating the figures. Also he allows for the role of youths under the age of 25, who are involved in nearly half the arrests made.

Reiss is aware of the change in regard to the coloured population, who now more often seek the law's protection and demand their 'rights'. He also sees many other factors operating to influence the crime figures. Reiss argues that rates based on total population are less useful than victimisation rates calculated in relation to persons or property at risk, e.g. women above the age of fourteen in regard to rape, dwellings and business premises in regard to burglary, and motor vehicles licensed in regard to auto theft. His main theme is that undoubtedly many times more crime is committed than is revealed by the F.B.I. Crime Index.

'What emerges . . . from an examination of both official statistics and from our sample survey studies is the clear picture that we live with far more major crime than that reported in official statistics' (p. 35). Reiss has many interesting things to say about why the official statistics should show an increase, and the role of police departments in recording and processing crime.

These studies lead to the conclusion that no firm conclusion can be reached about the increase in crime. As has been said in the text, no one denies that the raw figures have increased. The problem is how to interpret these increases, and what do they mean. What changes do they signify and portray regarding police practices, community expectations, and the actual experience of crime? As Reiss says, undoubtedly 'both the public and the police sense that crime has increased' (p. 40). Police authorities and departments are certainly more efficient than in the past. What consequences flow from this? A criminal judge in a mid-western American state who had been a prosecutor remarked to the author: 'Give the police department one more cop and I will guarantee one hundred more arrests next year'. Do we want more policing or less?

Victimology studies

1 Since the subject received attention from federally-supported surveys in the United States, arising out of the various crime commissions, it has received increasing attention from academic scholars. One reason for this was that the basic data required to undertake studies of criminal victimisation gradually became available. For example M. J. Hindelang's study of *Criminal Victimization in Eight American Cities: A Descriptive Analysis of Common Theft and Assault* (1976) was followed by M. J. Hindelang, M. R. Gottfredson and J. Garofalo *Victims of Personal Crime: An Empirical Foundation for A Theory of Personal Victimization* (1978). Sociologists have been interested in exploring the victim's role as a means or agent of social control: E. A. Ziegenhagen, *Victims, Crime, and Social Control* (1977). The five volumes emanating from the first world congress of victimology, held in Israel in 1973 edited by I. Drapkin and E. Viano, led to further congresses and a journal devoted to victimology.

2 A recent British study has been made by The Christian Economic and Social Research Foundation, Occasional Paper, Series C. No. 4 (August 1979): *The Victims of Theft from the Person, Robbery, Assault and Burglary in the Home*. This contains the results of a study of victims in the County of Bedfordshire carried out with the co-operation of the police. Among topics investigated are who the victims are, the age distribution, the time of the offences and the distribution by area. Although the subject is seen largely in terms of prevention and from a police angle, there is much here for the criminologist to ponder.

3 One feature of victimisation which deserves particular mention, if only because it ties in with the discussion of social class in relation to crime and belies the notion that there is an inter-class struggle which is reflected by the criminal statistics, concerns the findings of victimisation studies showing that frequently both in the case of crimes of violence and property crimes, those victimised come from the same socio-economic group or social class. Thus David Downes draws attention to the results of the field studies carried out for

the 1967 President's Commission on Law Enforcement and the Administration of Justice showing 'that the risk of victimization is highest among the lower-income groups for all Index offences except homicide, larceny and vehicle theft'. D. Downes 'Praxis Makes Perfect' in D. Downes and P. Rock, *Deviant Interpretations* (1979) p. 13.

4 With regard to personal violence, studies show that it is frequently intraracial not inter-racial, in other words, the victims come from the same ethnic group or social environment. Indeed, all the evidence seems to confirm the existence of high crime areas, and sensitive or high risk behaviour such as being in a certain place at a certain time, especially alone and particularly for the more elderly.

5 Marvin Wolfgang's study of the patterns of homicide in Philadelphia showed how frequently that crime occurred in the family setting, arising out of a domestic dispute or as a result of a bout of drinking: see M. E. Wolfgang, *Patterns in Criminal Homicide* (1958) and the article 'Victim-Precipitated Homicide' 48 Jo Crim L & Crim'ogy & Pol Sci, p. 1 (June 1957), reprinted in M. E. Wolfgang, L. Savitz and N. Johnston, *The Sociology of Crime and Delinquency* (1962) p. 388.

6 The focus on victims of crime has spawned a number of developments relating to the treatment of offenders in the penal system and the response to offences. In the attempt to restate and re-direct goals or objectives of the penal system, and replace what is now widely regarded as the outmoded and discredited 'treatment' goal based on rehabilitation and the medical model, there has come into prominence the consideration of the victim's situation. Chief among the results has been the development of schemes for compensating victims of crime. Laws have been re-cast or up-dated or freshly introduced to permit courts and indeed encourage them to make compensation orders against convicted offenders requiring them to make money payments in recompense to the victim for the damage done. In England and Wales the Powers of Criminal Courts Act 1973, s. 35 provides the relevant powers. Beyond that, in crimes of violence, there are state schemes, whether statutory or administrative, by which victims of crimes of violence may be compensated by the state from public funds. Such schemes have been widely adopted in recent years, and some believe that they help to take the edge off demands for severe retributive punishment. In addition, in Britain and the United States, voluntary organisations have been established to provide assistance, advice and support for victims of crime in a variety of ways. One specialised concern has been with the victims of rape, where the women's rights movement has developed aid and counselling services. The question how far the victim should be involved in the sanctioning process of the criminal trial, and sentencing, remains a rather vexed question, despite the suggestions made by some criminologists such as Norval Morris and Nils Christie that the case for the victim's participation and involvement cannot be denied. It may well be that the cause of reconciliation between the victim and the offender and between the offender and society may become a paramount consideration in the future. For some crimes it seems more suitable than for others. The dangers involved in handing over too much authority concerning sentencing to the victim must be balanced against the victim's need to feel satisfied about the result of the court proceedings. In the end, however, it is the community or society at large which must be 'satisfied' by the conduct of the case and its outcome, and it is perhaps fortunate that confidence in the work of the courts and the penal system does not depend entirely on a consumer's eye-view, or a victim's perception of the matter. The victim is perhaps too close to the event to reach a dispassionate judgment. When victims or their relatives stand up in court and abuse the judge for passing an inadequate sentence, one is bound to reflect upon the wisdom of victim-involvement in the sentencing process. See N. Morris, *The Future of Imprisonment* (1974); N. Christie, 'Conflicts as Property' BJC Vol. 17, No. 1, p. 1 (1977).

Chapter 8

Reports for the courts about offenders

Once an offence has been committed, and the alleged perpetrator identified, and a criminal prosecution has been launched against him or her, the question arises of what reports, if any, about the alleged offender's physical or mental state, his character, and his social and domestic circumstances, should be prepared and submitted to the court of trial. It is possible for reports of three different kinds to be prepared, viz. the police antecedents report, the probation service's social inquiry report, and a medical report, which usually means a psychiatric report. Only one of these, the police antecedents report, is routinely supplied in all cases[1]. Probation reports are frequently available, and we shall discuss the various problems which arise concerning their preparation and submission. Medical reports are more rare, since in most cases no question arises concerning the alleged offender's physical or mental health. Some criminological knowledge may assist the probation officer and the psychiatrist in preparing the report. It is believed that such persons would benefit from a background knowledge of criminological theory and explanation such as has been provided in the foregoing chapters. It is less clear that the police need such background knowledge, though their role in identifying crime, reacting to reports from members of the public, and deciding when a prosecution is merited and when the matter can be dealt with otherwise, whether by an official or an unofficial caution, or by reference to the social services or by treating the matter as a medical problem, requires the exercise of a considerable degree of discretion, which is a matter of training and experience. It is submitted that possession of some criminological knowledge would assist police officers in the exercise of their duties. The same applies to legally qualified prosecutors. Judges and magistrates clearly exercise discretion to a most significant degree in connection not only with the finding of guilt but in regard to sentencing. Here too one may dare to

1 For further details see R. Cross, *The English Sentencing System* (3rd edn., 1981), p. 95.

believe that some criminological knowledge might assist them in the exercise of this important part of their duties. In Chapter 9, post we shall discuss discretion in connection with decisions made by police, prosecutors, judges and magistrates. In this chapter we shall concentrate on reports prepared for the courts by probation officers and psychiatrists to assist them in the discharge of their sentencing function[1a].

1 Probation social inquiry reports

Reports are prepared in a variety of situations about alleged offenders facing trial, by members of the probation and after-care service. These are known as social inquiry reports (or S.I.R. for short). Considerable thought has been given to the subject of social inquiry reports in recent years, as the number of reports and the variety of situations in which they are prepared has increased. The law has required the preparation of such reports in a whole range of situations, and official advice goes even further. A substantial amount of research has been carried out into social inquiry reports, throwing considerable light on their utility.

The law and practice regarding social inquiry reports

Since 1933 in the juvenile court the position has been that by law a full social report has been required[2]. In the cases of adult and young adult offenders there has been a preference for leaving it open to the court's discretion whether or not to call for a social inquiry report. Although power was taken for the Home Office to make regulations requiring the preparation of social inquiry reports, in the Criminal Justice Act 1967 (now contained in section 45 (1) of the Powers of Criminal Courts Act 1973), no such regulation has in fact been made. Instead the Home Office prefers to rely on recommendations contained in official circulars[3]. At the same time one is bound to observe that the law has

1a See the author's articles on this subject: 'Legal Views of Psychiatric Evidence' Medicine, Science and Law (October 1980) Vol. 20, No. 4 and 'The Evaluation of the Personality of the Accused in the English System of Criminal Justice' Report of the International Seminar held at the International Institute of Higher Studies in Criminal Sciences, Syracuse Italy (September 1980), ed. G. Canepa.

2 Children and Young Persons Act 1933, s. 35.

3 Home Office circulars have been issued on this matter in 1968, 1971, 1974, and 1977.

required the preparation of social inquiry reports in a variety of situations by virtue of recent legislation.

Thus a social inquiry report is required or recommended in the following situations:

1 Before any sentence of borstal training or detention centre on a youth;

2 before passing a sentence of imprisonment of two years or less where the offender has not received a previous sentence of imprisonment or borstal training;

3 before any sentence of imprisonment on a woman;

4 before making a community service order;

5 before making any first sentence of imprisonment;

6 before making a probation order;

7 before making a probation order with a condition of residence;

8 before making a condition of attendance at a day training centre in conjunction with a probation order;

9 before making a psychiatric probation order under section 3 of the Powers of Criminal Courts Act 1973;

10 before passing a custodial sentence on a young person under 21.

In addition to the above situations the probation service are expected to report to the courts on any person who has previously been in touch with the probation service or has been the subject of a suspended sentence or a medical or psychiatric report. Prison governors should report on any offender who has previously been in custody, whether in prison, a borstal institution or a detention centre. A social inquiry report is also recommended where a magistrates' court commits an offender to the Crown Court for sentence. It has also been suggested by the Butler Committee in its Report on Mentally Abnormal Offenders (October 1975) that a social inquiry report should be obtained before making a mental health order under section 60 of the Mental Health Act 1959[4].

The growth in the number of social inquiry reports was highlighted by the Home Office in its Review of Criminal Policy (1976). A review

4 Home Office, Department of Health and Social Security, *Report of the Committee on Mentally Abnormal Offenders*, Cmnd. 6244 (October 1975).

of the situation over the ten years 1966–1975 showed that the number of social inquiry reports provided to adult magistrates' courts and to the Crown Court had more than doubled. By 1979 the annual number of such reports approached a quarter of a million[5]. Reports for juvenile courts have declined due to the fact that much of the work previously done there with offenders has been taken over by the social services departments of the local authorities, following the Children and Young Persons Act 1969. These figures have to be seen against the total number of cases tried each year, which in the case of indictable offences exceeds half a million, and in the case of summary offences (including traffic offences) exceeds a million and a half. The fact remains that the preparation and submission of social inquiry reports takes up a substantial proportion of the time of probation officers. It has been estimated that about one-fifth of the time of a probation officer is taken up with such matters in an average week[6].

The growth in this aspect of a probation officer's work received some impetus from the Report of the Streatfeild Committee in 1961 on *The Business of the Criminal Courts*[7] which made several recommendations on this matter, which constituted part of their Terms of Reference. They thought that courts were nowadays entitled to expect such reports to contain comprehensive, relevant and reliable information. They discussed how this information was obtained, the relationship of the probation report to the police antecedents report, access by the probation service to information in the possession of the police, the stage at which the report is prepared, i.e. whether before the finding of guilt or only after a person has been convicted, and whether the report should contain recommendations as to disposal.

Since Streatfeild there have been many developments. Sentencing has moved more and more in the direction of the individualised sentence based on the needs of the offender and the prospects for his rehabilitation, and away from the traditional goals of retribution, protection of society, and deterrence. However, in more serious cases, where the offence is a grave one or the offender has already failed on many occasions, the court will choose a sentence based on 'tariff' considerations, according to the current law and practice[8]. In such

---

5 Home Office, *Probation and After-care Statistics, England and Wales* (1979).
6 Martin Davies and Andrea Knopf, *Social Enquiry Reports and the Probation Service*, (1973) Home Office Research Studies No. 18, pp. 12 and 36.
7 Home Office, Lord Chancellor's Department, *Report of the Inter-departmental Committee on the Business of the Criminal Courts*; Cmnd. 2289 (February 1961).
8 See D. A. Thomas, *Principles of Sentencing*, (2nd edn., 1979).

cases there is less need to know about the offender's personality and social and domestic circumstances.

Clearly there is much room for consideration of the use to which social inquiry reports are put, the assumptions on which they are based, and their value for different purposes. Research on social inquiry reports has shown that probation officers in preparing such reports follow their own particular penal and social philosophy. In selecting the items of information for attention and in writing the report, they are reflecting their own personality and experience[9]. This should be no surprise, since it has been shown that judges and magistrates do much the same in sentencing. However, where so-called experts are involved it does raise questions about their expertise and impartiality. Little wonder that some have doubted the wisdom of allowing probation officers to make recommendations as to disposal of the case. *The Departmental Committee on the Probation Service*[10] (known as the Morison Committee) had in 1962, shortly after the Streatfeild Report, expressed the view that it was not desirable for probation officers to 'assume a general function of expressing opinions to courts'[11], and the Home Office agreed. By 1971, however, the climate of opinion had changed, and the Home Office accepted that probation officers should feel free to express opinions, including the likely response of the offender to any form of treatment[12]. The Court of Appeal has set the seal of its approval on this development[13].

It is now widely accepted that sentencing is such a complex task, with so many different considerations to be taken into account, that assistance from those with special skills or experience is to be welcomed, and the probation officer is in a good position to assist courts in this connection. Much will of course depend upon the relationship of the probation officer to the sentencer. In the Crown Court, where liaison probation officers co-ordinate the presentation of social inquity reports, the officer who made the report is not often called upon to give evidence and is rarely present in person. Moreover in busy courts there is less chance for the probation officer to know in advance which judge or magistrate will decide the case, so the

---

9 See the papers by L. Wilkins and A. Chandler and R. M. Carter, summarised in R. Hood and R. Sparks, *Key Issues in Criminology* (1970) pp. 164 et seq.

10 Home Office, *Report of the Departmental Committee on The Probation Service*, Cmnd. 1650 (1962).

11 Para. 41.

12 See Jennifer Thorpe, *Social Inquiry Reports: A Survey* (1979) Home Office Research Study No. 48, p. 5, citing the Home Office circular issued in 1963.

13 See D. A. Thomas, op. cit.

possibility of this knowledge influencing the content and direction of the report is reduced. Nevertheless it should be clear from what has been said that something of a dyadic relationship exists between the reporter and the sentencer: the one is communicating with the other in a relationship which is professional and not casual but likely to be repeated. Probation officers need to secure the confidence of courts, which is best ensured by reliable reporting and sensible recommendations. The crucial question is who decides what is sensible.

Courts frequently follow probation officers' recommendations in favour of probation, and research shows that when they do so, there is a high level of successful outcome[14]. However, when no such recommendation is made, or there is a recommendation against probation, the courts sometimes place the offender on probation in spite of this, and the research also shows a fair degree of success is obtained in such cases. It is also true that, as F. G. Perry observes 'it is inevitable that many people made the subject of a probation order will offend again'[15]. Many probation officers 'would prefer to take on a challenge rather than have to nominally supervise someone who is unlikely to get into trouble again and they continually take such risks in their recommendations to court'. It is a matter for regret that there has been a decline in the use of the simple probation order (without conditions) in the last decade or two. The Home Office has acknowledged this, and so have the representatives of the probation service. The *Fifteenth Report of the Expenditure Committee* expressed the hope that probation would continue to be regarded as one of the main alternatives to prison[16]. The fact is however that the development of several new alternatives to prison such as community service, and the increased use of fines, has often been at the expense of probation rather than prison. The 'displacement effect' of these new measures, in terms of reducing the use of prison, has not been as great as had been hoped or expected.

The stage of the trial at which the social inquiry report is prepared has been a matter for discussion. The Streatfeild Committee recommended that such reports should be prepared before the trial took place, whether or not the accused person intended to plead guilty. This was because, in the old days of courts of assize and quarter sessions, it was vital that there should be no delay in proceeding to sentence following a conviction, otherwise the court might have completed its

14 F. V. Jarvis, 'Inquiry before sentence' in *Criminology in Transition* (1965), ed. T. Grygier.
15 F. G. Perry, *Reports for Courts* (1979) p. 5.
16 H. C. 622–I, Session 1977–78 (July 1978).

business for the moment and there would be no court to which the report could be presented. The same situation does not arise in magistrates' courts, of course, but these were not within the Terms of Reference of the Streatfeild Committee. It was suggested in the Committee's Report that where an accused person intended to plead 'not guilty' the situation should be explained to him fully, including the possibility that the court of trial might order a social investigation which would lead to a serious delay in sentencing. It should then be left to the defendant to decide whether or not to agree to the preparation of a social inquiry report. The Courts Act 1971, which created the Crown Court in place of courts of assize and quarter sessions, altered the situation radically, and there is no longer the same need to prepare social inquiry reports before trial. Many probation officers found it difficult to prepare reports on a person pleading 'not guilty'. They avoided discussing in the report the offender's guilt, but this was an uneasy situation. It is not surprising therefore that since 1977 the professional organisation which represents the probation service (the National Association of Probation Officers) has recommended its members not to prepare social inquiry reports on an accused person until guilt has been established. There is an exception where the defendant is already known to the probation service as having been under supervision in the last twelve months, when, with the consent of the defendant, a report may be submitted. Even in such instances as this, however, the report will be withheld until the finding of guilt. There is some anxiety about the use to which such reports might be put by defending counsel. The matter is still the subject of discussion between the probation service and the Lord Chancellor's Department, representing the courts.

There remains to discuss the purpose for which probation social inquiry reports are used. Jennifer Thorpe's research[17] shows that such reports often receive a wide circulation, being supplied to the prison authorities (where the offender is in custody), the parole administration, colleagues in the probation service and other social agencies. Concern has been expressed about the implications of such a wide and uncontrolled circulation of the reports on the grounds of breach of confidentiality and civil liberty. This should certainly be a matter for further discussion. One may be permitted a personal observation here, as a former Parole Board member. Social inquiry reports are sought in the case of all persons to be considered by the

17 See note 12, ante.

Parole Board. Where available, the insight they give about the offender and his social and domestic situation at the time of the offence is invaluable when comparing it with his current attitude and situation, as revealed in the parole dossier, which should include a further probation report (known as a home circumstances report) prepared by the probation officer who is likely to be the offender's supervisor if he is granted parole. No arrangement for limiting the circulation of social inquiry reports should preclude the parole administration from having access to such reports.

The discussion of social inquiry reports has revealed that there are several important and sometimes rather delicate questions which need to be faced in this connection. We may conclude with a list of such questions and by making a proposal. The questions requiring investigation and solution are as follows:

1 Are too many social inquiry reports prepared?

2 Should probation officers make recommendations as to sentence, other than about probation?

3 What should be the relationship between the reporting officer and the sentencer?

4 What part should the individual probation officer's own character and personality be allowed to play in the preparation of the social inquiry report? If it is true, as the research seems to indicate, that these factors do influence the content and conclusions of the report, how might this be remedied?

5 Should reports be prepared before the finding of guilt, and if so on what offenders, and with what safeguards?

6 Should there be more control over the use made of social inquiry reports after sentence?

All these questions lead to the suggestion that the time has come for a fresh review of the whole matter. The recommendations of the Streatfeild Report of 1961 need re-examining in the light of the current situation, and these new concerns of the present day demand discussion and resolution. A committee should be set up without delay to carry out this task.

2 Psychiatric reports

A⁺ several points in the trial of a criminal offence it is possible that medical evidence will be called, or a medical report received in evidence. Bearing in mind the division of the English criminal trial into two stages, the finding of guilt, and the sentencing stage, the evidence may be called at either stage because it is relevant to the questions the court has to decide. We shall discuss these questions separately in relation to the two stages of the trial.

Before the finding of guilt

What is relevant in an English trial is narrowly circumscribed by the strict English rules of evidence. At the first stage (finding of guilt) the focus is entirely on the deed alleged to be a crime and the offender's part in its commission, together with his state of mind. For all practical purposes the accused person is assumed to be a normal person with the responses and intentions of an ordinary person, which means that it is left to the defence where the issue of guilt is contested to bring forward any evidence suggesting mental abnormality. When this is done it must be done in relation to certain specific legal defences which are well established, and not in general terms of a global kind. The prosecution will not lead with such evidence unless the defence has pleaded guilty and it is agreed that the evidence in the possession of the prosecution shall be placed before the court. The prosecution may however contest defence assertions that a particular defence is made out on mental grounds, and may reply with contradictory evidence[18]. All these aspects of practice are well known to criminal lawyers but are mentioned here at the outset for the sake of clairity of the following discussion, and as a reminder of the underlying situation.

The questions which arise on the issue of guilt and which may call for medical evidence relate to six legal issues or defences which involve the state of mind of the accused at the time of the offence (or in (i), below, the time of the trial). They are:

(i)   Fitness to plead;

(ii)   The insanity defence;

18 There is provision for this in the Criminal Procedure (Insanity) Act 1964, s. 6.

(iii) Diminished responsibility (in murder cases only);

(iv) Automatism;

(v) Provocation;

(vi) Drunkenness.

Prison medical officers and consultants may be called to give evidence on these matters, and the defence may call its own medical witnesses. There is sometimes a degree of overlapping between these defences, which causes difficulty and confusion.

(i) *Fitness to plead*

This arises rather rarely in practice, but when it does arise the matter is governed by the common law test, namely, the ability of the accused to understand the charge, to distinguish between the plea of guilty and not guilty, to exercise the right to challenge jurors, to examine witnesses, to instruct counsel on all these matters, and generally to understand the proceedings. In Scotland, according to the Royal Commission on Capital Punishment in 1953, there is much more flexibility about this question than occurs south of the border[19]. The English procedure was amended by the Criminal Procedure (Insanity) Act 1964 in order to allow the question of fitness to plead to be delayed or postponed until the strength of the prosecution's case has been disclosed, if the court thinks this course is expedient. The purpose of this provision is to allow a case to be thrown out on grounds such as the weakness of the evidence of identification, thus avoiding the danger of injustice being done to the accused who might otherwise be found unfit to be tried and be dealt with accordingly. Only a jury can determine the issue of fitness to plead, and the jury will be specially convened for this purpose. If the trial proceeds because the accused is found fit to plead, then another jury must be empanelled for the purpose of the trial proper. The effect of a finding of unfitness to plead is the same as in the case of an insanity verdict, viz. admission to a hospital specified by the Secretary of State. Since 1964, there is a right of appeal against such a decision.

(ii) *The insanity defence*

Here the outdated rules known as the M'Naghten Rules continue to

19 Cmd. 8932 (1953).

apply[20]. These were promulgated by the judges in their advice to the House of Lords in 1843, and, despite a constant barrage of criticism and many proposals for amendment, have remained unchanged to the present day. They have the effect of limiting the evidence to the question of cognition, and leave out of account any form of emotional insanity, irresistible impulse or a failure to control the will. The result is that few persons are mad enough to qualify for this defence when it is strictly construed. However, in the past there can be no doubt that judges and juries combined to make a liberal interpretation of this law in suitable cases. There remained some cases where undoubtedly the severity of the law led to injustice.

Proposals for reform were made by the Royal Commission on Capital Punishment in 1953[1], and by the Butler Report on Mentally Abnormal Offenders in 1975[2], but so far nothing has been done to change the law, except, as we shall see, in the case of homicide. The insanity defence is rarely used in English trials today: in 1979 there was only one finding of not guilty on the grounds of insanity[3]. Since 1957 there has been a shift over to the defence of diminished responsibility, which is available in murder trials to reduce the charge of murder to manslaughter. Sparks and Walker have shown how this innovation has worked out. Roughly the same overall total of cases are now dealt with as before: adding together the cases of diminished responsibility defences which succeed and successful insanity pleas, the proportion of what one might term psychiatric acquittals has not changed very much[4].

(iii) *Diminished responsibility*

The defence of diminished responsibility was made available, in murder cases only, by section 2 of the Homicide Act 1957, an Act which also sought to restrict the application of capital punishment in other ways. It applies where the accused person's mental responsi-

---

20 These provide a two-pronged test: by reason of defect of reason stemming from disease of the mind, did the accused person know what he was doing, i.e. the physical nature of the act? or, alternatively, did he know that what he was doing was wrong, i.e. contrary to law?

1 Loc. cit.

2 Cmnd. 6244 (October 1975).

3 Home Office; Criminal Statistics (England and Wales) 1979 Cmnd. 8098 (November 1980).

4 Richard F. Sparks, '"Diminished Responsibility" in Theory and Practice' MLR Vol. 27, No. 1, p. 9 (January 1964) at pp. 31–32. See also Nigel Walker, 'The Mentally Abnormal Offender in the English Penal System', in *Sociological Studies in the British Penal Services* (1965), ed. P. Halmos, p. 133.

bility has been substantially impaired due to disease or injury or arising from some inherent cause. If the jury so find then they must bring in a verdict of manslaughter, the effect of which is to avoid the fixed penalty for murder (life imprisonment) and to enlarge the judge's power over sentencing so that, as for any other manslaughter, a wide range of orders can be made, including a probation order, a psychiatric probation order, a hospital order under the Mental Health Act 1959, or imprisonment or a fine. The imprisonment may be for a definite term of years or for life.

The actual terms of section 2 of the Homicide Act 1957 require careful scrutiny. The section applies whether the accused person was the actual killer or was merely a party to the killing by another, in other words, an aider and abettor. The abnormality of mind must be shown to have arisen from a condition of arrested or retarded development or some inherent cause, or to have been induced by disease or injury. It has been held that drunkenness is not a condition covered by this section[5].

The interpretation of the section has been very wide in regard to the mental conditions which qualify for acceptance. The case of *Byrne*[6] in 1960 showed just how wide the defence is, and how it differs from the insanity defence. There Lord Parker C J explained that the phrase 'abnormality of mind' in the section refers to something wider than would satisfy the test under the M'Naghten Rules of 'disease of the mind'. It covers the mind's activities in all aspects, including not only the perception of physical acts or matters and the ability to form a rational judgment as to whether an act was right or wrong, but also the ability to exercise will-power to control physical acts in accordance with that rational judgment. Thus the notion of irresistible impulse, which had been resisted for so long in connection with the insanity defence, was accepted unquestionably in connection with the defence of diminished responsibility.

The whole area of emotional insanity was recognised as being included. Concerning the phrase 'mental responsibility for his acts' used in the section, Lord Parker said it points to a consideration of the extent to which the mind is answerable for the behaviour – which must necessarily include the question of the extent of the accused's ability to exercise will-power to control his physical acts.

Several other important points were clarified by the judgment in

5 *R v Di Duca* (1959) 43 Cr App Rep 167; *R v Fenton* (1975) 61 Cr App Rep 261.
6 [1960] 2 QB 396.

Byrne. It was made clear that the question of substantial impairment being clearly a matter of degree, this was a question of fact for the jury to decide. Medical men could advise on the question of the aetiology of the mental condition, explaining how it arose and its true nature and operation. Whether in fact the defence applied was a question for the jury to decide. But if the jury were faced with unanimous medical evidence, and there was no other evidence pointing to normality, then they were obliged to accept that the defence of diminished responsibility applied. This had already been made clear in the case of *Matheson* (1958)[7].

Further points of clarification have emerged in subsequent cases. For example, if the accused claims that he acted under a delusion (e.g. that his wife was committing adultery) it must be relevant to discover whether there was any factual basis for his suspicions, and the prosecution should cross examine witnesses with this in mind: *Ahmed Din* (1962)[8].

It has also been decided that when doctors have prepared reports on a defendant in prison on remand, pointing towards a defence of diminished responsibility, they may be called to give evidence on an entirely different question such as the defence of automatism when the accused prefers to run this defence rather than that of diminished responsibility: *Smith* (1979)[9].

(iv) *Automatism*

Automatism is a relative newcomer to the list of legal defences to crime, having been developed by means of case law in the last 25 years. The effect of the defence if it is successful is an acquittal. The defence now has quite an extensive application to situations where some physical condition of a medical kind leads a person to unconscious acts which are criminal, or criminal behaviour occurs in a condition of semi-consciousness[10]. It is not surprising that the defence is quite popular with defendants, but courts are reluctant to accept it, and juries are often sceptical or disbelieving.

A distinction is made between the type of automatism we are discussing here, viz. sane automatism leading to an acquittal if made

7 [1958] 2 All ER 87.
8 [1962] 2 All ER 123.
9 [1979] 3 All ER 605.
10 For a description of the medical situations which may arise, see T. C. N. Gibbens and J. E. Hall Williams, 'Medico Legal Aspects of Amnesia' in *Amnesia* (1979), eds. C. W. M. Whitty and O. L. Zangwill (2nd edn., 1979) p. 245.

out, and insane automatism, leading to an insanity verdict[11]. If all the evidence tends towards an insanity verdict or, in the case of homicide, a verdict of manslaughter by reason of diminished responsibility, then only that kind of verdict is appropriate. Where, however, there is some evidence which could support a finding of sane automatism, such as a blow on the head or some medical condition, then the defendant is entitled to have the defence of automatism considered by the jury if he so desires[12].

As in the case of the insanity defence, it is for the accused person to provide evidence to support the claim he is making, and in the case of automatism this means something more than his own story, e.g. a history of mental blackouts or some medical condition such as a brain tumour, or arteriosclerosis[13]. The most common cases concern the diabetic who is taking insulin, and for some reason fails to heed the warning signals of shortage of sugar in the blood and take some sugar, so that a state of clouded consciousness occurs, or, in common parlance, he has a blackout[14]. Frequently the defence has been raised in prosecutions for road traffic offences, where it has been held to have a limited application. Whether the prior negligence of the accused, in failing to take proper precautions, such as taking regular meals or imbibing alcohol, is sufficient to deprive him of the defence has not yet been decided, but it has been suggested that this should be a factor to take into account tending towards negativing the defence of automatism[15].

(v) *Provocation*

Provocation is available as a defence only in murder trials, and if successful it has the effect of reducing murder to manslaughter. The result is similar to that in the case of a successful plea of diminished responsibility, in that the judge's power in sentencing is enhanced by making available a wide range of choices instead of the fixed penalty for murder. Since the Homicide Act 1957, s. 3, which introduced changes in the law relating to provocation, the scope of this defence has been considerably enlarged. A wide range of situations previously excluded may now lead to a successful defence of provocation.

11 See the House of Lords decision in *Bratty* [1963] AC 386.
12 *R v Quick and Paddison* [1973] 3 All ER 347.
13 *Hill v Baxter* [1958] 1 QB 277.
14 See *Watmore v Jenkins* [1962] 2 QB 572.
15 *R v Quick and Paddison*, ante, note 12. But see the criticism of Ms Jennifer Temkin, MLR Vol. 37, p. 199 (March 1974).

From the point of view of the defence lawyer, this sometimes poses a problem. Supposing that the client has killed under provocation but is also a person who might qualify for a defence of diminished responsibility, then a choice has to be made. If provocation is chosen then the test has to be whether a reasonable person of the same sex and age as the defendant would have been provoked and reacted in this way[16]. The abnormally jealous or sensitive person might find it hard to qualify under the law of provocation. In such situations it is likely that a defence of diminished responsibility would be more advantageous, for, as we have seen, there is great flexibility in connection with the application of diminished responsibility.

A point which has arisen in connection with provocation is whether a psychiatrist can be called upon to testify to the propensity of the accused to be provoked. It has been made clear in two decisions of the Court of Appeal that psychiatric evidence is not admissible on the question of the accused's responsibility in general or his intent, except as allowed under the various specific defences to crime. This is because such matters are for the jury to decide, and the role of the expert witness in the English trial is severely limited. Expert evidence is regarded as opinion evidence, and is not allowed in matters of common knowledge. Lord Justice Lawton put it this way in *Turner*[17]:

'Jurors do not need psychiatrists to tell them how ordinary folk who are not suffering from any mental illness are likely to react to the stresses and strains of life'.

If it were the case that psychiatric evidence were admissible, he said, 'trial by psychiatrists would be likely to take the place of trial by jury and magistrates'. . . 'Psychiatry has not yet become a satisfactory substitute for the common sense of juries or magistrates on matters within their experience of life'.

In the case of *Chard*[18] the prison medical officer at Exeter Prison had not been allowed to be questioned on passages in his report bearing on the accused's ability to form the intent to murder – there being nothing to show that Chard was suffering from mental abnormality. In the case of *Turner*, counsel was not allowed to call a psychiatrist to show that the accused was not violent by nature but was likely to have been provoked into killing the girl by reason of what she had said.

16 See the House of Lords decision in *Director of Public Prosecutions v Camplin* [1978] 2 All ER 168.
17 [1975] 1 All ER 70 at 74.
18 (1971) 56 Cr App Rep 268.

(vi) *Drunkenness*

Drunkenness at the time of the crime is unlikely to be of much assistance to a defendant in a criminal prosecution. In general we can say that drink is no defence to crime. Indeed, being in a drunken state in certain situations itself amounts to a crime. Historically the common law has been reluctant to allow any room for drunkenness to affect the question of criminal responsibility. It is quite another matter in connection with the appropriate sentence, after the finding of guilt, where drunkenness is frequently urged in mitigation. A tiny wee gap has been forced in the common law position by the recognition, more clearly and strongly in recent years, but with a history going back to the nineteenth century cases, that drunkenness may in extreme cases negative intent, and that where the commission of the crime requires the formation of a complicated state of mind (or mens rea, to use the legal term) drunkenness may assist towards negativing that intent or mens rea[19]. If you ask the lawyer which crimes require a complicated state of mind—what the lawyer calls *specific intent*—at the present time, the reply may well be that since the decision in *Majewski* (1976)[20] it is impossible to give a clear answer. Some crimes like murder, theft, fraud, burglary are known to require a specific intent. Other crimes such as assault and rape do not. The definition of a crime of specific intent is usually provided in a statute where the precise state of mind required is spelled out. This is all very unsatisfactory, but for the time being must be accepted as the law.

Some crimes then may be negatived because the accused was drunk at the time, and could not form the necessary intent to commit the deed. Drunkenness will not, however, as we have seen, be recognised as a condition qualifying for a defence of diminished responsibility. The disposition of English law is against its recognition in connection with any defence. The situation can best be seen as partaking of the nature of a policy rule against making any allowance for drunkenness as a defence to crime.

A dramatic example of this posture occurred in *Majewski* (1976)[1] where the defendant had mixed alcohol and drugs with disastrous results. He got involved in a disturbance in a pub, when his friend was put out by the landlord and he intervened on his friend's behalf. He butted the landlord, punched a customer, and was evicted only to re-

---

19 *Director of Public Instructions v Beard* [1920] AC 479, as applied in *Ruse v Read* [1949] 1 All ER 398.
20 [1976] 2 All ER 142. The position is still more unclear following *R v Caldwell* [1981] 1 All ER 961.   1 Loc. cit.

enter waving a piece of broken glass. He assaulted a policeman called to arrest him. Even the next day he was far from normal. The doctor called for the defence said he had treated Majewski for drug addiction for many years, and that he had a personality disorder. Drugs mixed with alcohol were known to lead sometimes to rapid intoxication, even unconsciousness in rare cases. The police doctor gave evidence that Majewski was completely out of control both mentally and physically the next morning when he examined him. The trial judge ruled that it could not be a defence to the crimes charged that the accused was suffering from the effect of alcohol and drugs. This ruling was upheld in the House of Lords, the Lord Chancellor, Lord Elwyn-Jones, saying that it would be irresponsible and would undermine the criminal law to hold otherwise.

At the sentencing stage

Of the many alternative dispositions available to the sentencing court, several may involve a medical question and require medical evidence. As a preliminary, however, it is worth noting that some scholars[2] would like to see postponement so far as possible of such medical issues, in particular those relating to the state of mind of the accused, until the finding of guilt, thus avoiding many of the intellectual, philosophical and practical issues which arise when one is relating medical evidence to the question of legal responsibility at the first stage of the criminal trial.

(i) *A hospital order, with or without a restriction order*[2a]

Under sections 60 and 65 of the Mental Health Act 1959 a court may under certain conditions order that a convicted offender receive hospital treatment as an in-patient, on the ground that he is suffering from a mental disorder within the meaning of section 4 of that Act. Section 4 covers mental illness, subnormality, severe subnormality and psychopathic disorder. There must be evidence from two doctors suitably qualified in the field of mental disorder. The offence must be one punishable with imprisonment (excluding murder, for which a fixed penalty applies). The effect of the order is that the offender becomes a patient at a named mental hospital for at least a year, a period which may be extended later. A patient may obtain his release by consent of the responsible medical officer, or by decision of the

2 Nigel Walker.
2a see Hall Williams (1970) Chap. 15, p. 223 for further explanation.

Mental Health Review Tribunal, in the case of a section 60 order[3].

The purpose of adding a restriction order under section 65 is to limit the discretion to release, so that only the Secretary of State (the Home Secretary) has the power to sanction discharge. The restriction order may be made by the Crown Court in one of two ways, either for a fixed period of time or for an unlimited period.

A hospital order does not guarantee that the offender will be detained in hospital for any length of time. Moreover, mental hospitals are notoriously lacking in security, since they prefer to operate an 'open door' policy. Courts have been aware of these aspects of the situation, and have stressed that sometimes the duty to protect the community must prevail over the interests of the patient. The Court of Appeal in *Gardiner* (1967)[4] laid down that a restriction order should be made in all cases where the public requires protection from violence or sexual molestation, and that it should be indefinite in duration except where it is clear that a cure can be effected within a fixed time.

The 'special hospitals' at Broadmoor, Rampton, Moss Side and Park Gate, and in Scotland at Carstairs, exist to provide more secure detention for patients under the National Health Service who 'require treatment under conditions of special security on account of their dangerous, violent or criminal propensities'. These patients include those committed from the courts directly because of a finding of unfitness to plead or insanity. Also some found to be of diminished responsibility will be sent to a special hospital. Release procedures from these places are more elaborate, and involve careful screening in the case of patients considered to be dangerous. An independent tribunal examines each case and makes recommendations. This is known as the Aarvold Committee, since its establishment followed the recommendations of a committee under Judge Aarvold[5].

Prisoners who are considered to be mentally ill or who become so during their sentence may be transferred to a mental hospital under section 72 of the Mental Health Act 1959. Such transfers are not easily arranged, and it is a well-recognised fact that the prisons contain many mentally disordered prisoners, whose presence in the prison population causes difficulties[6].

3 See R. Cross, *The English Sentencing System* (3rd edn., 1981) pp. 70 et seq.
4 [1967] 1 All ER 895.
5 Report on the review of procedures for the discharge and supervision of psychiatric patients subject to special restrictions, Cmnd. 5191 (January 1973).
6 See the Fifteenth Report from the Expenditure Committee, House of Commons, H. C. 662–I, Session 1977–78, (July 1978); Fourth Report from the Home Affairs Committee, House of Commons, Session 1980–81, H. C. 412–I (July 1981).

(ii) *A psychiatric probation order*

It has been possible since 1948 to attach to a probation order a condition that the offender should undergo psychiatric treatment. The present law is contained in section 3 of the Powers of Criminal Courts Act 1973. Originally there was a limitation of one year to the condition concerning psychiatric treatment, but now it may endure for the duration of the probation order, or the court may specify a shorter period. The probation order may be for any period not less than six months nor more than three years. There has been some decline in the number of psychiatric probation orders in recent years, but it still remains 'the most-used court order for the mentally disordered'[7].

(iii) *Mitigation of punishment*

Psychiatrists sometimes find that their written reports or oral evidence are used by defence counsel as part of the argument in mitigation of punishment. Here the strict rules of the law of evidence are somewhat relaxed, and there is more freedom to develop a dialogue with the judge about the best course to take. It should not be assumed that a diagnosis of mental disorder will necessarily lead to any mitigation of punishment. Persons found guilty of serious crimes of violence are frequently imprisoned. This is mandatory in the case of murder where the fixed penalty of life imprisonment applies. Persons found guilty of manslaughter on grounds of diminished responsibility will frequently be imprisoned, sometimes for a substantial term. Manslaughter by provocation also usually attracts a prison sentence of several years.

At this point it may be useful to say something about the *life sentence*. This is mandatory for murder, and discretionary or optional for a wide range of serious crimes.

(*a*) *The mandatory life sentence for murder.* Here the judge has power to recommend a minimum period which in his view should elapse before the offender is released. Some judges are more inclined than others to impose such a minimum. Such a recommendation is not essential, and when made, it is not binding on the Home Secretary, who has the last word concerning the release of all life prisoners, or the Parole Board, which advises the Home Secretary. There is no appeal

---

7 Rupert Cross, op. cit., p. 70.

against such a recommended minimum, though the Criminal Law Revision Committee believe there should be a right of appeal[8].

(b) *The discretionary or optional life sentence.* This is available for robbery, serious wounding, rape, manslaughter and some other crimes such as buggery and arson. Where there is some evidence that the convicted person is suffering from a mental disorder a choice may have to be made between a life sentence, a hospital order or a psychiatric probation order. The courts may well choose a life sentence not simply to protect society but in order to allow an opportunity for the treatment of the offender and his release when he has responded to such treatment[9]. However one should not be too sanguine about the chances of early release from a life sentence. An informal tariff appears to apply. This is operated by the Home Secretary on the advice of the Lord Chief Justice who must be consulted in every case, and the Parole Board which must also have the case referred to it. Some would argue that it is much easier to be released from a special hospital such as Broadmoor than from prison on a life sentence.

Through a series of decisions the Court of Appeal has developed a policy about life sentences. They are seen as desirable only where there is a probability that the offender will commit grave offences in the future. David Thomas has observed that the nature of the mental condition required to justify a life sentence eludes precise definition. In some cases the offender is suffering from mental disorder within the meaning of section 4 of the Mental Health Act 1959, in other cases, though he is suffering from a condition which is clinically recognisable it may not be within the statutory definition. Life sentences have been upheld on the basis that the offender is emotionally immature, subject to abnormal sexual drives and fantasies, or impulsive and unstable. What is important is not that the offender's condition can be accurately described by a recognised psychiatric term, but whether it can be predicted with a sufficient degree of confidence that the offender will, unless restrained, commit further grave offences in the future, and that his propensity to do so will not decline within a foreseeable period.

Thomas believes that a sentence of life imprisonment should not be passed without a full psychiatric investigation of the offender. The test to be applied is 'the continuation of a state of dangerousness' rather

8 Home Office, Criminal Law Revision Committee, Twelfth Report, *Penalty for Murder*, Cmnd. 5184 (January 1973); Fourteenth Report, *Offences against the Person*, Cmnd. 7844 (March 1980).
9 See D. A. Thomas, *Principles of Sentencing* (2nd edn., 1979).

than 'amenability to treatment'[10]. The danger for the future need not be of the same kind of offence for which the sentence was imposed.

(iv) *On appeal*

The appeal court may take a fresh look at the sentencing choice made in any case before it. Here psychiatric evidence or a probation report has sometimes led the court to take an entirely different view of the matter from that taken by the trial court, and this has led to the variation of the sentence. It should be borne in mind that the Court of Appeal may no longer increase the sentence, and that any variation or substitution must not mean that the offender is dealt with 'more severely'. Some difficulty has arisen over the application of these words. It has been held, for example, that a fixed term of imprisonment may not be varied to life imprisonment even where the effect might well be to shorten the time spent in custody, but a hospital order may be substituted for imprisonment[11].

10 p. 303.
11 D. A. Thomas, op. cit., p. 397.

Chapter 9

Discretion in the criminal justice process

Modern studies of the administration of justice have drawn attention to the significant part played by discretion in the criminal justice process. By this is meant that choices between different courses of action are deliberately entrusted to different kinds of person at successive stages in the process, and that such choices are not governed completely by a code of rules of law and procedure, but that much scope is left to the individual vested with responsibility for making the choice in question. Concern about the implications of this, legal and social if not political, has led to increasing scrutiny of these aspects of the criminal process, with some justification, and growing anxiety is felt in some quarters about the apparent arbitrariness of such discretionary powers.

Administrative lawyers have underlined the dangers inherent in such arbitrary powers. Chief among these has been the American Professor K. C. Davis[1]. Criminologists have turned their attention to this aspect of the penal process, particularly A. K. Bottomley[2]. His choice of topics to scrutinise from this angle, is, on his own admission, incomplete[3]. We shall develop a slightly different selection of topics, on the basis of their relationship to the steps by which an alleged offender is dealt with up to his trial and possible conviction, and afterwards, through the sentence and its administration. These steps are concerned with:

1 the role of the police;

2 the role of the prosecutor;

3 the role of the court, in relation to trial and sentence;

4 the role of the Home Office, in relation to the prerogative power and parole.

1 K. C. Davis, *Discretionary Justice: A Preliminary Inquiry* (1969).
2 A. K. Bottomley, *Decisions in the Penal Process* (1973).
3 p. xvi.

1 The role of the police

Here we should start by recalling the discussion of the criminal statistics, and the way offences become 'known to the police', and their role in defining whether behaviour which comes to their notice should be regarded as criminal, and be processed as such. There is no need here to repeat that discussion. What has not been discussed is the various choices open to the police once a crime has been recognised to have occured, and a suspect has been identified. We shall briefly describe these choices, dealing with the relevant considerations in outline only, since they belong more appropriately to books on police powers and criminal procedure. The single exception where the discussion will be more elaborate is that of cautioning by the police, which has received the attention of some criminologists and may well be regarded as an extremely important part of modern criminology, since it provides such an excellent opportunity for 'diversion'. The various choices can be listed as follows, in terms of the decisions which have to be made:

A.   Arrest or summons;

B.   Charge;

C.   Bail by the police or upon appearance in court when police may object to bail;

D.   Legal aid and advice;

E.   Caution.

A.   Arrest or summons

The law is quite clear that when a police officer has evidence which points to a crime having been committed by a particular person, he should take steps to place the evidence before a court of law, which in the first instance will be a magistrates' court. The first decision required is whether to arrest the suspect, or invite him to go to the police station for further inquiries to be made. A person's attendance at court can be achieved by way of summons to appear, and in many minor cases this will seem to be the appropriate course. In more serious offences, however, process may commence by way of arrest, and this may be effected without a warrant in pursuance of the police officer's common law and statutory powers, or, in some cases, a warrant may be obtained first from a magistrate, empowering the police to arrest the suspect. The suspect arrested will then be taken to a police station and formally charged. There is another stage which frequently precedes arrest, viz. interrogation, and the relation of this to the two stages of arrest and charge is partly governed by the Judges' Rules, and partly a matter of police practice[4].

B. Charge

Considerable latitude exists in many cases in choosing what charge or charges to bring against an accused person. There is room here for the exercise of discretion. More serious charges may be dropped in favour of charges of lesser offences. There may be a degree of over-charging, i.e. 'piling on the agony', as it were, by preferring the maximum number of charges which the evidence will support. This is frequently done in order to induce a confession of guilt or plea of guilty, the accused person being happy to plead to the lesser of several offences. Additional charges may be added later, and where the case goes for trial by jury on indictment in the Crown Court, not infrequently there may be the addition of fresh counts in the indictment once counsel has studied the evidence. Decisions about what to charge, made by the police, may be arrived at after consultation with senior officers, and sometimes after obtaining legal advice from a lawyer employed or retained by the police.

One feature is clear, and that is that in respect of offences known to the police, it is not realistic or expedient to expect that there should be arrest or summons or that charges should be brought in all cases where there is evidence against someone of having committed an offence. Decisions are constantly made by the police not to enforce the law in particular matters or on particular occasions. Provided there is no general direction but that each case is viewed on its merits, there is no legal objection to this. The appeal court has recognised the necessity of this type of discretion[5]. Professor Joseph Goldstein once characterised such decisions made by police officers as 'low visibility decisions' in

4 On these matters, see L. H. Leigh, *Police Powers in England and Wales* (1975).
5 *R v Metropolitan Police Comr, ex parte Blackburn* [1968] 2 QB 118; *R v Metropolitan Police Comr, ex parte Blackburn (No. 3)* [1973] QB 241.

the criminal process[6]. He argued that so much discretion ought not to be left to police officers. Other scholars have shown how great a part is played by such decisions in determining who comes to court and is eventually judged to be delinquent or criminal[7]. Even radical critics of the system, like Quinney, recognise the need for such discretion[8]. Full enforcement of the law is neither possible nor desirable[9]. Those senior police officers who have written on the subject appear to agree. John Alderson in discussing different styles of policing, believes that to adopt the opposite view, and hold that the law should be enforced in every possible case, 'is a barren, unimaginative approach which can bring both law and police system into disrepute and fails to exploit the potential of the law for soothing rather than irritating social maladies'[10].

Alderson goes on to say that while there can be no tolerance of serious offences, 'setting those aside, there are large areas where the police may use their discretion, and, for the minor offences, police can, as a deliberate policy, operate within local levels of tolerance'[11]. By this he means that every part of our society adopts its own expectations and evaluations in regard to criminal behaviour. There are certain general attitudes and values, and there are also local variations. The police have to come to terms with this situation. Their goals are rarely complete law-enforcement. 'Situational control' often has priority in operational terms. The police officer's involvement in the community he polices requires him to some degree to reflect its tastes and standards. However there are occasions, for example, when public order or decency are violated, where there is little choice but to intervene. The relationship between reactive and proactive policing (previously referred to in Chapter 7) is recognised by Alderson, and carefully examined[11]. Also recognised is the extremely difficult problem of adjusting police methods of operating to the needs and demands of a multi-racial and pluralistic society, and to changing patterns of living. A similar theme comes through in the autobiography of Sir Robert Mark[12].

6 J. Goldstein, 'Police Discretion Not to Invoke the Criminal Process: Low-visibility Decisions in the Administration of Justice' Yale L Jo Vol. 69, p. 543 (1960).

7 W. La Fave, *Arrest: The Decision to Take a Suspect into Custody* (1965); A. J. Reiss Jr., *The Police and The Public* (1971); J. M. Skolnick, *Justice Without Trial* (1966).

8 R. Quinney, *The Social Reality of Crime* (1970).

9 A. K. Bottomley, op. cit., p. 37.

10 J. Alderson, *Policing Freedom* (1979) p. 24.

11 Chapter 5, 'Styles of policing' p. 35.

12 Sir Robert Mark, *In the Office of Constable* (1978).

C. Bail

Bail may be allowed by the police to any person charged with a criminal offence, under section 38 of the Magistrates' Courts Act 1952, provided that he has been taken into custody for an offence without a warrant. This may be done when it is impracticable to bring him before a magistrates' court within 24 hours, and the accused person must enter into a recognizance or bond, with or without sureties, for a reasonable amount, to guarantee his appearance in court. An alternative is to bail the offender to re-appear at the police station in order that the inquiries may be completed. There are stronger provisions in favour of releasing children and young persons under seventeen on bail[13]. Clearly the police are in a position to put considerable pressure on an accused person by threatening to withhold bail. This part of bail procedure was not examined by the Home Office Working Party on Bail Procedures in Magistrates' Courts[14]. Leigh believes that it should be possible 'to provide guidance of an inclusive character concerning the sorts of offences and circumstances of commission which would justify exclusion of bail. It is at least arguable that police officers interpret s. 38 narrowly'[15].

When the offender is brought before the magistrates' court, where he has not been bailed by the police but has been in custody, at this stage the police may object to bail. In the past magistrates' courts have too readily acceded to police objections to bail and have remanded the accused in custody. The Working Party Report proposed that there should be an obligation placed on magistrates to examine the basis of any police objection to bail, and that this should be achieved by enacting a presumption in favour of bail. These recommendations have been implemented by the Bail Act 1976.

Now the objection is heard from some police sources, including Sir Robert Mark[16], and the Chief Constable of Liverpool, Mr Kenneth Oxford[17], that too many persons are committing fresh offences while released on bail, and sometimes quite serious offences are committed. On the other hand, the civil liberties lobby argues that the Act has made very little difference, and that too many people are still remanded in custody. Usually the point is made that of those

13 Leigh, pp. 56 et seq.
14 Report (1974).
15 pp. 58–59.
16 Mark, op. cit., pp. 276–278.
17 *Sunday Times*, 7 May 1978, report by Michael Pye.

remanded in custody before trial, a large proportion do not receive a custodial sentence following conviction, and indeed a much smaller proportion but a significant number are acquitted.

The criminologist should be able to offer some guidance on the chances of a person committing a fresh offence while on bail, which is one of the considerations which a court must bear in mind in granting or refusing bail. Some categories of offence and offender are less likely to re-offend than others. Contrary to popular belief and conventional wisdom, this includes sexual offenders. Further research would be useful here, however, regarding those categories of offender who actually do offend while on bail.

D. Legal aid and advice

When a person is being interrogated on suspicion of having committed an offence, the police frequently receive requests for access to a lawyer. The Judges' Rules provide that a person in custody should be allowed to speak to his solicitor on the telephone, and that a person 'should be able to communicate and to consult privately with a solicitor' at any stage of an investigation. Both these statements are subject, however, to the qualification that access to the solicitor is only to be allowed provided that no unreasonable delay or hindrance is caused to the processes of investigation or the administration of justice. In practice it is often difficult for an alleged offender who is being interrogated but has not yet been charged to gain access to a solicitor. Many excuses are offered why this should not be possible. The Criminal Law Act 1977, s. 62 has given a person who has been detained in custody the right to notify someone such as a member of his family of his whereabouts. This may be some protection, but the situation is not so satisfactory as it is in some other European countries[18].

Usually the question of legal aid is dealt with at the magistrates' court. Unlike applications for legal aid in civil cases, criminal legal aid is a matter for judicial discretion. Here the police have no reason or power to intervene. It is of interest to note, however, that research has shown that defendants remanded in custody and not legally aided stand a greater chance of a custodial sentence and that being legally represented greatly increases one's chance of bail[19].

18 See L. H. Leigh and J. E. Hall Williams, *The Management of Prosecutions in Denmark, Sweden and The Netherlands* (1981).
19 A. K. Bottoms and J. D. McClean, *Defendants in the Criminal Process* (1976).

E. Caution

We have said that the most significant part of police discretion concerns their power to administer a caution instead of processing the case by way of prosecution in court. Criminologists have carried out several studies of the practice of police cautioning, the results of which are summarised in J. A. Ditchfield's excellent Home Office research study[20]. A careful examination of the police practice reveals considerable differences in policy between different police forces. This may reflect differences in the pattern of crime in urban and rural areas, but it also seems to be the result of different views about expediency in terms of the time and trouble which would be involved in taking a case to court.

Excluding motoring offences, the majority of cases cautioned consist of minor theft and breaking offences; some sexual offenders are also dealt with in this way. Often the offenders are very young, and the Children and Young Persons Act 1969 gave a strong impetus in favour of more cautioning of juveniles. Cautioning of adult offenders is much less frequent, and some police forces such as those in metropolitan areas seem to follow a policy of using cautions hardly ever for adults. The Home Office research suggests that the different pattern of crime, for example, in regard to shoplifting and minor theft, to some extent explains the observed differences in cautioning. It seems likely, however, that differences in police force policies do influence the situation more powerfully. Where cautioning rates are low, it seems to follow that rates of discharge of offenders prosecuted are high, since the courts are presented with many weak and unnecessary prosecutions. Those who criticise the courts for too many discharges and acquittals should reflect on these findings and consider whether sufficient care is taken in screening out these weak and unnecessary prosecutions and thus saving much time, expense and anxiety. The Home Office research suggests that it is because prosecution is a much easier course to take that this course is followed so invariably, yet an experienced chief constable like John Alderson regards cautioning as 'considerably cheaper than mounting prosecutions'[1].

It should be observed that the general rule for administering cautions is that the offender admits the offence, that it is a first offence, and is not a serious one. Also that the police are satisfied they have a

20 J. A. Ditchfield, *Police Cautioning in England and Wales* (1976), Home Office Research Study No. 37.
1 Alderson (1979) p. 121.

provable case, and the complainant does not insist on a prosecution. Official cautions are usually administered by a senior police officer, in uniform at the police station, though in motoring offences this may be done in writing. Unofficial cautions administered on the spot or at the police station informally are not recorded in the criminal statistics, but figures are kept for the number of official cautions. The statistics do not include cautions for motoring offences, however. Ditchfield suggests that there is room for a considerable increase in the use of cautions which would help to relieve the pressures on the courts and penal institutions. 'Considerable numbers of minor adult offenders could indeed be diverted from the system by increased cautioning, particularly in the cities'[2]. Arrangements would have to be made for more information to be gathered about adult offenders, as with juveniles, on a systematic basis from the social services and other agencies, in order to inform those who would have the responsibility of making the decision to caution[3]. In the absence of a full-blooded prosecutor service, there would be an extra burden placed on the police, but it is one which should be borne with cheerfulness bearing in mind the considerable advantages flowing from such a development. Judging by the experience with motoring offenders, Alderson believes there would be gains in respect for the law. There might well be less recidivism. Cautioning of juveniles is not only cheaper than prosecutions, says Alderson, but 'the rates of recidivism following police cautions are low'. His conclusion, which we are happy to share, is that 'there is room for further studies of cost-effective aspects' of this matter[4].

2   The role of the prosecutor

The police do not always prosecute cases themselves, in the magistrates' courts, though very frequently it is a police officer who is deputed to do so. Lawyers are employed by some police authorities or local government authorities to represent the police. In the Crown Court, barristers will be briefed to appear for the prosecution (in the name of the Crown). The discussion of police discretion overlaps that of prosecutor's discretion, but there are a few features which appertain specially to prosecutors which deserve special attention.

2 p. 20.
3 p. 25.
4 Alderson (1979) p. 121.

We have already mentioned that there is often room for some choice to be made in regard to the offence or offences to be charged. When it comes to bringing the case to court, prosecutors exercise considerable discretion over the way in which this is done, for example, whether to press certain charges or offer no evidence, whether to ask for a case to go to trial (assuming it is one which is triable by jury), whether to seek to amend the indictment in the Crown Court, and whether to seek the judge's permission at the end of the trial to leave certain matters 'on the file'. All such matters of discretion are well known to prosecutors, in addition to their discretion as to what evidence to call, what written reports or expert evidence to require, and matters connected with the proof of the case. Here is the place where discussion of the so-called 'plea-bargain' focusses. A notion well known and generally accepted in the United States, the 'plea-bargain' resulting in a deal between prosecutor and the defence, is claimed to be unacceptable in England and Wales, and largely non-existent. That informal understandings may be reached prior to a trial, concerning the defendant's willingness to plead guilty to certain offences and not to others, is well recognised. The extent to which the trial judge can be involved in any discussion of the likely sentence in the event of a guilty plea is dubious. The official view is against any such consultation in private, though in open court the judge may indicate the way his mind is working in this connection where he deems it would be helpful[5]. There can be little doubt, however, that some forms of negotiation between prosecutor and defendant, or more often, his legal representative, do take place, and that these have a powerful bearing on the outcome of the trial[6].

The idea that prosecutors can waive a prosecution or forego it without conditions or upon some condition being fulfilled, which is a very common practice in some European countries possessing a full-time corps of legally qualified prosecutors separate from the police, is an alien idea unacceptable at present to English notions of the roles and relationships involved in the criminal process. However, research into some of these European systems has suggested that there might well be some advantage in providing a structure or framework of procedures and rules within which prosecutor's discretion might operate. In such a system a considerable number of trials would be avoided, with corresponding gains in terms of relieving the pressure on the courts[7].

5 *R v Turner* [1970] 2 All ER 281. See also R. Cross, *The English Sentencing System* (3rd edn, 1980) p. 115. There are strict limitations which must be observed.
6 J. Baldwin and S. McConville, *Negotiated Justice* (1979).
7 L. H. Leigh and J. E. Hall Williams, op. cit.

Indeed, since some of those tried would be convicted and might receive prison sentences there would be some relief also accruing to the sorely pressed penal institutions. The Royal Commission on Criminal Procedure[8] has recommended in favour of the development of a locally-based professional prosecution system. It is submitted that building into this a recognised procedure for the exercise of waiver of prosecution would be a great advantage[9].

3 The role of the court, in relation to trial and sentence

In this section we shall be concerned primarily with the subject of sentencing discretion, but first it should be noted that the trial court, by its decision concerning the offender, and for which offence or offences he is found guilty, powerfully affects the choice of the sentence. For example, a court which finds a defendant charged with murder guilty of manslaughter, as has already been explained, avoids the fixed penalty for murder being applied, and greatly enlarges the range of sentences from which the sentencer can choose. A court which finds a person charged with a serious assault guilty of a less serious form of assault, restricts the choice of the sentencer to some sentence within the maximum provided by the law for the offence in question. Thus both the finding of the trial court concerning the offender's guilt and the legal rules concerning the maximum penalty for the offence in question set limits to the exercise of discretion by the sentencer in his choice of sentence.

Nevertheless the provision by the law of many different kinds of sentence, together with the movement away from a narrowly conceived retributive/deterrent policy towards sentencing based more on the needs of the offender and the possibility of his reform, has meant in modern times that a completely different set of considerations has to be embraced and evaluated as part of the exercise of the sentencing function. This development was high-lighted by the Report of the Streatfeild Committee[10]. The result was, in that Committee's view, that courts needed more information and better advice in order to enable them properly to discharge their sentencing responsibilities.

8 Cmnd. 8092.
9 Leigh and Hall Williams, op. cit., p. 77.
10 Report of the Interdepartmental Committee on The Business of the Criminal Courts, Cmnd. 1289 (February 1961).

While the Streatfeild Committee was more concerned to see the courts adapt to the new emphasis on rehabilitative goals, today the climate of opinion has changed dramatically, and, as we shall see, there is great suspicion of attempts to sentence with a view to the rehabilitation or reform of the offender, and a trend back towards classical or neo-classical views of punishment, based on ideas of fairness and proportion, with deterrence and retribution as the underlying aims.

One factor which contributed towards the re-assessment of the goals of sentencing has been the research on sentencing which has revealed so many discrepancies. This is not the place to recapitulate the findings of sentencing research in detail[11]. It is sufficient to remark that a more rounded view of the subject sees discrepancy as inevitable, if not desirable, and views the differences which have been observed between different judges as being the result of the application of different sentencing philosophies which in turn do no more than reflect differences in the personality and beliefs of individual judges. Moreover, judges have been found to be remarkably consistent in themselves with their own standards and values[12]. The attention to the needs of individual offenders, moreover, necessarily means that differences will occur in the sentencing choices made for different defendants[13]. What should be a source of concern would be totally irrational and inexplicable differences. So far there is not much sign of such discrepancies being uncovered. Once it is recognised, as John Hogarth puts it, that sentencing is an essentially human process, we can then understand it better, and even accept the inevitability of variations occurring. Machinery should exist, however, to challenge and review sentences. Thankfully, in England and Wales this does exist in the form of the extremely extensive powers of review of sentences in Crown Courts exercised by the Court of Appeal and by an equally extensive appeal jurisdiction from sentences by magistrates' courts.

If the foregoing discussion sounds complacent, one can offset that impression by now describing the various attempts which have been made to restructure the sentencing powers of courts and improve the practice of sentencing.

11 For further details of sentencing research, see R. Hood and R. Sparks, *Key Issues in Criminology* (1970) pp. 141 et seq. A. K. Bottomley, *Decisions in The Penal Process* (1973) pp. 130 et seq.

12 See, for example, J. Hogarth, *Sentencing as a Human Process* (1971).

13 M. H. Tonry and N. Morris, 'Sentencing Reform in America' in *Reshaping the Criminal Law*, Essays in honour of Glanville Williams (1978), ed. P. R. Glazebrook, p. 434.

Structuring sentencing discretion

Various techniques are available whereby the exercise of sentencing discretion might be restricted or influenced. These we may describe as structural changes in regard to sentencing discretion.

(i) *Minimum terms and fixed terms*[14]

These can be used to prevent sentencers from giving too lenient sentences. The practice of providing minimum terms has been widespread in America, and exists elsewhere, but in Britain there has been a marked reluctance to fetter the discretion of sentencers by this means. Only in the case of murder and certain very minor statutory offences such as road traffic offences does the law insist on a fixed or mandatory penalty. Also when a court is sentencing a young adult offender to a custodial sentence, by virtue of section 3 of the Criminal Justice Act 1961 it is precluded from choosing anything other than a sentence of borstal training between the lower limit of six months and the upper limit of three years, with certain exceptions for recidivist offenders. This limitation proved so unpopular that it is to be abolished.

One type of power which deserves mention here is the power of a trial court in the case of a conviction for murder, but not in any other case, to make a recommendation concerning the minimum period the offender should be detained in custody. This power, which was introduced by the same Act which abolished the death penalty[15], has been reviewed by the Criminal Law Revision Committee[16], which has recommended that there should be a right of appeal regarding the exercise of the power. The Committee however declined to follow the example of the Emslie Committee in Scotland[17] and make it mandatory for the judge to recommend a minimum period in custody. The recommendation of such a minimum period in sentences for murder is not binding on the Home Secretary, but clearly carries considerable weight when release is being considered by the Secretary of State following consultation with the Lord Chief Justice and the Parole Board for England and Wales.

---

14 See Colin Howard, 'An Analysis of Sentencing Authority' in *Reshaping the Criminal Law* (1978), ed. P. R. Glazebrook p. 404, at p. 408.

15 Murder (Abolition of Death Penalty) Act 1965, s. 1(2).

16 Criminal Law Revision Committee, The Penalty for Murder, Cmnd. 5184 (1973) and Fourteenth Report, Offences against the Person, Cmnd. 7844 (1980).

17 The Penalties for Homicide, Cmnd. 5137 (1972).

Another example of a mandatory sentence was the mandatory suspended sentence which applied to certain sentences of imprisonment up to six months by virtue of the Criminal Justice Act 1967. This proved so unpopular with the courts that it was abolished in 1972. A further example of a mandatory sentencing requirement is to be found in the provisions relating to the disqualification of motorists from driving, under the Road Traffic Act.

The power to make a restriction order in connection with a hospital order is available in the Crown Court by virtue of section 65 of the Mental Health Act 1959. This again has the effect of restricting the release of a convicted offender by providing that only the Secretary of State may sanction his discharge.

Beyond these few examples of fixed and minimum penalties, there is no inclination to go, so far as England and Wales are concerned. American jurisdictions, however, have in recent years favoured the adoption of fixed penalty provisions, as part of the reaction against indeterminate sentencing which has been widespread. The wisdom of this development is already being doubted in view of the overcrowded prisons and the consequences in terms of the inability of the authorities, such as parole boards, to sanction executive release. The techniques employed sometimes preclude parole for specified categories of prisoner or abolish parole altogether. They have the effect of transferring discretion over sentencing to prosecutors[18].

(ii) *Sentencing guidelines*

Another solution which has been adopted by some American jurisdictions is what can be described as the guidelines approach[19]. The idea is for the legislature or some agency empowered thereby to set up parameters within which judges must fix the sentence, and to provide that sentences outside those fixed limits must be justified or indeed are prohibited altogether. These parameters or limits would be chosen to reflect current sentencing patterns as revealed by research studies. An alternative procedure is to provide that each judge on coming to

18 M. H. Tonry and N. Morris, loc. cit.; Albert W. Alschuler, 'Sentencing Reform and Prosecutorial Power, A Critique of Recent Proposals for "Fixed" and "Presumptive" Sentencing' in *Criminology Review Yearbook* (1979), eds. S. L. Messinger and E. Bittner, Vol. 1, p. 416.
19 Leslie Wilkins, 'Sentencing Guidelines to Reduce Disparity?' [1980] Crim LR 201. L. Radzinowicz and R. Hood, 'The American Volte-Face in Sentencing Thought and Practice' in *Crime Proof and Punishment: Essays in Memory of Sir Rupert Cross* (1981), ed. C. Tapper, p. 127.

sentence a case should be supplied with a statistically derived average of all the sentences given for that particular kind of case in that jurisdiction in the recent past, and be required to follow that in sentencing or give his reasons for not doing so. Then the choice could be tested on appeal.

The Home Office Advisory Council on the Penal System, in its important Report on Sentences of Imprisonment (1978) found the guidelines approach of considerable interest, but doubted whether such a sophisticated formalisation of the 'tariff' would be acceptable in the English context[20]. They did ask for the progress of this new concept to be monitored. They remarked that:

'The system of sentencing guidelines, now making headway in the United States as a compromise between indeterminate sentencing and a system of more or less fixed penalties, was of special interest to us, both because the philosophy of steering a middle course between a wide and a narrow discretion in sentencing was the one which most appealed to us, and because the practical solution of adopting a penalty system based on the existing practice of the courts was that which we ourselves ultimately decided to recommend'[1].

(iii) *The Advisory Council's recommendations*

Instead of trying to revise the existing maximum penalties for different crimes, a task which would have involved making difficult value judgments concerning the relative seriousness of different kinds of criminal behaviour, the Advisory Council preferred to recommend the adoption of a scheme in two parts, based largely on existing sentencing practice. A new scheme of penalties for ordinary cases would be adopted, fixing the maximum penalty for each offence at the point below which 90 per cent of prison sentences have fallen in the last three years. This would involve a substantial reduction in existing maxima, which is no doubt what the Advisory Council saw as desirable in order to achieve its goal of shorter sentences, expressed in its Interim Report on The Length of Prison Sentences[2]. This was the first part of the package. The second part concerned making provision for the exceptional case where the maximum provided in the first part was inadequate. These exceptional cases were defined as those involving

20 Report, Appendix C, para 20, p. 167.
1 Report, para. 17 p. 8.
2 Home Office, Advisory Council on the Penal System, Interim Report, *The Length of Prison Sentences* (1977).

the threat of serious harm in the future, 'serious harm' being defined as normally comprising 'serious physical injury, serious psychological effects, exceptional personal hardship, or damage to the security of the State or to the fabric of society'. In such cases as this, the sentencer would be empowered, subject to complying with certain conditions, to impose a determinate sentence of any length.

The Advisory Council's proposals encountered a storm of criticism in the press, which unfortunately concentrated on such details as the maximum penalty for rape. In ordinary cases under these proposals this would be reduced from life imprisonment to seven years. Academic criticism was directed towards other aspects of the proposals, including the failure to revalue maximum penalties, and the astonishing breadth of the judge's power in the case of exceptional sentences[3]. It seems unlikely that sufficient support can be found for these proposals to warrant their implementation.

There are many other important recommendations in the Advisory Council's Report, such as those concerning the extended sentence, the life sentence, and the penalty for murder, which deserve careful scrutiny. There is also some discussion of combined sentences (e.g. prison plus fine), suspended sentences, and criminal bankruptcy.

(iv) *Other means of influencing or modifying sentencing*

There are several other means whereby sentences could be influenced or modified. These include requiring the prosecutor to make a recommendation to the court concerning the appropriate sentence for the case in question. This is a practice widely adopted in European legal systems, but is not thought to be compatible with the impartial role expected of the prosecutor in English legal practice[4]. Another device, whereby the administration of a sentence might be influenced or modified, is that of the supervising judge, deputed to concern himself with the details of the actual conditions in which the sentence is served, and the progression towards release[5]. This is known in France as the *judge de l'execution des peines*, and the institution is known also in Italy. Reports concerning its effectiveness in practice do not suggest that great advantages would ensue for prisoners. In

---

3 See L. Radzinowicz and R. Hood, 'A Dangerous Direction for Sentencing Reform' [1978] Crim LR 713. J. E. Hall Williams, BJC Vol. 18, No. 4, p. 396 (review article) (October 1978).
4 See M. H. Tonry and N. Morris, loc. cit.
5 See European Committee on Crime Problems, Council of Europe, Report on *Sentencing* (1974).

England and Wales some of the functions carried out by the supervising judge are entrusted to the prison administration, some to the Parole Board.

Influencing the exercise of sentencing discretion

Several means exist or might be adopted whereby the exercise of discretion by sentencing judges might be influenced other than by structural or institutional means. These include:

(i) *The development of the 'tariff'*

In England and Wales a common approach towards sentencing, or 'tariff' is derived from the results of decided cases, as known by lawyers and judges and as expressed in the decisions of the Court of Appeal in sentence appeals. David Thomas has shown how the principles of sentencing may be derived from a study of sentencing decisions of the Court of Appeal[6]. There is now a separate series of law reports on sentencing. The 'tariff' may also be derived from a perusal of the criminal statistics published by the Home Office, which gives much information about sentencing practice throughout the length and breadth of England and Wales. Judges are supplied with these figures, but until now it seems unlikely that they have been greatly influenced by such statistical information. It may be however that it provides a better guide to what courts actually do than the study of the results of appeal cases. A careful study of these statistics such as that written by Ian McClean[7] should do much to remedy the situation.

(ii) *Training judges.*

There is nowadays general agreement with the view that lawyers who are appointed to be judges require some form of training to equip them for their new responsibilities. This includes some knowledge and guidance concerning sentencing options. So far as concerns England and Wales the matter was put beyond doubt by the Report of the Working Party on Judicial Studies and Information (1978). The Working Party reached the conclusion that:

6 D. A. Thomas, *Principles of Sentencing* (2nd edn., 1979). David Thomas has also addressed himself to the subject of this chapter in his essay 'The Control of Discretion in the Administration of Justice' in *Crime, Criminology and Public Policy: Essays in Honour of Sir Leon Radzinowicz* (1974), ed. R. Hood, p. 139.
7 I. McClean, *The Crown Court – Patterns of Sentencing* (1981).

'there is a need, widely accepted among the judiciary and elsewhere, for programmes of study to equip the judiciary for their functions in relation to criminal trials, and of sentencing in particular, and that something more than the present level of provision is called for'[8].

The present level of provision referred to includes a week-long residential seminar for newly appointed judges and recorders, and occasional one-day conference held in the Lord Chief Justice's Court in London.

The Working Party made proposals for the provision of judicial studies programmes to be organised by a Judicial Studies Board, together with a salaried Director of Studies, and for information services to be provided for the judiciary, as well as continuing opportunities to confer. Because of doubts about the implications of the notion of 'training' judges, the term 'judicial studies' is preferred.

In other countries efforts have been made to develop study programmes. Appexdix B of the Report of the Working Party gives a summary of the arrangements in Commonwealth countries, in the United States, and in other European countries. Of particular interest are the sentencing institutes organised in America for the federal judiciary.

(iii) *Consultation*

Some American jurisdictions have established machinery for consultation between judges sitting in the same jurisdiction concerning each other's sentencing choices[9]. The idea can be useful where many judges sit together in one large complex of courts exercising criminal jurisdiction. However most criminal court judges sit in some degree of isolation from each other in separate geographical locations. While no doubt a certain amount of informal consultation takes place, it is unlikely that this needs to be formalised into an institution such as a 'sentencing council'.

(iv) *Exhortation*

Successive Lords Chancellor and Lords Chief Justice have made speeches from time to time exhorting courts, particularly magistrates' courts, to use their sentencing powers in a particular way. In recent

---

8 Report, para. 3.22, p. 13.
9 S. S. Diamond and H. Zeisel, 'Sentencing Councils: A Study of Sentence Disparity and Its Reduction' 43 U Chi L Rev p. 109 (1975).

years this has usually been in the direction of reducing the use of imprisonment. In the past however, courts were recommended to increase the level of fines, and to take harsher measures against motoring offenders. Whether these injunctions from on high had any effect on the practice of the courts is not known, but we do know that in respect of magistrates' courts local conditions vary so much that it seems difficult to lay down a general rule or policy, and that the main culprits seem too often to be immune to such criticism or totally insensitive to such advice, viz. judges in Crown Courts.

(v) Information

The last method whereby sentencing choices might be controlled or influenced is by the dissemination of information to the courts. This comes in the form either of reports to the courts, a subject discussed already in Chapter 8, or in the form of Home Office circulars giving guidance and advice, and the research bulletins of the Home Office Research Unit, which summarise the results of recent research. The Judicial Studies Working Party recommended that a bulletin specifically directed to sentencers should be published presenting in easily digestible form all current material of interest to sentencers[10].

The House of Commons Expenditure Committee in its Fifteenth Report recommended that courts should be supplied with up-to-date status reports concerning the availability of places in Prison Department institutions[11]. This suggestion was thought to be impractical by the Home Office[12], but the House of Commons Home Affairs Committee in its Fourth Report has renewed the demand for an information bulletin 'containing information on the accommodation available in custodial institutions, but supplemented with brief digests of recent research findings and policy discussions'. The Home Office in their reply to the Expenditure Committee had questioned the value of supplying courts with regular and detailed reports on penal accommodation[13]. Many judges take the view that it should be none of their concern whether accommodation is available for offenders whom they sentence to custody. Realistically, however, their intentions may be thwarted by conditions of overcrowding and shortage of staff, and it

10 Report (1978) pp. 26 et seq., and para. 8.7, p. 34.
11 H. C. 662–I, Session 1977–78.
12 Home Office, Observations on the Fifteenth Report from the Expenditure Committee, The Reduction of Pressure on the Prison System, Cmnd. 7948 (June 1980).
13 H. C. 412–I, Session 1980–81, para. 84, p. xxxv.

is just as well they should be made aware of the true state of affairs in the penal institutions.

A sentencing tribunal?

The alternative to judicial sentencing would be some form of sentencing tribunal. This would take some part or the whole of the responsibility away from the trial judge and vest it in some body of experts or committee which would be charged with deciding on the appropriate sentence after assembling all the relevant information and studying reports about the offender.

Some criminologists have espoused such a sentencing tribunal, and others have supported the idea momentarily or in some abridged form[14]. Distinguished judges and magistrates, probation officers and chief constables have expressed such views[15]. There is an inherent attractiveness in the notion since it is thought it would solve the problem of discrepancies in sentencing. The price to be paid, however, is generally regarded as unacceptable, since it would remove from the courts and public view an essential part of the criminal process, viz. the decision about the disposal of the convicted offender. Even if such a sentencing tribunal were to operate, there would have to be a right of appeal against its decisions, and as Colin Howard has pointed out, that appeal would bring the case back into the public arena.

'It would be distinctly paradoxical to remove sentencing from the courts to a tribunal whose operations became subject to review by the very courts which are supposed to lack the expertise to carry out sentencing themselves. The only alternative is to free such a tribunal from judicial supervision or review altogether, and this is unthinkable'[16].

As we shall see, the operations of the Parole Board partake in part of the nature of re-sentencing, and there is no provision for an appeal. This is because parole in England and Wales is viewed entirely as a matter of administrative discretion. It is worth remarking that the expertise represented in the membership of the Parole Board

---

14 See J. E. Hall Williams (1970) pp. 40–41, (1975) pp. 44 et seq.
15 Sir Leo Page, *The Sentence of the Court* (1948); Henry Cecil, *The English Judge* (1970) Hamlyn Lectures; James Anderton, Chief Constable of Greater Manchester, *The Times*, 23 April 1980.
16 Colin Howard in *Reshaping the Criminal Law* (1978), ed. P. R. Glazebrook pp. 413–414.

(psychiatrists, probation officers, criminologists) frequently feel poorly equipped to discharge this part of their responsibilities, and some members object to the role cast upon them in this respect, on the ground that there is nothing in their training and experience to equip them to make what are essentially value-judgements about such matters as the appropriateness of the length of time served in relation to the gravity of the offence. This is a matter best left to judges.

Another objection to the sentencing tribunal is a logistic one. Where would one find sufficient persons able and willing to devote enough time to this activity? It seems unlikely that many psychologists, psychiatrists, social workers and criminologists, would be willing to leave their present jobs and responsibilities and sit more or less full-time as members of a sentencing tribunal. Moreover, to cover England and Wales several tribunals could be required, and there would be variations between them, so that the vexed problem of discrepancy would recur. Whichever way one looks at this proposal it seems impractical, and the best course seems to be to bury it.

The current sentencing scene

We have referred to the concern about the use of prison. It is worth stressing that not only are sentence lengths in England and Wales unnecessarily long, but that many short terms of imprisonment are repeatedly imposed on what have come to be known as 'petty inadequate offenders'. The Home Office research findings have shown that a high proportion of such offenders is to be found in our prisons[17]. The intervention of the Court of Appeal in this matter, in two decisions discouraging the use of prison for inadequate offenders, is greatly to be welcomed[18]. The real difficulty appears to be the absence of any acceptable alternative disposal or measure.

Alternatives to prison have been developed dramatically in recent years, both by the probation and after-care service and by voluntary agencies[19]. There is some concern, however, whether the true 'displacement effect' of such measures is as great as it should be, in terms of displacing a custodial sentence. Often the new measure is used for persons who would not have been sentenced to imprisonment in

---

17 *Persistent Petty Offenders* (1981) Home Office Research Study No. 66; see also C. Banks and S. Fairhead, *The Petty Short-term Prisoner* (1976).
18 *R v Upton* [1980] Crim LR 508; *R v Bibi* [1980] Crim LR 732.
19 For a description see the Fifteenth Report from the Expenditure Committee, H. C. 662–I, paras. 182 et seq., pp. lxviii et seq.

any event, but who might have been fined or placed on probation or given a suspended sentence. There is also a body of academic opinion which fears the long-term consequences of the widespread introduction of alternatives to prison[20]. Many offenders are likely to fail on such programmes and they will increase the proportion of bad risks appearing in court, for whom custody appears to the courts as the only solution. Another concern is about the many mentally disordered offenders in custody. Both the Fifteenth Report from the Expenditure Committee of the House of Commons[1] and the Fourth Report from the Home Affairs Committee[2] stressed the importance of ensuring that such mentally disordered offenders be accommodated in mental hospitals rather than prison. Remanding in custody to await trial is also another subject of great concern, since many of those remanded do not in the end receive custodial sentences. Indeed some are acquitted.

In all these areas of contemporary concern, it is open to courts to use the discretion which is entrusted to them creatively and intelligently to provide acceptable solutions. The more sentencers know about the true nature of the problems, and understand the personality and character of the offenders appearing before them, the less likely is it that their exercise of discretion in these matters will be criticised, and suggestions made for the removal from them of these wide powers. The last decades of the twentieth century should be marked by the creative and enlightened use by sentencers of their extensive discretion, as well as the development of alternative measures to custody.

4 The role of the Home Office in relation to the exercise of the prerogative power of pardon and remission, and in relation to parole release

When we reach the stage in the criminal process where there has been a conviction and sentence, once again we find that wide discretionary power is vested in the Home Office over matters concerning the prisoner's release. On some of these matters, knowledge and

---

20 A. Scull, *Decarceration: Community Treatment and the Deviant* (1978).
1 H.C.662–I, Session 1977–78, paras. 69, pp. xxxviii et seq.
2 H.C. 412–I, Session 1980–81, paras. 45 et seq., pp. xix et seq.

understanding of offenders might well contribute towards better exercise of these powers.

The powers fall into three categories:

1 The prerogative power of pardon and remission;

2 The power to refer a case to the Court of Appeal;

3 The power to release on parole.

The first two of these concern mainly matters regarding the correctness of the conviction and sentence, where subsequent developments in the evidence throw doubt upon the justice of the original decision. The Crown has always enjoyed the power to pardon altogether or to remit sentences in part[3]. Under recent legislation there is now a wide power to refer a case for decision to the Court of Appeal (Criminal Division) under the provisions of the Criminal Appeal Act 1968 and the Criminal Justice Act 1972[4].

Parole discretion

The most common exercise of discretion by the Home Office is in respect of early release of a prisoner on licence, or what is commonly known as parole. The parole system was introduced by the Criminal Justice Act 1967, and took effect from 1 April 1968. Thousands of prisoners have been paroled each year since then, with a remarkably high success rate—or low failure rate—judged in terms of reconviction or recall during the period of operation of the parole licence. Approximately 10 per cent of parolees fail judged by this standard, and the scheme has commanded a high degree of respect for this reason[5].

Parole decisions are made by a tri-partite system which divides responsibility between the Local Review Committee (LRC), a body constituted at each prison where parole-eligible prisoners are held, the Parole Board for England and Wales, a statutory creation independent from the Home Office, and the Home Secretary advised by his officials and responsible to Parliament. The LRC makes more or less final decisions for a wide range of short term offenders, subject only to

---

3 See J. E. Hall Williams (1970) pp. 180 et seq.

4 See D. A. Thomas, *Principles of Sentencing* (2nd edn., 1979).

5 See J. E. Hall Williams, 'Ten Years of Parole – Retrospect and Prospect', The Sixth Denis Carroll Memorial Lecture, I.S.T.D. (1978); 'Parole in England and Wales: A Success Story' Toledo LR Vol 10, No. 2, p. 465 (1979).

scrutiny by the Home Office[6]. Some categories of offender, however, cannot be paroled solely on the authority of the LRC's recommendation, as backed by the Home Office. These are cases of violence, sex, drugs and arson where the sentence is in excess of two years, and all cases where the sentence is in excess of four years. Such cases must be referred to the Parole Board[7]. Also referred are cases where the LRC decision was not unanimous. The Parole Board sits in panels usually consisting of four or five members. The membership of over 40 includes judges and recorders, psychiatrists, probation officers, criminologists, and other persons such as lay magistrates, social workers, businessmen and trade union representatives. The panels sit three or four times a week, mostly in London, but with regular panels meeting in Manchester, and occasional panels meeting elsewhere.

Parole decisions involve making choices. The risks of early release on licence have to be balanced against the advantages of the prisoner being released under the supervision of a probation officer at a time when he may benefit and in circumstances which are the most favourable. Inevitably mistakes are made, though there have been remarkably few bad parole failures, in the sense that a prisoner released on a parole licence has committed a serious offence during the licence period. Critics say the Board errs on the side of caution. Yet two out of three of those eligible are granted parole at some stage in their sentence. Selection is the essence of the operation. It should not become an automatic consequence of serving a prison term that one is released on a parole licence. The prisoner has to make an application for parole. He is required to set down in writing his reasons for wanting parole. He has to be interviewed by one member of the local review committee, who will try and clarify the prisoner's reasons, and write a report of the interview. The prisoner can decline to write down his reasons, preferring to wait until the interview, and this occurs not infrequently where the prisoner feels difficulty in explaining things on paper. He may decline to be interviewed. He may even decline to be considered for parole, which is known as 'opting out' in which case the matter is not brought before the Parole Board or the LRC. Only a minority of prisoners 'opt out', 6.4 per cent in 1980[7].

6 These prisoners are released by the Home Secretary without consulting the Parole Board, on the recommendation of the LRC, by virtue of s. 35 of the Criminal Justice Act 1972.
7 See the Report of the Parole Board for England and Wales for details of the statistics: Parole Board Report for 1980, H. C. 340 Session 1980-81.

The prisoner granted parole has to agree to various conditions of the parole licence, including the supervision by a probation officer. Occasionally special conditions are added to the licence, concerning work and residence – to work where approved and reside where approved. There may be conditions concerning access to his family, for example, in a case of a sexual nature such as incest. The prisoner is made aware of these conditions and given a copy of the licence before his discharge. The supervisor will ensure that the prisoner makes early contact with him, and will go over the conditions of the licence with the prisoner to make sure that he understands what is expected of him. He may receive visits from the supervisor at his home or place of residence, but most contacts occur by the parolee reporting at the office of his supervisor. Difficulties frequently arise when there is a break in the supervision, such as when the supervisor is on holiday, or when the parolee moves to another area. Naturally efforts are made to prevent any breakdown in the relationship, for once an offender is 'out of touch' with his supervisor, and this appears to be confirmed, then the proper course is to ask for the recall of the offender and if this is sanctioned, the offender will then be arrested. All applications for recall will be put before a panel of the Parole Board for decision except where an emergency has arisen. It is one aspect of the Parole Board's work that it is charged with the responsibility for recalls. Where an emergency has arisen, officials may sanction a recall, but the case must be reported immediately to the Parole Board for them to confirm the recall. Since panels of the Board are sitting three or four days a week, it is rarely necessary for officials to use the emergency power. Once recalled, a prisoner has a right to appeal against the recall, by making written representations, and if he wishes, being interviewed by an LRC member. A Board panel will then be asked to consider the appeal, and it may make an order directing the offender's release immediately or within a short time.

It will be seen from the above account of the working of parole decision-making, both at the sanctioning stage and when recall is under consideration, that a number of checks and balances exist in regard to the exercise of discretion. Despite these safeguards, there is considerable anxiety about parole decisions, and academic criticism of the way the system works[8]. It is argued that a more just system would

8 P. Cavadino et al., *Parole: The Case for Change* (1977) NACRO; *Parole: Its Implications for the Criminal Justice and Penal Systems* (1974), ed. D. A. Thomas; R. Hood, *Tolerance and the Tariff* (1974) NACRO, reprinted in *Criminal Justice: Selected Readings* (1978) eds. J. Baldwin and A. K. Bottomley, p. 269; *Freedom on Licence*, Report of a Howard League Working Party (1981).

be one where discretion was eliminated, and sentences were for fixed terms, with early release on licence being available to all prisoners without exception, thus avoiding selection altogether, and replacing parole by some other concept such as automatic supervision of all persons released. The wide support for such notions in America which has been a feature in recent years has led to their adoption is states like California and Maine. Whether the result will prove satisfactory in terms of the consequences for prison and for the community is a debateable question. Norval Morris and Michael Tonry, Albert Alschuler and others are already doubting the wisdom of these developments[9].

Young adult offenders (17–21)

Meanwhile the Home Office has been re-examining proposals for young adult offenders which were developed in recent years, originating with the Advisory Council's review of imprisonment for young adult offenders[10]. The result of this re-examination[11] was new proposals involving all such young adult offenders being subject to release on licence under supervision, or a statutory licence, although the discretionary element of a flexible release date which was a feature of the borstal system will be abolished. One is bound to doubt the assumptions underlying these proposals. Presumably they are premised on the needs of young persons under 21 for continuing supervision after release. Nothing is said about their amenability or suitability for such supervision, yet it is widely accepted that many young adults actively resent supervision in this form, and the failure rate of this age group is likely to be much wider than for the rest of the adult population. They are as a group exceedingly difficult to deal with. Challenging as this may well be to certain probation officers, it is submitted that they would prefer to be charged with a more limited responsibility for supervising those who are selected for supervision, ask for it, consent to it, and need it, rather than for an unselected population, some of whom are rather unwilling and unsuitable customers.

---

9 M. H. Tonry and N. Morris (1978). A. W. Alschuler (1979). See pp. 211 and 213, ante.
10 Home Office, Report of the Advisory Council on the Penal System, *Young Adult Offenders* (1974).
11 Home Office, *Youth Custody and Supervision: A New Sentence*, Cmnd. 7406 (December 1978); Home Office, White Paper, Cmnd. 8045 (October 1980). The new proposals are contained in the Criminal Justice Bill 1981.

The same argument can be applied to proposals canvassed involving granting automatic release on licence to prisoners serving sentences of between eighteen months and three years. Large numbers of unsuitable offenders, in terms of the risk of their re-offending and their amenability to supervision, would be•released in this way, with the consequence that there would be a high failure rate. It is no answer to say that the supervision expected from the probation service would be similar to that under a suspended sentence supervision order, the sole obligation on the offender being to keep in touch with his superviser and notify any changes of address, and to say that many reports now required for the parole review would no longer be necessary[12]. One benefit alone would have flowed from this change, a most welcome reduction in the prison population, estimated to be in the region of 7,000.

However, when the proposal was mooted by the Home Office for inclusion in the 1981 Criminal Justice Bill, and the judiciary and magistrates were consulted, the result was the withdrawal of the proposal because of the grave reservations expressed by those consulted. Instead the Home Office now prefers to rely on activating the idea of the partly-suspended sentence, already provided for in the Criminal Justice Act 1972, but not yet brought into force.

Criminologists and penal reform

Criminologists who have turned penal reformers frequently carry with them in their interpretation of the evidence concerning the outcome of penal measures, both in this country and elsewhere, a sizeable measure of crusading and reforming zeal, prejudice against prisons and many preconceived ideas. This, it is submitted, is inimical to clarity and complete impartiality and represents a betrayal of the scientific tradition. If indeed one has such strong feelings, e.g. against prison, one should declare them, and strenuously try to safeguard one's judgment against the bias this is likely to introduce, for example, in interpreting the evidence concerning the success or failure of penal measures. The cause of penal reform may well have been promoted by such interventions and support by criminologists. In trying to wear two hats, however, they do seem at times to lack that complete objectivity which is the mark of true scholarship. The speed with

---

12 These arguments appear to have persuaded the House of Commons Home Affairs Committee: see House of Commons Home Affairs Committee, Fourth Report, H. C. 412–I, Session 1980–1981, July 1981, paras. 88–98, pp. xxxvi–xxxix.

which criminologists embraced the evidence concerning the failure of reformative measures, especially in the United States, is one example of what we have been referring to. Since the early days of this attack on liberal and reformist penological measures, there has been time for second thoughts. One at least of the major protagonists of the 'nothing does any good' school has retracted from the position originally taken, and has now admitted that reform of offenders can take place for some prisoners in some situations[13]. A more careful look at the criteria chosen to establish success or failure of rehabilitation might have alerted criminologists much sooner to the possibility that one was either using the wrong criteria or asking the question in an inappropriate form.

This mention of research leads to the suggestion that the results of research and the deliberations of advisory committees should figure more prominently among the considerations which determine the direction of penal policy. Too often one has seen in recent years the adoption of a penal measure or the introduction of a new policy regarding the treatment of offenders without any regard to previous research findings or the recommendations of an advisory committee relevant to the subject in question. Examples include the introduction of the suspended sentence, and the introduction of the 'short sharp shock' regime in some detention centres. Twice the Home Office was advised by its committees not to introduce the suspended sentence. A more educational basis of the regime in detention centres was recommended by the Advisory Council. Scant regard seems to be paid to such recommendations when certain policy decisions commend themselves to government for reasons often quite unconnected with the likelihood of the success or failure of the measure in question, such as the reduction of the prison population or the carrying out of election promises to be tough on crime.

Notes. Police cautions

1 David Steer's research on police cautions, *Police Cautions – A Study in the Exercise of Police Discretion* (1970) Oxford University Penal Research Unit, Occasional Paper Number Two, remarks that the police in England and Wales have used some form of cautioning since the very beginning of their existence. In Scotland it is known as a police warning. Some types of offender are more

13 R. Martinson, 'It Has Come to Our Attention' Federal Probation Vol. 43, No. 1, p. 86 (March 1979). See also R. Martinson 'New Findings, New Views: A Note of Caution regarding Sentencing Reform (1979) 7 Hofstra L Rev No. 2, p. 243.

likely to be cautioned than others, in particular females and young offenders. The older an offender is the less likely is he or she to be cautioned. With regard to juveniles, even before the Children and Young Persons Act 1969 many police forces had established juvenile liaison schemes, under which police officers supervised selected young offenders who had been cautioned instead of being prosecuted. Ditchfield (1976) shows how the 1969 Act radically altered the situation regarding children and young persons, increasing the number cautioned dramatically. Dickehs in 1970 showed that local government authorities sometimes preferred to caution offenders rather than prosecute, B. M. Dickens, 'Discretion in Local Authority Prosecutions' [1970] Crim LR 618. The statistics published by the Home Office since 1954 about cautions show a steady rise in the number of persons cautioned for both indictable offences and non-indictable offences other than motoring, but a decline in the use of cautions for motoring offences. The decline in the number of cautions for motoring offences is probably linked with the introduction of fixed penalty offences: Steer (1970) p. 11.

2 Steer's study expressed concern about variations in cautioning policy between different police forces. Sebba's study of juvenile offenders cautioned was designed to test out various possible explanations for such variation: L. Sebba, 'Decision-Making in Juvenile Cases – A Comment' [1970] Crim LR 347. No relationship was found between cautioning rates and high levels of juvenile delinquency, or high clear-up rates, or size of population. F. H. McClintock and N. H. Avison in 1968, *Crime in England and Wales*, had concluded that the variations in 1962 were too great to be explained in terms of differences in types of crime or sex and age of offenders in the different local areas (Ditchfield (1976) p. 2). One was led to conclude that the differences might be attributable to the different policies adopted by senior police officers and their chiefs, a conclusion supported by Steer: (1970) p. 17, and J. G. Somerville, 'A study of the preventive aspect of police work with juveniles' [1969] Crim LR 407.

Differences were observed in Sussex between different divisions of the same police force: D. Rainton, 'Police discretion: a study of how it works in Sussex' (1974) Police Review pp. 878 et seq., 912 et seq. 945 et seq. However, any suspicion that this may be due to differential law enforcement or some form of discrimination against certain areas should be allayed by Mawby's study of the situation in Sheffield, where on the face of it different rates of caution operated in different areas: R. Mawby, *Policing the City* (1979). He submits that the findings tending to show discrimination by the police in certain areas are not supported (p. 176). So far as official cautioning for indictable and non-indictable offences is concerned, comparisons made in nine different police areas of Sheffield, when allowance is made for the different types of offender living in different areas, showed no significant difference for juveniles or offenders under 21. There may be differences for adult offenders but even here the differences are minimal. Factors such as age, sex and previous convictions appear to be more strongly related to cautioning patterns than do more general factors such as area of residence (p. 172).

3 On a broader front, as Professor Bottoms points out in his Foreword, Mawby's study demonstrates that differences in official crime rates between selected areas are not the result of differential law-enforcement processes (p. viii). The conclusion is inescapable that, as Bottoms puts it 'there are "real" differences between the high crime rate and the low crime rate areas in the extent of criminal behaviour actually occuring in the districts, and being committed by residents of the districts' (p. ix). This is a conclusion relevant both to the study of criminal statistics (Chapter 7) and to the area study of crime.

Prosecutor's discretion

1 The literature on prosecutor's discretion is of fairly recent origin and mostly comes from the United States where the trial scene allows, indeed compels, the exercise of considerable power by the prosecutor (the district attorney) to negotiate plea bargains and influence the progress and result of cases by securing guilty pleas. Donald Newman was one of the first to draw attention to the prosecutor's discretion: Donald J. Newman, 'Pleading Guilty for Considerations: A Study of Bargain Justice' 46 Jo Crim L & Crim'ogy & Pol Sci p. 780 (1956) reprinted in *The Sociology of Punishment and Correction* (2nd edn., 1970); eds. N. Johnston, L. Savitz and M. E. Wolfgang, p. 172; see also his *Introduction to Criminal Justice* (1975) Chap. 5, pp. 187 et seq., and his study carried out for the American Bar Foundation, *Conviction: The Determination of Guilt or Innocence Without Trial* (1966).

2 Other studies include W. F. McDonald, *The Prosecutor* (1979); Brian A. Grosman, *The Prosecutor: An inquiry into the exercise of discretion* (1969) which is a Canadian study; see also Brian Grosman's article, 'The Role of the Prosecutor: New Adaptations in the Adversarial Concept of Criminal Justice' Canadian Bar Journal Vol. 11, p. 580 (November 1968); A. F. Wilcox, *The Decision to Prosecute* (1972); D. G. T. Williams, 'Prosecution, Discretion and the Accountability of the Police' in *Crime, Criminology and Public Policy: Essays in Honour of Sir Leon Radzinowicz* (1974), ed. R. Hood, p. 161. See also Lord Justice James, 'A Judicial Note on the Control of Discretion in the Administration of Justice' in *Crime, Criminology and Public Policy* (1974), ed. R. Hood, p. 157.

3 The Royal Commission on Criminal Procedure commissioned and has published several important reports on the subject of the organisation and management of prosecutions, both in the public sector and private prosecutions: No. 10, Prosecutions by private individuals and non-police agencies, by K. W. Lidstone et al. (1980); Nos. 11 and 12, The prosecution system: survey of prosecuting solicitors' departments; organisational implications of change, by Mollie Weatheritt, David R. Kaye et al. (1980).

Chapter 10

Crime and the community

We now address ourselves to a veritable rag-bag of subjects relevant to the understanding of crime, all of which are of great topical interest and importance.

Crime and opportunity

Recent studies by the Home Office Research Unit have focussed on the relevance of physical opportunities to commit crime and physical or technological measures of crime prevention[1]. Leslie Wilkins in 1964 drew attention to the relationship between certain features of the so-called affluent society and the rise in property crime:

'In any stable social system the increase in economic activity and affluence would lead to increased opportunities – opportunities for honest and dishonest practices'[2].

Wilkins observes that as the amount of money being transferred legitimately increases so do the opportunities for crime. As the number of motor cars increases, so do the opportunities for car theft or stealing from cars. He found a relationship between motor vehicle ownership and theft from motor vehicles, the two sets of data following each other extremely closely between 1938 and 1961[3]. This example may be multiplied in many directions. Thefts from shops and supermarkets may be related to the number of shops and supermarkets and the volume of open-counter trading. Changes in marketing methods may affect the opportunities for crime. Changes in banking methods and security in banks have undoubtedly affected the pattern of robbery, re-directing it into attacks on money in transit, rather than at the place of

1 P. Mayhew, R. V. G. Clarke, A. Sturman and J. M. Hough, *Crime as Opportunity*, (1976) Home Office Research Study No. 34.
2 L. T. Wilkins, *Social Deviance* (1964) pp. 51 et seq. See also L. Radzinowicz, 'Economic Pressures' in *Crime and Justice* (1971) eds. L. Radzinowicz and M. E. Wolfgang, Vol. 1, p. 420.
3 Table 1 and Figure 2, pp. 54 and 55.

business. Crime prevention policies are frequently directed towards urging people to take more care of the security of their homes and belongings, but common experience shows that an enormous variety of opportunities for theft are provided by members of the public in the ordinary business of everyday living, and there seem to be those who are always at hand, ready and willing to seize such opportunities.

Other studies have focussed on situational inducements to criminality but there are considerable difficulties in forging a theory of crime in terms of situational variables, as the Home Office review of such studies points out. The best one can do is ask that 'greater prominence might be given in criminological explanation to how the inducements of the situation operate in different instances of criminality'[4]. One might also add that the relevance of deterrent punishment to such situations needs to be evaluated in this connection, as well as the chances of detection.

One advantage of approaching the study of crime in these terms is that it requires no grand theory concerning the etiology of criminal behaviour. One might settle for the mundane view that people are motivated by greed and that this more than need inspires much crime in a modern western society. There is also the hope that one can influence the pattern of crime by restricting opportunities for its commission, and here the Home Office studies of various experiments prove instructive.

Thus the effectiveness of installing steering locks on cars in preventing car theft has been studied. At first sight the result of making the fitting of such locks in steering columns compulsory, which has been mandatory for all new cars since January 1971, had not been so great as had been anticipated, judged by the broad figures of car theft in the Metropolitan Police District. Fitting a steering column lock does not altogether prevent a car theft, however, since the car owner may leave the key in the lock or the thief may supply himself with a key. Closer examination of the situation based on a sample drawn from 1973 compared with 1969 showed that fitting steering locks had in fact considerably reduced the risk of such cars being stolen or taken without authority. The risk to old cars had nearly doubled in the period in question, which explains the general rise in car thefts mentioned above. The study concludes by questioning the Wilkins' hypothesis that autocrime is fairly closely related to the number of

4 Home Office Research Study No. 34, p. 3.

vehicles registered[5]. Wilkins chose to use thefts *from* motor vehicles rather than theft *of* motor vehicles or unauthorised taking, but even this measure of autocrime has not related well to the increase in vehicle registration since 1961, as the Home Office study points out[6]. In Germany, where since 1963 all cars, both old and new, are required to be fitted with anti-theft devices, there has been a very marked decrease in car theft, which suggests that increasing car security decreases the incidence of car theft. To be balanced against this gain there is the 'displacement effect' that intending thieves will transfer their attentions to unprotected vehicles.

Another study concerned the effects of the level of supervision on buses by drivers and conductors on the incidence of damage to buses. Single man and two deck buses suffer more damage than when there is a conductor or the bus is a single decker. These findings, the study admits, are hardly surprising[7]. This was a very limited study of an exploratory kind. The study did point to there being 'powerful situational determinants of the behaviour'[8] which could have some bearing on bus design and manning policy.

Vandalism is a subject which has invited research along similar lines. Inspired by American studies like those of Oscar Newman into 'defensible space', the Home Office Research Unit looked into the extent to which vandalism is influenced by building design and layout. Results from a survey of London municipal housing estates provided limited support for Professor Newman's ideas and also showed the relevance for vandalism of the densities at which children are accommodated on estates[9].

Further studies which have been carried out into the effect of surveillance by residents and employees on rates of vandalism suggest that limited success is likely to attend such schemes. Hopes of reducing crime dramatically by such means seem unrealistic. There may well be a displacement effect, by transferring the incidence of such crimes elsewhere. Some improvement may be achieved by increasing the likelihood of crimes being seen by those members of the public most likely to intervene, e.g. residents and employees[10]. The two studies

5 p. 13.
6 p. 13, footnote 2.
7 p. 26.
8 p. 27.
9 *Tackling Vandalism* (1978) Home Office Research Study No. 47, ed. by R. V. G. Clarke, contributors F. J. Gladstone, A. Sturman, Sheena Wilson.
10 P. Mayhew, R. V. G. Clarke, J. N. Burrows, J. M. Hough, and S. W. C. Winchester, *Crime in Public View* (1979) Home Office Research Study No. 42.

here reported concerned vandalism to telephone kiosks in Greenwich, and the impact of closed circuit television on crime in the London Underground. Mawby also studied telephone kiosk vandalism in Sheffield[11].

Other studies of vandalism have since been published, including a study of a programme designed to combat vandalism in schools[12]. A Home Office Standing Committee on Crime Prevention has published recommendations on protection against vandalism[13]. The working party which prepared this report described vandalism as 'a national disgrace' affecting the lives and pockets of citizens in many different ways. The cost to the community was far higher than is generally suspected. Vandalism also attracted the attention of the Central Policy Review Staff of the Cabinet Office[14]. The document issued by them in September 1978 said there was some risk of getting the problem out of proportion, and that in most parts of the country public property, however vulnerable, is not vandalised. There was however, a great deal of public concern about it, and there seemed to be no easy remedies. They made various suggestions for government action to combat vandalism.

The results of an anti-vandalism campaign mounted in the North West in 1978 and a publicity campaign asking motorists to pay more attention to car security, mounted in the North of England in 1979, have been monitored[15]. The disappointing conclusion is reached that crime prevention publicity had little success in modifying the behaviour of either potential victims or offenders in ways which may reduce crime.

The community and crime prevention

The foregoing discussion leads to the question whether one can involve the community more in crime prevention and with what hope

11 R. I. Mawby, 'Kiosk vandalism: a Sheffield study' BJC Vol. 17, p. 30 (1977).
12 F. J. Gladstone, *Co-ordinating Crime Prevention Efforts* (1980) Home Office Research Study No. 62.
13 Home Office Standing Committee on Crime Prevention, *Protection against Vandalism* (November 1975).
14 Cabinet Office, *Vandalism: A Note by the Central Policy Review Staff* (September 1978).
15 D. Riley and P. Mayhew, *Crime Prevention Publicity: An Assessment* (1980) Home Office Research Study No. 63. Many of the separate Home Office Research Unit studies have been collected together in *Designing Out Crime* (1980), eds. R. V. G. Clarke and P. Mayhew.

of success. The U.S. Commission which reported in 1973 (the Peterson Commission) made many recommendations about ways and means whereby different crimes might be combated by what is described as 'citizen action' and the development of community crime prevention efforts. They found numerous examples where crime and delinquency prevention programmes had been developed which had reduced crime[16]. There had also been previous reports which touched on the desirability of involving the community in preventing crime[17]. No previous report had given this matter so much prominence, however. Since its publication, community action programmes have intensified, and some states have adopted elaborate arrangements for citizen participation in crime prevention efforts.

In the United Kingdom, efforts in this direction have been patchy and less well developed. Although there is a formidable tradition of voluntary activity and service to the community, with some exceptions this has so far not been harnessed to the need for crime prevention. Attention has been given to the needs of convicted offenders, especially in connection with alternatives to prison and the after-care of those released from custody. A major initiative in crime prevention has been lacking, however.

Some police forces have developed programmes directed towards involving the community in partnership with the police in crime prevention. Outstanding is the contribution in this direction of the Chief Constable for Devon and Cornwall, John Alderson. In his book Alderson sets out a programme for the introduction of a scheme of community policing, and demonstrates from a practical example how this development can be achieved[18].

John Alderson admits that creating a sense of community in some parts of our inner cities may be difficult if not impossible. He believes that 'where a community exists it should be strengthened; where it does not exist it should be created'[19]. He has much to say about the 'village in a city', which his superior police will be able to police without repression or resort to the seductive attractions of new technology.

'In most city areas, there are tightly-knit communities in existence which would lend themselves to a resurgence of village organisation.

16 U.S. National Advisory Commission on Criminal Justice Standards and Goals, Report on *Community Crime Prevention* (1973).
17 See the references cited in the Report, p. 1 and p. 7.
18 J. Alderson, *Policing Freedom* (1979).
19 p. 48.

There are others more loosely-knit which could be drawn together, and there are those where little or no social identity exists and where a good deal of effort would be needed to create any kind of unity'[20].

With almost prophetic insight, Alderson writes about the problems of 'policing in a hostile environment'. He believes that relations between the police and the policed in those situations can only be strengthened if the demeanour of the whole organisation is sympathetic[1]. The problems of policing in a conflict situation are a severe challenge to the imagination and initiative of the police, who must develop new responses to modern conditions.

The desirability of enrolling the community, including many of the existing agencies and institutions, in the effort to control and prevent crime is underlined and reinforced by the proposals of the House of Commons Expenditure Committee in its Fifteenth Report, Session 1977–78, relating to the need for a partnership between official and unofficial agencies, between professionals and volunteers, in providing for the needs of offenders discharged from custodial institutions and those who are sentenced by the courts to some alternative to prison[2]. This approach was endorsed by the Home Office in its reply to the Expenditure Committee's Report[3] who pointed out that already there existed a wide range of local arrangements involving co-operation between different agencies and voluntary organisations.

In May 1981 a government minister, Lord Belstead described as a particularly promising development in this direction 'The New Initiative in Penal Treatment' which was being jointly sponsored by the Central Council of Probation and After-Care Committees and The Magistrates Association. The New Initiative encourages local probation committees to bring together all those involved in the sentencing process to look at the various options available to the courts and see if a better understanding can be reached of the part each can play in promoting non-custodial measures[4]. This development must surely be in line with the thinking behind the Expenditure Committee's recommendations. One further step would be to involve the police in these discussions.

20 p. 191.
1 p. 26.
2 House of Commons, *Fifteenth Report from the Expenditure Committee*, H. C. 662-I Session 1977–78, (July 1978) paras. 209–216, pp. lxxv–lxxvii.
3 Home Office etc. Observations on the Fifteenth Report from the Expenditure Committee, Cmnd. 7948 (June 1980), paras. 107–111, pp. 25–27.
4 Home Office News Release, 1 May 1981.

At the national level too there should be a policy advisory committee, as the House of Commons Home Affairs Committee has suggested in its Fourth Report, Session 1980–81[5]. This suggestion belongs more to the discussion of criminal policy formation (see post) but it is of interest to note here that the membership of the National Criminal Policy Committee which is proposed would include, apart from representatives of the central government bodies closely concerned, representatives of the senior judiciary, the magistracy, the police, probation and after-care committees and local authorities[6].

The Home Office Research Study No. 50 by John Croft, addresses the topic of Crime and the Community[7]. One conclusion which emerges from this review of the situation is 'the need for some carefully controlled experiment and exploration in which the involvement of the community would be encouraged'[8].

The Home Office Research Unit has reviewed the evidence so far available concerning the effectiveness of programmes designed to promote greater involvement of the community in crime prevention and detection[9]. The constraints working against the success of such methods are recognised. These arise not only from the different roles played by the police (social help versus social control) but from the diverse and pluralistic character of the communities policed and the overlapping of police with other agencies serving the community. That there are benefits flowing from such schemes in terms of an increased flow of information to the police regarding criminal activities, and a reduction of public anxieties about crime, cannot be denied. The effect on crime itself is less clear. It could well be that more crime comes to the knowledge of the police. The police themselves are by no means all agreed about the value of this 'community' approach. An illustration of this is provided in the evidence submitted to the Scarman Inquiry into the Brixton riots in 1981, and the public discussion of policing methods. Policing in a riot situation demands a response of a different character. The effect of introducing community policing methods must only be evident in the long-run, probably over a span of several years.

5 House of Commons, *Fourth Report from the Home Affairs Committee, The Prison Service*, H. C. 412-I, Session 1980–81, paras 117–119, p. xlvi.
6 Para. 117.
7 John Croft, *Crime and the Community* (1979) Home Office Research Study No. 50.
8 p. 7.
9 P. Morris and K. Heal, *Crime Control and the Police: a review of research* (1981) Home Office Research Study No. 67.

Public opinion

One of the constant factors in the crime/society equation is the state of public opinion about crime. Public attitudes and values are, however, by no means uniform, nor indeed are they constant in the sense of never changing. Such matters resemble ladies' fashions in that there are fairly rapid switches of opinion or emphasis. Different topics attract attention at different times. At one time anxiety is focussed on 'mugging'. At another time attention is concentrated on baby snatchers, or the battered child syndrome or battered wives. Capital punishment and the need for it represents a subject which recurs from time to time in different connections, e.g. should it be available for terrorist crime? The sources of such 'public opinion' needs to be considered, as well as its fickleness, in evaluating how reliable it is as a guide to policy making.

Public opinion surveys provide one source for gauging the state of public opinion, much favoured by psephologists. Their notorious unreliability as a prediction of voting choices should alert us to the intrinsic dangers of over-reliance upon them. More scientific surveys conducted over a longer time with sophisticated measurement techniques may be helpful. W. A. Belson's study of the London police and their public image is one example[10]. One may measure such matters as the residents' fear of crime in relation to the frequency of policing by means of footpatrols[11]. One may measure the effect of adopting alternative strategies to fight crime not only in terms of the reduction of crime itself but also in terms of the reduction of anxieties about crime. Anxieties about crime are often unrealistic, and based on hearsay, rumour, and press and media reporting. Stan Cohen has written convincingly about the public tendency to look for folk devils and indulge in moral panics[12]. It is possible that we all need reassuring from time to time about our values by measuring them against some unspeakable behaviour currently in the public view. This is not intended to depreciate the seriousness of crime in any way, particularly what has come to be known as street crime. Its consequences for the victims who are often poor, elderly, lonely people, are traumatic and deplorable. One way to alleviate these matters is to develop schemes designed to meet the needs of such victims for comfort and support,

10 W. A. Belson, *The Public and the Police* (1975).
11 P. Morris and K. Heal, *Crime Control and the Police: A Review of Research* (1981) Home Office Research Study No. 67.
12 S. Cohen, *Folk Devils and Moral Panics: The Creation of the Mods and Rockers* (1972).

including financial compensation. When, however, the actual behaviour is examined in the clear light of day, as for instance, has been
done in the case of football hooliganism, it is found that the amount of
physical injury caused is minimal, though the behaviour apparently
has a ritualistic element, and is more designed for internal consump-
tion by the peer group members than anything else[13].

The influence of the media

The role of the media in reflecting or creating and instigating public
opinion about crime is very important. Studies of hooliganism and
vandalism, drug-taking, 'mugging', all suggest that the press and
television and radio do more than simply reflect in a mirror-like
fashion the response of the public to such deviant behaviour. To a very
large degree, the media are trend-setters, and help to stimulate and
expand opinion to a significant degree. The mirror becomes a mag-
nifying glass, and inevitably there is some distortion. The selective
process of news-gathering, the emphasis on a good story line, the need
to provide excitement and titillation, all these are well-known features
of modern media operations.

A slightly separate question concerns the role of the media not so
much in creating public opinion about criminal behaviour but in
stimulating criminal behaviour itself. This has been studied mainly in
relation to the influence of television on juvenile delinquency[14]. Here
it seems likely there can be harmful effects especially on those viewers
predisposed towards delinquent behaviour. The possibility of being
stimulated has to be offset against the cathartic effect which must
frequently occur. The stimulation is usually in the direction of violent
and aggressive behaviour. There is less concern about the promotion
of dishonesty, since most TV features appear to find that subject less
interesting. So the major concern is about a type of crime which we
know to be rare in our society, viz. violent crime. The possibility that
television promotes our abhorrence of violence has to be considered.

It seems however to be accepted by both the BBC and Independent

---

13 See the studies of crowd behaviour by Peter Marsh and Eugene Trivizas.
14 See the studies by H. Himmelweit, A. N. Oppenheim, P. Vince, *Television and the
child* (1958); W. A. Belson, *The Impact of Television* (1967); *Television violence and
the adolescent boy* (1978); Stephen Brody, *Screen Violence and Film Censorship*
(1976) Home Office Research Study No. 40. Report of the Pilkington Committee on
Broadcasting Cmnd. 1753 (June 1962); B. Wilson, 'Mass Media and the Public
Attitude to Crime' [1961] Crim L R 376.

Television in Britain that there should be limits to the portrayal of violent incidents, and a code of practice has been worked out to govern this aspect of television production[15]. At one time there was great public concern over horror comics, which were mostly imported, and the harmful effects these were thought to have upon children led to legislation[16]. Concern over obscene publications and pornography has also led to amendments of the law, though here the main thrust of reform has been in the direction of liberalisation from anything which looks like censorship[17]. There is very little evidence that people are influenced in the direction of deviant behaviour including crime by what they see or read. Just occasionally one comes across an instance of imitation or stimulation by the printed word[18], but even there, one must evaluate the evidence carefully, to see what led to the depravity and the kind of personality involved. Much research has been sponsored into the effect of television on viewers but like John Ebdon's research into the BBC sound archives, this has reached no very solid conclusions.

Public policy

Policy in relation to the prevention and control of crime cannot depend solely or mainly on public opinion. Otherwise we should still have capital punishment, public execution and corporal punishment. In a democracy, the true repository of opinion upon which legislation is to be based resides in the elected representatives of the people. They must decide what policy to pursue, whether by legislation or otherwise. Many years ago that distinguished student of the British constitution A. V. Dicey, made this abundantly clear[19]. Moreover the views of legislators cannot be governed solely by the mandated votes of party caucuses. They must be free to listen to and respond to the solicitations of the various pressure groups which will try to engage

15 See Pilkington Report, Cmnd. 1753 (June 1962) para. 117, p. 38. The ITA adopted a code in 1964, but the BBC already had one.
16 Children and Young Persons (Harmful Publications) Act 1955.
17 Obscene Publications Acts 1959 and 1964; Roy Jenkins, 'Obscenity, Censorship and the Law', Encounter (October 1959); Home Office, Report of the (Williams) Committee on *Obscenity and Film Censorship* Cmnd. 7772 (November 1971).
18 The former Metropolitan Police Commissioner, Sir Joseph Simpson said on 24 November 1964 that when a teenager saw himself reflected on television as doing criminal, unpleasant and vicious things, there was a very grave risk that he will copy it.
19 A. V. Dicey, *Law and Public Opinion in England during the Nineteenth Century* (1914) (reprinted 1962).

their support. In penal reform we know of the excellent work done by the Howard League for Penal Reform and NACRO (The National Association for the Care and Resettlement of Offenders). There are also bodies which represent the police, magistrates, probation officers and social workers, and prison staff. Policy is developed out of a wide range of consultations and considerations. It is not plucked from the air or invented by civil servants, though the influence of the latter should not be under-estimated.

In 1977 the Home Office published a Review of Criminal Policy covering the ten years 1966–1975[20]. This was one result of the setting up inside the office of a criminal policy planning unit. In addition to the historical review of achievements in the ten-year period, policy objectives were identified and elaborated, and some evaluation of the situation was attempted. Some relevant research findings were also reviewed.

The Home Office Research Unit has also published several essays by the Head of the Unit, John Croft, on the relation of research to criminal policy, the problems of managing criminological research, and the relevance of comparative studies[1]. Cost effectiveness is one subject to which attention is now being directed, as is evidenced by Stephen Shaw's NACRO study, *Paying the Penalty: An Analysis of The Cost of Penal Sanctions* (1980)[2].

The equivalent agency to the Home Office Research Unit in France has published studies of the cost of crime, the nature of public opinion in relation to criminal justice, and the public image of collective violence[3]. One might venture to conclude that research studies of the kind carried out by the French and British researchers may assist in the better understanding of crime and the problems connected with crime prevention and control[4]. There must be a research input into criminal policy-making. Most governments now recognise this. The creation of strong research departments signifies as much.

20 Home Office Working Paper, *A Review of Criminal Justice Policy 1976* (1977).
 1 *Research in Criminal Justice* (1978) Home Office Research Study No. 44; *Crime and Comparative Research* (1979) Home Office Research Study No. 57; *Research and Criminal Policy* (1980) Home Office Research Study No. 59; *Managing Criminological Research* (1981) Home Office Research Study No. 69. All by the Head of the Home Office Research Unit, Mr. I. J. Croft.
 2 NACRO (1980).
 3 P. Robert, T. Lambert and C. Faugeron *Image du Viol Collectif et Reconstruction d'Objet* (1976); P. Robert and T. Godefroy, *Le Cout du Crime ou L'Économie Poursuivant le Crime* (1978); P. Robert and C. Faugeron, *La Justice et Son Public: Les représentations sociales du système pénal* (1978).
 4 See the proceedings of the one-day conference held in Paris; reported in International Annals of Criminology (1979–80) Vol. 18, No. 2, pp. 49 et seq.

What the objectives of crime research should be is a matter for consideration. In the past too much attention was given to the study of offenders at the expense of neglecting study of the offence and the society in which it occurs. Since the development of the modern sociological approach that state of affairs has changed radically, and interest has shifted to the study of how offences and offenders come to be perceived and dealt with.

What seems to be required now is a balancing of the various emphases and marrying them with the needs of policy makers and administrators. As Croft puts it:

'If empirical research is to be seen as a reliable guide to social policy, it is important that there should be some sort of consensus about the purpose of a programme, the priority to be assigned to individual projects and the methods by which objectives are to be achieved'[5].

In this matter Croft sees it as highly desirable that care be taken to accommodate a variety of conceptual approaches to the subject. In choosing a research subject it is inevitable that much will depend on the concept the researcher has of crime itself[6].

We have seen that there are many different views on this subject. Some derive essentially from the tradition inherited from a particular scientific discipline, some are essentially inspired by certain views of the nature of society and the way it operates. Criminological study will endure only if it is approached in a sufficiently eclectic and catholic way. This is not the same as saying one must have no views or show no commitment. The failure to understand this has weakened many recent studies. Yet its full comprehension and realisation present a major challenge and provides countless opportunities for the future of criminological study. There is here plenty to occupy criminology in the last quarter of the twentieth century.

5 *Research in Criminal Justice* (1978) Home Office Research Study No. 44, p. 9.
6 p. 9.

Bibliography

Abbott E. and Breckinridge S. P. *The Delinquent Child and the Home* (1912)
Abrahamsen D. *Crime and the Human Mind* (1944)
  The Psychology of Crime (1960)
Aichhorn A. *Delinquency and Child Guidance: Selected Papers* (1964)
  Wayward Youth (1925)
Ainsworth Mary D. et al. *Deprivation of Maternal Care: A Reassessment of its Effects* (1962) W.H.O.
Alderson J. *Policing Freedom* (1979)
Alexander F. and Healy W. *Roots of Crime: Psychoanalytic Studies* (1935)
Alexander F. and Staub H. *The Criminal, The Judge and the Public* (1931)
Alihan M. A. *Social Ecology: A Critical Analysis* (1938)
Allport F. H. *Social Psychology* (1924)
Andry R. G. *Delinquency and Parental Pathology* (1960)
Antilla I. and Jaakola R. *Unrecorded Criminality in Finland* (1966)
Baer A. *Der Verbrecher in Anthropologischer Beziehung* (1893)
Baldwin J. and Bottoms A. E. *The Urban Criminal* (1976)
Baldwin J. and McConville S. *Negotiated Justice* (1979)
Bandura A. *Aggression* (1973)
  Social Learning Theory (1977)
Bandura A. and Walters R. H. *Social Learning and Personality Development* (1963)
Banks C. and Fairhead S. *The Petty Short-term Prisoner* (1976)
Beccaria C. *Dei delitti e delle pene* (1764)
Becker H. S. *Outsiders* (1963)
Bell D. *The End of Ideology* (1960)
Belson W. A. *The Impact of Television* (1967)
  The Public and the Police (1975)
  Television Violence and the Adolescent Boy (1978)
Bentham Jeremy *Introduction to the Principles of Legislation* (1780)
Bloch H. A. and Niederhoffer A. *The Gang: A Study in Adolescent Behaviour* (1958)
Blom-Cooper L. (ed.) *Progress in Penal Reform* (1974)
Bonger W. A. *An Introduction to Criminology* (1936)
Bottomley A. K. *Decisions in the Penal Process* (1973)
Bottoms A. K. and McClean J. D. *Defendants in the Criminal Process* (1976)
Bovet Lucien *Psychiatric Aspects of Juvenile Delinquency* (1951)
Bowlby J. *Attachment and Loss* (1969), (1973), (1980) 3 Vols.
  Child Care and the Growth of Love (2nd edn., 1965)
  Forty-Four Juvenile Thieves: Their Characters and Home Life (1946)
  Maternal Care and Mental Health (2nd edn., 1952) W.H.O.

Braithwaite J. *Inequality, Crime and Public Policy* (1979)
Burgess E. W. and Bogue D. J. *Contributions to Urban Sociology* (1965)
Burt Sir Cyril *The Young Delinquent* (1925)
Cabinet Office, *Vandalism: A Note by the Central Policy Review Staff* (September 1978)
Cambridge Department of Criminal Science, Report, *Sexual Offences* (1957)
Carlen P. and Collison M. *Radical Issues in Criminology* (1980)
Carr-Saunders A. M., Mannheim H., Rhodes E. C. *Young Offenders* (1942)
Carson W. G. and Wiles P. *Crime and Delinquency in Britain* (1971)
Carter M. P. and Jephcott P. *The Social Background of Delinquency* (1954) (unpublished manuscript)
Cavadino P. et al. *Parole: The Case for Change* (1977) NACRO
Cecil H. *The English Judge* (1970) Hamlyn Lectures
Chambliss W. H. *Crime and the Legal Process* (1969)
Chassell C. F. *The Relation between Morality and Intellect* (1935)
Chesser E. *The Sexual, Marital and Family Relationships of the English Woman* (1956)
Christian Economic and Social Research Foundation *The Victims of Theft from the Person, Robbery, Assault and Burglary in the Home* (August 1979) Occasional Paper, Series C. No. 4
Christiansen K. O. (ed.) *Scandinavian Studies in Criminology* (1965) Vol. 1
Cicourel A. V. *The Social Organisation of Juvenile Justice* (1968)
Clarke Ann M. and Clarke A. D. B. *Early Experience: Myth and Evidence* (1976)
Clarke R. V. G. and Mayhew P. (eds.) *Designing Out Crime* (1980)
Clinard M. B. *Sociology of Deviant Behaviour* (1957)
Cloward R. and Ohlin L. *Delinquency and Opportunity* (1960)
Cohen A. K. *Delinquent Boys: The Culture of the Gang* (1955)
Cohen A., Lindesmith A., Schuessler K. (eds.) *The Sutherland Papers* (1956)
Cohen S. *Folk Devils and Moral Panics: The Creation of the Mods and Rockers* (1972)
    Crime and Punishment: Some Thoughts on Theories and Policies (May 1979) (RAP)
Cohen S. (ed.) *Images of Deviance* (1971)
Cohen Y. A. *Man in Adaptation: The Bio Social Background* (1968)
Conrad J. P. and Dinitz S. *In Fear of Each Other* (1977)
Conrad K. *Der Konstitutionstypus* (1963)
Cortes J. B. and Gatri F. M. *Delinquency and Crime: A Biopsychosocial Approach* (1972)
Council of Europe, European Committee on Crime Problems, *Collected Studies in Criminological Research* (1970) Vol. V
Council of Europe, European Committee on Crime Problems, *The Index of Crime: Some Further Studies* (1970)
Council of Europe, European Committee on Crime Problems, *Report on Sentencing* (1974)
Cressey D. R. *Other People's Money* (1953)
Cross R. *The English Sentencing System* (3rd edn., 1981)
Davis K. C. *Discretionary Justice: A Preliminary Inquiry* (1969)
de Greef E. *Introduction à la Criminologie* (1946)

de Reuck (ed.) *The Mentally Abnormal Offender* (1968)
de Wit J. and Hartup W. W. (eds.) *Determinants and Origins of Aggressive Behaviour* (1974)
Debuyst C. *Criminels et valeurs vécues* (1960)
Department of Health and Social Security, Report on the review of procedures for the discharge and supervision of psychiatric patients subject to special restrictions. Cmnd. 5191 (January 1973)
Di Tullio B. *Horizons in Clinical Criminology* (1969)
Dicey A. V. *Law and Public Opinion in England during the Nineteenth Century* (1914) (reprinted 1962)
Ditton J. *Controlology: Beyond the New Criminology* (1979)
Ditton J. *Part-time Crime: an ethnography of fiddling and pilferage* (1977)
Douglas J. W. B. and Blomfield J. M. *Children under Five* (1958)
Downes D. *The Delinquent Solution* (1966)
Downes D. and Rock P. (eds.) *Deviance and Social Control* (1979)
Downes D. and Rock P. (eds.) *Deviant Interpretations* (1979)
Drapkin I. and Viano E. *Victimology: A New Focus* (1973)
Drapkin I. and Viano E. (eds.) *Victimology* (1974)
East Sir Norwood *The Adolescent Offender* (1942)
　　　　　　Medical Aspects of Crime (1936)
　　　　　　The Roots of Crime (1954)
　　　　　　Society and the Criminal (1949)
Eissler K. R. (ed.) *Searchlights on Delinquency* (1949)
El Saaty H. *Juvenile Delinquency in Egypt* (1946) (Unpublished doctoral dissertation, University of London)
Empey, Lamar T *American Delinquency: Its Meaning and Construction* (1978)
Eysenck H. J. *Crime and Personality* (1977)
　　　　　　Dimensions of Personality (1947)
　　　　　　Fact and Fiction in Psychology (1965)
　　　　　　The Scientific Study of Personality (1952)
　　　　　　Sense and Nonsense in Psychology (1957)
　　　　　　The Structure of Human Personality (1960)
Eysenck H. J. (ed.) *Handbook of Abnormal Psychology* (1973)
Eysenck H. J. and Eysenck S. B. G. *Personality Structure and Measurement* (1969)
Faugeron C. *La Justice et Son Public: Les représentations sociales du système pénal* (1978)
Feldman M. P. *Criminal Behaviour: A Psychological Analysis* (1977)
Ferdinand T. N. *Typologies of Delinquency: a critical analysis* (1966)
Ferguson T. *The Young Delinquent in his Social Setting* (1952)
Ferri E. *Criminal Sociology* (1884) (English edn., ed. Rev. W. D. Morrison (1897; American edn., translated from the French edn. of 1905, (1917) reprinted 1967)
Foulkes S. H. *Psycho-Analysis and Crime* (1944)
Friedlander K. *The Psychoanalytical Approach to Juvenile Delinquency* (1947)
Fyvel T. R. *The Insecure Offender* (1961)
Gall F. G. and Spurzheim G. *Recherches sur Le Systeme nerveux* (1809)
Gibbens T. C. N. *Psychiatric Studies of Borstal Lads* (1963)

Gibbens T. C. N. *Trends in Juvenile Delinquency* (1961) W.H.O. Public Health Papers No. 5
Gibbens T. C. N. and Ahrenfeldt R. H. *Cultural Factors in Delinquency* (1966)
Gibbens T.C.N. and Prince J. *Shoplifting* (1962)
Glaser D. (ed.) *Handbook of Criminology* (1974)
Glass R. *Newcomers* (1960)
Glazebrook P. R. (ed.) *Reshaping the Criminal Law: Essays in Honour of Glanville Williams* (1978)
Glover E. *The Roots of Crime* (1960)
Glueck S. and Glueck E. T. *Family Environment and Delinquency* (1962)
         Physique and Delinquency (1956)
         Predicting Delinquency (1959)
         Unraveling Juvenile Delinquency (1950)
Goddard H. H. *Feeblemindedness* (1914)
      Feeble-mindedness: Its Causes and Consequences (1962)
      Human Efficiency and Levels of Intelligence (1920)
      Juvenile Delinquency (1921)
      The Kallikaks (1912)
Goffman E. *Asylums* (1961)
    Stigma (1963)
Goring C. *The English Convict* (1913) (abridged edn. HMSO, 1919)
Gould J. and Kolb W. F. (eds.) *Dictionay of the Social Sciences* (1964)
Gouldner A. *The Coming Crisis of Western Sociology* (1971)
Gove W. R. (ed.) *The Labelling of Deviance: Evaluating a Perspective* (1975)
Grosman B. A. *The Prosecutor: An Inquiry into the Exercise of Discretion* (1969)
Grünhüt M. *Penal Reform* (1948)
Grygier T. et al. (eds.) *Criminology in Transition* (1965)
Gunn J. *Epileptics in Prison* (1977)
Gunn J. et al. *Psychiatric Aspects of Imprisonment* (1978)
Hall, Calvin S. *A Primer of Freudian Psychology* (1954)
Hall J. *General Principles of Criminial Law* (1947)
Hall S. and Jefferson T. (eds.) *Resistance through Rituals: Youth Subcultures in Post-War Britain* (1976)
Hall Williams J. E. *The English Penal System in Transition* (1970)
Hart H. L. A. *Punishment and Responsibility* (1968)
Haskell M. R. and Yablonsky L. *Crime and Delinquency* (1971)
Healy W. and Bronner A. F. *Delinquents and Criminals, Their Making and Unmaking* (1926).
         New Light on Delinquency and its Treatment (1936)
Hebb D. O. *The Organization of Behaviour* (1949)
Herbert D. *Urban Geography: A Social Perspective* (1972)
Herbert H. L. and Jarvis F. V. *Dealing with Delinquents* (1961)
Himmelweit H., Oppenheim A. N., Vince P. *Television and the Child* (1958)
Hinde R. E. *Animal Behaviour* (1970)
Hindelang M. J. *Criminal Victimization in Eight American Cities: A Descriptive Analysis of Common Theft and Assault* (1976)
Hindelang M. J., Gottfredson M. R., Garofalo J. *Victims of Personal Crime:*

An Empirical Foundation for a Theory of Personal Victimization (1978)
Hirschi T. *Causes of Delinquency* (1969)
Hirschi T. and Gottfredson M. *Understanding Crime: Current Theory and Research* (1980)
Hirschi T. and Selvin H. C. *Delinquency Research: An Appraisal of Analytic Methods* (1967)
Hogarth J. *Sentencing as a Human Process* (1971)
Home Office *Committee on Homosexual Offences and Prostitution* (1957) Report, Cmnd. 247
Home Office *Committee on Obscenity and film Censorship* (the Williams Committee) (November 1979) Report, Cmnd. 7772
Home Office *Criminal Statistics (England and Wales) 1979* (November 1980) Cmnd. 8098.
Home Office *Departmental Committee on Criminal Statistics* (December 1967) Report, Cmnd. 3448
Home Office *Departmental Committee on the Probation Service* (1962) Report, Cmnd. 1650
Home Office *People in Prison* (1978)
Home Office *Probation and After-Care Statistics, England and Wales* (1979)
Home Office *Statistics of the Criminal Justice System (England and Wales) 1969-79* (December 1980)
Home Office *Youth Custody and Supervision: A New Sentence* (December 1978) Cmnd. 7404
Home Office, Advisory Council on the Penal System, Interim Report *The Length of Prison Sentences* (1977)
Home Office, Advisory Council on the Penal System, Report *Sentences of Imprisonment* (1978)
Home Office, Advisory Council on the Penal System, Report *Young Adult Offenders* (1974)
Home Office, Criminal Law Revision Committee, Twelfth Report *Penalty for Murder* (January 1973) Cmnd. 5184
Home Office, Criminal Law Revision Committee, Fourteenth Report *Offences against the Person* (March 1980) Cmnd. 7844
Home Office, Department of Health and Social Security *Committee on Mentally Abnormal Offenders* (October 1975) Report, Cmnd. 6244
Home Office, Lord Chancellor's Department, Interdepartmental Committee on *The Business of the Criminal Courts* (February 1961) Report, Cmnd. 2289
Home Office News Release, 1 May 1981
Home Office, Observations on the Fifteenth Report from the Expenditure Committee, *The Reduction of Pressure on the Prison System* (June 1980) Cmnd. 7948
Home Office Research Studies No. 7 *Prediction Methods in Criminology* (1971) by F. H. Simon
Home Office Research Studies No. 18 *Social Enquiry Reports and the Probation Service* (1973) by M. Davies and M. Knopf
Home Office Research Study No. 34 *Crime as Opportunity* (1976) by P. Mayhew, R. V. G. Clarke, A. Sturman and J. M. Hough
Home Office Research Study No. 37 *Police Cautioning in England and Wales* (1976) by J. A. Ditchfield

Home Office Research Study No. 40 *Screen Violence and Film Censorship* (1976) by S. Brody
Home Office Research Study No. 42 *Crime in Public View* (1979) by P. Mayhew, R. V. G. Clarke, J. N. Burrows, J. M. Hough and S. W. C. Winchester
Home Office Research Study No. 44 *Research in Criminal Justice* (1978) by John Croft
Home Office Research Study No. 47 *Tackling Vandalism* (1978) R. V. G. Clarke (Ed.). Contributors F. J. Gladstone, A. Sturman, Sheena Wilson
Home Office Research Study No. 48 *Social Inquiry Reports: A Survey* (1979) by Jennifer Thorpe
Home Office Research Study No. 50 *Crime and the Community* (1979) by John Croft
Home Office Research Study No. 57 *Crime and Comparative Research* (1979) by John Croft
Home Office Research Study No. 58 *Race, Crime and Arrests* (1979) by P. Stevens and C. F. Willis
Home Office Research Study No. 59 *Research and Criminal Policy* (1980) by John Croft
Home Office Research Study No. 62 *Co-ordinating Crime Prevention Efforts* (1980) by F. J. Gladstone
Home Office Research Study No. 63 *Crime Prevention Publicity: An Assessment* (1980) by D. Riley and P. Mayhew
Home Office Research Studies No. 66 *Persistent Petty Offenders* (1981) by Suzan Fairhead
Home Office Research Study No. 67 *Crime Control and The Police: A Review of Research* (1981) by P. Morris and K. Heal
Home Office Research Study No. 69 *Managing Criminological Research* (1981) by John Croft
Home Office Research Study No. 70 *Ethnic Minorities, Crime and Policing* (1981) by M. Tuck and P. Southgate
Home Office Standing Committee on Crime Prevention *Protection Against Vandalism* (November 1975)
Home Office White Paper *Young Offenders* (October 1980) Cmnd. 8045
Home Office Working Paper *A Review of Criminal Justice Policy 1976* (1977)
Home Office Working Party on *Bail Procedures in Magistrates' Courts* (1974) Report
Honderich T. *Punishment: the supposed justifications* (1969)
Hood R. *Tolerance and the Tariff* (1974) NACRO reprinted in *Criminal Justice: Selected Readings* (1978) Baldwin J. and Bottomley A. K. (eds) pp. 296 et seq.
Hood R. (ed.) *Crime, Criminology and Public Policy* (1974)
Hood R. and Sparks R. *Key Issues in Criminology* (1970)
Hooton E. A. *The American Criminal* (1939) Vol. 1
            Crime and the Man (1939)
House of Commons, Fifteenth Report from the Expenditure Committee *The Reduction of Pressure on the Prison System* H.C. 622–I (Session 1977–78)
House of Commons, Fourth Report from the Home Affairs Committee, *The Prison Service* H.C. 412–I (Session 1980–81)

Howard League for Penal Reform *Freedom on Licence* (1981) Report of a Working Party

Hurwitz S. *Criminology* (1953)

Inciardi J. A. (ed.) *Radical Criminology: The Coming Crisis* (1980)

Institute of Criminology, The Hebrew University of Jerusalem, Proceedings of a Symposium on *Chromosome Abnormality and Criminal Responsibility* (1969)

Jahoda M. *Current Concepts of Positive Mental Health* (1958)

Jones H. *Crime and the Penal System* (1962)

Kaiser G. *Randalierende Jugend* (1959)

Karpman B. *Case Studies in the Psychopathology of Crime* (1944)

Kimball Young (ed.) *Social Attitudes* (1931)

Kinberg O. *Basic Problems in Criminology* (1935)

Klare H. J. and Haxby D. (eds.) *Frontiers of Criminology* (1967)

Klein M. W. (ed.) *Juvenile Gangs in Context: Theory, Research and Action* (1967)
  Street Gangs and Street Workers (1971)

Kornhauser R. *Social Sources of Delinquency: An Appraisal of Analytic Models* (1978)

Kretschmer E. *Physique and Character* (1921). English transl. W. J. H. Sprott (1925). 2nd English edn. revised, with appendix by Dr E. Miller (1936)

Krohn M. D. and Akers R. L. (eds.) *Crime, Law and Sanctions: Theoretical Perspectives* (1978)

La Fave W. *Arrest: The Decision to Take a Suspect into Custody* (1965)

Laing R. D. *The Divided Self* (1959)
  The Politics of Experience (1967)

Lambert J. R. *Crime, Police and Race Relations* (1970)

Lander B. *Towards an Understanding of Juvenile Delinquency* (1954)

Lange J. *Crime as Destiny: A Study of Criminal Twins* (1931)

Le Bon G. *Psychologie des foules* (1895)

Leigh L. H. *Police Powers in England and Wales* (1975)

Leigh L. H. and Hall Williams J. E. *The Management of the Prosecution Process in Denmark, Sweden and the Netherlands* (1981)

Lemert E. M., *Human Deviance, Social Problems and Social Control* (1967)

Lenz A. *Grundriss der Kriminalbiologie* (1927)

Lewis H. *Deprived Children* (1954)

Lindner R. M. *Rebel Without a Cause* (1944)

Little K. *Negroes in Britain* (1948)

McCabe S. and Sutcliffe F. *Defining Crime* (1978)

McClean I. *The Crown Court – Patterns of Sentencing* (1981)

McClintock F. H. *Crimes of Violence* (1963)

McClintock F. H. and Avison N. *Crime in England and Wales* (1968)

McClintock F. H. and Gibson E. *Robbery in London* (1961)

McCord W. and McCord J. *Origins of Crime* (1959)

McDonald L. *The Sociology of Law and Order* (1976)

McDonald W. F. *The Prosecutor* (1979)

McLennan B. N. (ed.) *Crime in Urban Society* (1970)

Mannheim H. *Comparative Criminology* (1965) 2 Vols
    Group Problems in Crime and Punishment (1955)
    Juvenile Delinquency in an English Middletown (1948)
    Social Aspects of Crime in England Between the Wars (1940)
Mannheim H. (ed.) *Pioneers in Criminology* (1960)
Mannheim H. and Wilkins L. T. *Prediction Methods in Relation to Borstal Training* (1955)
Mark Sir Robert *In the Office of Constable* (1978)
Marsh P. *Aggro: The illusion of violence* (1978)
    The rules of disorder (1978)
Martin J. P. *Offenders as Employees* (1962)
Mason P. *Race and Society* (1970)
Matza D. *Becoming Deviant* (1969)
    Delinquency and Drift (1964)
Mawby R. *Policing the City* (1979)
Mays J. B. *Crime and Social Structure* (1963)
    Growing up in the City (1954)
    On the Threshold of Delinquency (1959)
Mednick S. A. *Genetics, Environment and Psychopathology* (1974)
Mednick S. A. and Shoham S. G. (eds.) *New Paths in Criminology: Interdisciplinary and Intercultural Explorations* (1979)
Merton R. K. *Social Theory and Social Structure* (1957)
Messinger S. L. and Bittner E. (eds.) *Criminology Review Yearbook* Vol. 1 (1979), Vol. 2 (1980)
Metropolitan Police Commissioner, Report for 1963 (July 1964) Cmnd. 2408
Middendorff W. *New Forms of Juvenile Delinquency: Their Origin, Prevention and Treatment* (1960)
Moberly Sir Walter *The Ethics of Punishment* (1968)
Morris N. *The Future of Imprisonment* (1974)
Morris N. and Hawkins G. *The Honest Politician's Guide to Crime Control* (1970)
Morris N. and Tonry M. (eds.) *Crime and Justice: An Annual Review of Research* (1979)
Morris T. *Deviance and Control: The Secular Heresy* (1976)
Morris T. P. *The Criminal Area: A Study in Social Ecology* (1957)
NACRO, Report of Proceedings of Day Conference on *The Reduction of Pressure on the Prison System* (July 1980)
National Deviancy Conference *Permissiveness and Control: the fate of the sixties legislation* (1980)
Nebylitsyn V. D. and Gray J. A. (eds.) *Biological Bases of Individual Behaviour* (1972)
Nettler G. *Explaining Crime* (1974) (2nd edn., 1978)
Newman D. J. *Introduction to Criminal Justice* (1975)
Newman D. J., American Bar Foundation Report *Conviction: The Determination of Guilt or Innocence Without Trial*
Nye F. I. *Family Relationships and Delinquent Behaviour* (1958)
    Role Structure and Analysis of the Family (1976)
Nye F. T. and Berardo F. M. *The Family: Its Structure and Interaction* (1973)
Packer H. L. *The Limits of the Penal Sanction* (1969)

Page Sir Leo *The Sentence of the Court* (1948)
Pahl R. E. *Patterns of Urban Life* (1970)
Pahl R. E. (ed.) *Readings in Urban Sociology* (1968)
Parker H. *A View from the Boys* (1974)
Parker T. *The Frying-Pan* (1970)
　　　　The Twisting Lane (1969)
　　　　The Unknown Citizen (1963)
Parker T. and Allerton R. *The Courage of his Convictions* (1962)
Parole Board, Report for 1980, H.C. 340 (Session 1980–81)
Parliamentary All-Party Penal Affairs Group *Too Many Prisoners* (1980)
Parnell R. W. *Behaviour and Physique: An Introduction to Practical and Applied Somatotyping* (1958)
Parrot P. and Gueneau M. *Les Gangs d'adolescents* (1959)
Patrick J. *A Glasgow gang observed* (1973)
Patterson S. *Dark Strangers* (1963)
Pearce J. D. W. *Juvenile Delinquency* (1952)
Perry F. G. *Reports for Courts* (1979)
Phillipson M. *Sociological Aspects of Crime and Delinquency* (1971)
Polsky H. W. *Cottage Six – The Social System of Delinquent Boys in Residential Treatment* (1962)
Prins H. *Criminal Behaviour: An Introduction to its Study and Treatment* (1973)
Quinney R. *The Social Reality of Crime* (1970)
Radzinowicz L. *Ideology and Crime* (1966)
Reckless W. C. *The Crime Problem* (1955) (1967)
　　　　Criminal Behaviour (1940)
Redl F. and Wineman D. *Children Who Hate* (1951)
Rees W. L. Linford *A Short Textbook of Psychiatry* (1967)
Reiss A. J. Jr. *The Police and the Public* (1971)
Reiwald P. *Society and its Criminals* (1949)
Robert P. and Godefroy T. *Le Cout du Crime ou L'economie poursuivant le crime* (1978)
Robert P., Lambert T., Faugeron C. *Image du Viol Collectif et Reconstruction d'Objet* (1976)
Robert P. and Lascoumes P. *Les Bandes D'Adolescents: Une Theorie de La Ségrégation* (1975)
Robison, Sophia M. *Can Delinquency Be Measured?* (1936)
Robson B. T. *Urban Analysis: A Study of City Structure with Special Reference to Sunderland* (1971)
Rock P. *Deviant Behaviour* (1973)
Rock P. and McIntosh M. (eds.) *Deviance and Social Control* (1974)
Rose A. G. *Five Hundred Borstal Boys* (1954)
Royal Commission on Capital Punishment (1949–1953) Report, Cmd. 8932.
Royal Commission on Criminal Procedure (1981) Report, Cmnd. 8092.
Rutter M. *Maternal Deprivation Reassessed* (2nd edn., 1981)
Sainsbury P. *Suicide in London* (1955)
Salisbury, Harrison *The Shook-Up Generation* (1959)
Schafer S. *Theories in Criminology* (1969)
Schlapp M. G. and Smith E. H. *The New Criminology* (1928)

252   *Bibliography*

Schur E. M. *Labeling Deviant Behaviour: Its Sociological implications* (1971)
            The Politics of Deviance: Stigma Contests and the Uses of Power
            (1980)
Scull A. T. *Decarceration: Community Treatment and the Deviant* (1978)
Scottish Law Reform Commission *The Penalties for Homicide* (1972)
Cmnd. 5137
Sellin T. *Culture Conflict and Crime* (1938)
Sellin T. and Wolfgang M. E. *The Measurement of Delinquency* (1964)
(reprinted 1978)
Shaw C. *Brothers in Crime* (1938)
            The Jack-roller (1931)
            The Natural History of A Delinquent Career (1931)
Shaw C. R. and McKay H. D. *Juvenile Delinquency and Urban Areas*
(1942)
Shaw S. *Paying the Penalty: An Analysis of the Cost of Penal Sanctions* (1980)
Sheldon W. H. *The Varieties of Delinquent Youth* (1949)
                The Varieties of Human Physique (1940)
                The Varieties of Temperament (1942)
Sherif M. and Sherif W. *Problems of Youth: Transition to Adulthood in a
Changing World* (1965)
Shevky E. and Bell W. *Social Area Analysis: Theory, Illustrative Application
and Computational Procedures* (1955)
Shevky E. and Williams M. *The Social Area of Los Angeles: Analysis and
Typology* (1949)
Shields J. *Monozygotic Twins brought up apart and together* (1962)
Shonfield A. and Shaw S. (eds.) *Social Indicators and Social Policy* (1972)
Short J. F. Jr. (ed.) *Gang Delinquency and Delinquent Subcultures* (1968)
Short J. F. Jr. and Strodtbeck F. L. *Group Process and Gang Delinquency*
(1965)
Skolnick J. *Justice Without Trial* (1966)
Soddy K. *Clinical Child Psychiatry* (1960)
Sparks R. F., Genn H. G. and Dodd D. J. *Surveying Victims* (1978)
Spencer J. C. *Stress and Release in an Urban Estate* (1964)
Steer D. *Police Cautions – A Study in the Exercise of Police Discretion* (1970)
Oxford University Penal Research Unit, Occasional Paper Number Two
Stott D. H. *Delinquency and Human Nature* (1950) and 2nd edn. (1980)
                Saving Children from Delinquency (1952)
                Studies of Troublesome Children (1966)
                Unsettled Children and Their Families (1956)
Sutherland E. H. *The Professional Thief* (1950)
Sutherland E. H. and Cressey D. *Principles of Criminology* (6th edn., 1960)
(10th edn., 1978)
Szabo (ed.) *Criminology in Action: Inventory of Contemporary Criminology: its
principal fields of application* (1968)
Szasz T. *The Manufacture of Madness* (1973)
            The Myth of Mental Illness (1961)
Taft D. R. *Criminology* (3rd edn., 1956)
Tappan P. W. *Juvenile Delinquency* (1949)
Tappan P. W. *Crime, Justice and Correction* (1960)

Tapper C. (ed.) *Crime, Proof and Punishment: Essays in Memory of Sir Rupert Cross* (1981)

Taylor J., Walton P. and Young J. *Critical Criminology* (eds.) (1975)
                     The New Criminology (1973)

Taylor L. *Deviance and Society* (1971)

Taylor L., Morris A. and Downes D. *Signs of Trouble: Aspects of Delinquency* (1976) (B.B.C.)

Thomas D. A. *Principles of Sentencing* (2nd edn., 1979)

Thomas D. A. (ed.) *Parole: Its Implications for the Criminal Justice and Penal Systems* (1974)

Thrasher F. *The Gang* (1964) J. F. Short Jr. (ed.)

Timms D. *The Urban Mosaic: Towards a Theory of Residential Differentiation* (1971)

Tobias J. J. *Crime and Industrial Society in the Nineteenth Century* (1967)
              Nineteenth-Century Crime, Prevention and Punishment (1972)

Trasler G. *The Explanation of Criminality* (1962)

Turner J. W. C. and Radzinowicz L. (eds.) *The Modern Approach to Criminal Law* (1948)

U.S.A. *Criminal Victimization Surveys in 13 American Cities* (1975)

U.S.A. National Advisory Commission on Criminal Justice Standards and Goals, Report on *Community Crime Prevention* (1973)

U.S.A. National Advisory Commission on Criminal Justice Standards and Goals, Report on the *Criminal Justice System* (1973)

U.S.A. The President's Commission on Law Enforcement and Administration of Justice, *The Challenge of Crime in a Free Society* (1967)

U.S.A. Report on the Causes of Crime, National Commission on Law Observance and Enforcement Vol. II No. 13 (1931)

Vaz E. W. (ed.) *Middle Class Juvenile Delinquency* (1967)

Vervaeck L. *Syllabus du course d'anthropologie criminélle donnée à la prison de Forest* (1926)

Vold G. B. *Theoretical Criminology* (1958) (2nd edn., 1981)

Von Hentig H. *The Criminal and His Victim* (1948)

Walker N. *Behaviour and Misbehaviour: explanations and non-explanations* (1977)

Walker N. *Crime and Punishment in Britain* (1968), Revised edn.

Walker N. *Crimes, Courts and Figures* (1971)

Weihofen H. *Psychiatry and the Law* (1952)

Wertham F. *Show of Violence* (1949)

West D. J. *The Delinquent Way of Life* (1977)
              Present Conduct and Future Delinquency (1969)
              The Young Offender (1967)

West D. J. (ed.) *Criminological Implications of Chromosome Abnormalities* (1969)

West D. J. and Farrington D. P. *Who Becomes Delinquent?* (1973)

Whitty C. W. M. and Zangwill O. L. (eds.) *Amnesia* (2nd edn., 1979)

Whyte W. F. *Street Corner Society* (1943) (2nd edn., 1955)

Wilcox A. F. *The Decision to Prosecute* (1972)

Wilkins L. T. *Social Deviance: Social Policy, Action and Research* (1964)

Willemse W. A. *Constitution-Types in Delinquency* (1932)
Wilson H. *Delinquency and Child Neglect* (1962)
Wilson J. Q. *Thinking About Crime* (1975)
Wilson R. *Difficult Housing Estates* (1963)
Wing J. K. *Reasoning about Madness* (1978)
Wolfgang M. E. *Patterns in Criminal Homicide* (1958)
Wolfgang M. E. (ed.) *Crime and Culture: Essays in Honor of Thorsten Sellin* (1968)
Wolfgang M. E. and Ferracuti F. *The Subculture of Violence* (1967)
Wolfgang M. E., Savitz L. and Johnston N. *The Sociology of Crime and Delinquency* (1962)
Woodward M. *Low Intelligence and Delinquency* (1955) I.S.T.D. pamphlet reprinted from BJD Vol. 5 pp. 281 et seq. (April 1955)
Wootton B. *Crime and the Criminal Law: Refelctions of a Magistrate and Social Scientist* (2nd edn., 1981)
    Social Science and Social Pathology (1959)
World Health Organisation *Glossary of Mental Disorders and Guide to Their Classification* (1974)
Wright S. W., Crandall B. F. and Boyes L. (eds.) *Perspectives in Cytogenetics: The Next Decade* (1972)
Wyrsch J. *Gerichtliche Psychiatrie* (1955)
Yablonsky L. *The Violent Gang* (1962)
Ziegenhagen E. A. *Victims, Crime and Social Control* (1977)

Index

Hooton, E. A.
criticism of research of, 20
Lombroso criticised by, 25*n*
physique and behaviour, relationship
between, study of, 20, 25*n*, 75
Hospital
mental, 197
order, with or without restriction, 196,
197
special hospitals, 197
Howard, Colin
sentencing, 219
Hughes, E. W.
delinquency, study of, 92
Hyperactive children, 36

Immigration
culture conflict theory, 133–136
Intelligence
high, crime and, relation between, 51, 52
IQ tests, problems arising, 51
low
Cambridge Study in Delinquent Development, 50
crime and, connection between, 48,
49–51
sexual offences, connection with, 50
**Introversion and extraversion, 72, 73,
83**

Jacobs, P.
chromosome research, 33
Jahoda, M.
*Current Concepts of Positive Mental
Health*, 43
Jones, Howard
broken home, view on effect of, 92
Judicial Studies and Information
working party on, 216, 217, 218

Kahn, J.
chromosome research, 34, 35
Kleim, M. W.
'conflict' type gangs, research into, 120,
121, 129*n*, 130*n*
Kretschmer, Ernst
classification of physical types,
(somato types), 18, 19
mental illness and physical type, study
of links between, 19
Physique and character, 18, 75

Labelling
theory of, 144, 145
Laing, R. D.
mental disorder, view of, 44
Lange, Johannes
Crime as Destiny, 28
twins, study of, 28, 75
Le Bon, G.
crowd behaviour, study of, 131*n*
Legal aid and advice
provision of, 206
Lemert, E. M.
'deviancy amplification,' 143
labelling theory, 144
Lenz, Adolf
Grundriss der Kriminalbiologie, 25*n*
Lewis, Hilda
maternal deprivation, study of, 62
Life sentence
murder, for, 198, 199
optional, 199
Little, Alan
maternal deprivation, research into, 61,
62
personality dimensions tested by, 76,
77
Lombroso, Cesare
classification of criminal types, 17
Italian School of criminology, 11, 12
L'Uomo Delinquente, 11, 16
mental illness, study of, 17
neo-Lombrosian theories, 18 et seq.
physical types, study of, 11, 12, 16, 17
theory of crime, criticism of, 17

Mannheim, H.
Comparative Criminology, 131*n*
prediction of criminal behaviour, study
of, 14
Marsh, Peter
violence, studies in, 126
Maternal deprivation
'affectionless characters', 60
Bowlby's theory of, 59 et seq.
research contradicting, 61, 62
deprivation and privation distinguished, 65, 66
Rutter's review of, 64–66
Matza, David
drift, theory of
delinquent behaviour, 146
stages of delinquency, 146
Maudsley, H.
crime and insanity, study of, 11, 14*n*

Wolfgang, M. E.
  and Ferracuti, F., *The Subculture of Violence*, 38
  Patterns of Criminal Homicide, 178*n*
World Health Organisation
  mental disorders, classification of, 87*n*

Yablonsky, Lewis
  conflict gangs, research into, 119, 120

Yablonsky, Lewis – *cont.*
  'near groups', elements of, 120
Young adult offenders, 225
Young, Jock
  symbolic interaction, work on, 143

Zeleny, L. D.
  Feeble-mindedness and Criminal Conduct, 49